STANDOFF

STANDOFF

RACE, POLICING, AND
A DEADLY ASSAULT THAT
GRIPPED A NATION

JAMIE THOMPSON

Henry Holt and Company
New York

Henry Holt and Company
Publishers since 1866
120 Broadway
New York, New York 10271
www.henryholt.com

Henry Holt® and ® are registered trademarks of Macmillan Publishing
Group, LLC.

Library of Congress Cataloging-in-Publication Data

Names: Thompson, Jamie (Journalist), author.
Title: Standoff : race, policing, and a deadly assault that gripped a
nation / Jamie Thompson.
Description: First edition. | New York : Henry Holt and Company, [2020] |
Includes bibliographical references and index.
Identifiers: LCCN 2019055941 (print) | LCCN 2019055942 (ebook) |
ISBN 9781250204219 (hardcover) | ISBN 9781250756442 |
ISBN 9781250204202
(ebook)
Subjects: LCSH: Police—Violence against—Texas—Dallas. | Mass
Shootings—Texas—Dallas. | Hostage negotiations—Texas—Dallas. |
Police-community relations—Texas—Dallas. | Discrimination in law
Enforcement—United States.
Classification: LCC HV8148.D2 T46 2020 (print) | LCC HV8148.D2 (ebook) |
DDC 364.152/34097642812—dc23
LC record available at https://lccn.loc.gov/2019055941
LC ebook record available at https://lccn.loc.gov/2019055942

Our books may be purchased in bulk for promotional, educational, or business
use. Please contact your local bookseller or the Macmillan Corporate and
Premium Sales Department at (800) 221-7945, extension 5442, or by e-mail at
MacmillanSpecialMarkets@macmillan.com.

First Edition 2020

Designed by Meryl Sussman Levavi

Printed in the United States of America

1 3 5 7 9 10 8 6 4 2

Let us go into the dark
Not afraid, not alone.
Let us hope by some good pleasure
Safely to arrive at home.

—Texas folksinger Sam Baker

For the ones who didn't make it home.
And the ones who did.

Contents

A Note to the Reader

Four years before the death of George Floyd shook the nation, other videos of police officers killing black men sparked similar grief and anger. This book is about what happened on one night, July 7, 2016, when a young man opened fire on police officers at a Black Lives Matter rally in Dallas.

It is a true story, based on hundreds of hours of interviews with dozens of men and women who were there. I reconstructed dialogue from their recollections. But when possible—and it often was—I transcribed what was said from audio and video recordings. My notes on sourcing details are at the end of the book. Much of the narrative is told from the perspectives of the characters, as if from inside their heads. With a couple of exceptions detailed in the source notes, these thoughts and feelings were described to me by the people who experienced them.

The people in this story hold a variety of viewpoints. I wrote about them with the hope that readers might step into each of their shoes for a moment.

Prologue

There was no end to the killings, and no turning away from the videos that captured every death. Cameras were everywhere now, in purses and pockets, in the hands of every motorist and passenger pulled over by flashing lights. The police had their own cameras, fastened to uniforms and mounted in patrol cars. The images captured by all those lenses repeated on the news and online, over and over, and every time someone else died, another video surfaced to join the endless loop of blood and tears.

The videos burned the names of the dead and their final moments into the nation's collective memory. There was Eric Garner, the man on a Staten Island sidewalk who kept saying "I can't breathe" as he suffocated under the weight of officers. There was Tamir Rice, the twelve-year-old with a pellet gun who lay dying in a snowy Cleveland park, shot by a cop who had just pulled up in his cruiser. There was Walter Scott, the man in North Charleston, South Carolina, running away as an officer shot him in the back. Eventually the footage blurred into one long and never-ending movie that forced the country to stare into its brokenness.

Deep into the summer of 2016, another video emerged. It was taken by a woman sitting in the passenger seat of an Oldsmobile, talking to her boyfriend as he lay bleeding behind the wheel. "Stay with me," she begged him as he moaned. A police officer stood just outside the car, still pointing his gun at the driver. "You shot four bullets into him, sir," the woman said. "He was just getting his license and registration, sir." They'd been on their way home from the grocery store with frozen potpies and chocolate swirl ice cream before being pulled over for a broken brake light. The officer could only stand there shouting, "Fuck!" By the next morning, millions had watched Philando Castile die on their phones.

In a suburb of Dallas, inside a two-story house on a tree-lined block, a twenty-five-year-old black man studied the Castile video, growing more and more angry. He was a five-foot-six loner, drummed out of the Army in disgrace. Now he was living in his mother's house, working on a plan he'd been churning over for a while. As the Castile video went out across the country, he felt a deepening resolve. He put on khaki military pants and a long-sleeve camouflage shirt, covering a tattoo on his upper left arm that said SEIZE THE DAY. He laced up his tan high-top boots. Neighbors had seen him in his mother's backyard, doing push-ups and drills. In his bedroom he kept a journal of tactics, recording his progress at reloading more efficiently, learning how to lay down suppressive fire, reminding himself to be aware of muzzle flash and how it could reveal his position to enemies. He was honing a method called "shoot and move," practicing how to surprise and dominate. He sketched images of soldiers and wrote himself words of encouragement. He told himself there was no shame if he had to pee on himself during battle. As he headed out the door, his mother looked up. Her son rarely went out.

"I'm going to a protest rally," he said.

"What are you protesting?" his mother asked.

"All the shootings," he said. "Mom, you've got to listen to the news."

"Stay out of trouble," she said.

He climbed into his mother's black SUV and headed toward downtown. He arrived just as the sun slipped out of sight, bathing the city in a dark, dusky blue. He parked on Lamar Street, in front of a bone-colored building that housed a community college, switched on the SUV's hazard lights, and got out. On the streets around him, a slight breeze was moving through the oak trees, a late reprieve from the ninety-seven-degree day. Above, glass and steel skyscrapers were coming aglow with lights. A police helicopter swooped low over the buildings, its rotors thumping across the sky. The protest, organized in the wake of Castile's shooting, had already begun. Hundreds of people marched through the streets, and the emotion in their chants carried on the wind. The sound infused the streetscape with the same unsettled air felt that evening in cities across the nation.

The young man slipped on his bulletproof vest and picked up a Saiga AK-74 rifle. He walked toward a group of police officers, their backs turned to him as they focused on the marchers. He raised his rifle and took aim at his first target.

An officer's body camera captured what happened when the first shots roared out, shocking and deafening. The camera was pointed at another officer, the first to fall. It recorded the officer letting out a primal cry, the sound of life leaving his body. He folded and dropped facedown. Then the camera's angle shifted violently, as the officer wearing it fell, too. Now the camera pointed directly upward and recorded a passenger jet flying high above, glistening in the day's last sunlight as it drifted peacefully across the frame. There the camera's gaze remained for many long seconds, recording gunfire and the darkening sky.

STANDOFF

I

_____

The Negotiator

Summer was always the busiest time for Dallas police. The heat would declare itself at sunrise and grow unbearable by noon, working on patience and nerves. People's will to hold things together would fail. There would be a betrayal or grudge or heartbreak, and someone would start waving a gun or climb to some precipice.

That's when Senior Cpl. Larry Gordon, a negotiator on the Dallas police SWAT team, would get a call. He'd be headed along one of the city's looping highways, toward some air-conditioned assignment, and learn that another poor soul had let go of the rope, abandoning the notion that everything was okay or ever would be again. Gordon would turn the wheel and head toward another unraveling.

Over the years, he'd grown used to meeting people on their worst days. A call early in his negotiating career, one that would stick with him for years, took him downtown to one of the city's oldest skyscrapers, a stone-paneled, 1920s-era former bank building. A young woman had climbed to its highest ledge, twenty stories above Main Street. Police barricaded a city block, and Gordon made his way to the roof. A crowd from Jason's Deli gathered on the sidewalk, heads tilted back.

Gordon cut an imposing figure in his navy-blue uniform, at six feet two and 230 pounds, with bulging muscles. Although his body implied sheer force, he moved with the agility of a high school quarterback, which he had been, and the coiled readiness of a kid who'd grown up in a rough neighborhood.

From the building's roof, Gordon took in the immense blue Texas sky. It was surprisingly noisy; the wind whipped, and the sounds of traffic echoed. The knot of fear inside his chest was partly caused, he knew, by being up so high, but also because he still, at that point in his career, believed outcomes depended on whether he could find the right words.

One of Gordon's teammates held a rope and looked around for a place to tie it. He settled on a large metal pole. Gordon fastened the rope to his harness and studied his teammate's knot. *That ain't gonna hold me*, he thought. The teammate was black, like him. Gordon would have preferred one of his white partners tying him off—someone who'd grown up around boats and Boy Scouts. Most brothers, he thought, had not been schooled in the varieties of hitch knots.

He gave the rope a tug and hoped for the best. The men walked toward the edge of the roof, the rope unspooling as they went. Gordon stopped at a waist-high concrete wall, steadied his hands on it, and peered over the ledge. About six feet below sat the young woman, her delicate frame perched at the edge of the building. The sight made Gordon's hands sweat. Any tiny nudge, shift of weight, or gust of wind could send her on a three-hundred-foot free fall.

The woman looked to be in her mid-twenties, with her knees pressed together girlishly, as if she were on a playground swing. She wore a white T-shirt, blue jeans, and sneakers. Her brown hair fell across her face as she looked down. A pack of cigarettes and a wallet rested on the ledge beside her. The serious jumpers often emptied their pockets to leave identification behind.

Gordon called out to the woman, trying to sound friendly, casual. "I'm Officer Gordon with the Dallas Police. What's going on today?" No response. He called out again, raising his voice. Still nothing. The woman was making what Gordon called "target glances" toward the street, as if she were thinking, *Where am I going to jump? How am I going to miss that tree? Am I going to fall on that car?* Gordon made his own plan for when she jumped. He knew his instinct would be to grab her. But she was too far away to safely catch. If he lost his balance, he'd fall until the rope caught him, probably about ten feet, provided the knot held. Then he'd slam into the concrete building, maybe breaking a leg or his back. So he steeled himself. If the woman jumped, he'd let her go. He didn't want to watch her fall or see what happened when her body hit the pavement. *Just turn around and walk away.*

Several long minutes dragged by as he kept shouting to the woman while she ignored him. Finally, in frustration, he shouted, "Why won't you talk to me?"

That's when he saw her lips move. He leaned in closer, straining to hear her over the wind. "Say it again?"

"I don't want to live anymore," she said.

"Why?" Gordon asked.

"He took my daughter."

"Who is 'he'?"

Finally, Gordon had something to work with. He kept her talking and learned she'd lost custody of her child. Gordon told his partner to get the cops below to find the baby. He kept her talking about her daughter, about the man who'd betrayed her, about what she'd miss if she slipped off the ledge. They talked for what felt like an eternity, until a squad car arrived and parked a block away. "Your child is here," Gordon told her. "I don't want her to see you fall."

He watched the woman's every move. Now she began to fidget. She had her palms on the ledge and quickly pushed up, raising herself into a standing position. *Fuck, here she goes*, Gordon thought. He held his breath as the woman stood still for a moment, her back turned, her body swaying at the ledge.

Then she rotated and faced Gordon, lifting her arms into the air. It took Gordon a second to understand what was happening. She wanted to come up. He stretched his upper body over the wall as far as he could and reached toward her wrists. If she changed her mind and resisted, tried to pull him down, he'd overpower her. He was also nervous he would drop her. Once his grip was secure, he pulled as hard and fast as he could, fueled by a surge of adrenaline. He lifted her small body into the air and over the wall. The momentum sent them tumbling backward onto the roof, Gordon still clenching her wrists as she fell on top of him. Another police officer grabbed the sobbing woman as Gordon lay there on his back, breathing hard.

* * *

He never knew exactly who he needed to be until he got there. Hard or soft, commanding or gentle, deferential or aggressive. Every call was a new riddle. Sometimes he had hours to work, but often only minutes to decide what piece of himself to summon at the crucial moment, when someone had become the focus of a couple dozen heavily armed men dressed in black. Most of these troubled souls would emerge alive but some would not. If they let him, Larry Gordon would bring them out safe. Who did they need him to be?

Sometimes it was Larry from the hood, the black kid who grew up with holes in his sneakers and had to sift through his Sugar Smacks to make sure he didn't eat a roach. Other times he needed to be middle-class Larry, a professional with a college degree. He could spend hours discussing Bible passages, debating social influence theory, detailing the weaknesses of the Cowboys' defensive line. He could be athlete Larry, husband Larry, father-of-three Larry, funny Larry, big mean Larry, or a soft teddy bear. Usually Shrink Larry showed up at some point and called out one of his favorite lines: "Right now it's a question of, how much do you love yourself?" Cheesy, but he found it resonated. Most people did love themselves. Most did not want to die. He said it again and again, even though every single time it made his SWAT partners stifle laughter as they stared down the barrels of their M4s. Most days he was just rolling the dice, hoping his would not be the last voice in a stranger's ear.

Gordon had joined Dallas SWAT in 2004, after nine years on the force. He took a typical path to the unit—a couple of years on patrol, then to narcotics, where he'd battled the crack trade, the same one that during his childhood had taken over his neighborhood and sent two older brothers to prison. He'd wanted to join SWAT for the same reason as most other officers, because men on the team were held in prestige as the city's toughest. He was not the team's fiercest warrior, nor its fastest runner, nor its best marksman. Gordon's gift, the skill that made him indispensable, was that he could talk.

Each SWAT officer was assigned a specialty. The more cerebral were drawn to sniping. The more energetic liked busting through doors with steel rams and blasting through walls with explosives. Supervisors assigned Gordon to the crisis and hostage negotiating team, one of the less desirable posts. While others got to rush in with M4s, negotiators sat back in command posts, sipping coffee and talking into headsets. They had to be compassionate and empathetic. One officer begged his supervisors to assign him any job but negotiating. As he put it: "I don't want to spend all day talking to shitheads on the phone."

But Gordon did. He loved to talk. About politics and religion, children and wives, nothing and everything. About the Mavericks or *Big Bang Theory* or race in America. Most of the cops Gordon knew were Republicans. He was the rare Democrat; he'd voted for Barack Obama. Teammates called him "Liberal Larry."

Gordon once read a quote from a Hollywood actress who said she fell in love a little with each of her costars. That's how he felt about the people he negotiated with. They were smart, Gordon thought, and could tell if you really cared about them. He called it "the music behind the words," a concern that was genuine. Negotiating wasn't like other jobs in the police department, where officers were expected to be dispassionate behind their badges and shields. Good negotiators had to lean in and connect.

This came naturally to Gordon. He'd grown up in one world and crossed over into another. He knew people were more than their worst moments. Everybody, when you got down to it, was a complicated mess of one sort or another. But inside every person was a relatable piece of humanity, Gordon believed, and his job on every call was to find it.

* * *

Gordon had been a negotiator for eleven years in 2015 when an unemployed mechanic with a cache of firearms unloaded on Dallas police headquarters, a call Gordon assumed would be the most memorable of his career. The man had bought a makeshift armored van on eBay, where it was advertised as a "Zombie Apocalypse Assault Vehicle." One midsummer night, he sprayed the headquarters building with bullets, shattering the glass windows and sending cops ducking for cover. Officers fired back, and the man took off in his van. He made it to the highway, where an officer shredded his tires with spike strips, and he pulled off at a Jack in the Box. From its parking lot, he called 911 and let loose a tirade about how authorities had arrested him and taken away his son. "You took everything I worked for, everything I fucking loved, every goddamn thing," he said. He claimed to have explosives with him. "If you come near this van, I'll blow the fuck out of it. Do you understand me now?"

Gordon had been off duty, working a second job as security for a nightclub, when he heard the call. Soon he was crouched beside a building near the Jack in the Box with his M4, prepared for a shoot-out. Suspects occasionally fired at the SWAT team, but usually while barricaded inside a house and usually because they wanted officers to go away. This man had come for the cops.

A supervisor summoned Gordon to negotiate with the guy. He ran back to his Tahoe, pulled out his phone, and took a couple of deep breaths, trying to slow his heart rate. He dialed the number and began as he always did. "I'm Officer Gordon with the Dallas police. What's going on today, man?"

When the guy first answered, he sounded so calm that Gordon thought he'd dialed the wrong number. Then the man launched into a litany of grievances. He told Gordon cops had arrested him for domestic violence, then a family court judge had taken away his eleven-year-old son. He'd lost his job, his house, everything. This was payback. Gordon listened for an hour, then two, trying to empathize, working to make some connection. By this point in his career, he'd come to believe outcomes depended little on what he said. More than anything, what Gordon did was listen. He'd focus on the voice coming over the line, using minimal encouragers to keep people talking. "Uh-huh, tell me more," he'd say. He'd reflect suspects' emotions back to them: "So what I hear you saying is . . ." He gave them something they often couldn't get from people in their own lives: sympathy, validation, compassion. "I understand," Gordon said again and again.

The man vacillated between calm and rage. He said he had twenty pounds of C4 with him. He said he'd tried to tell them where Osama bin Laden had been hiding. Every so often, supervisors walked by Gordon's Tahoe as the conversation played over its speakers. They told Gordon to keep talking; eventually, he'd wear the guy down. Gordon began to think that wasn't going to happen. Most people can't stay angry that long. They get tired. But crazy people are not on the same time line as everyone else, Gordon knew. They could remain in high emotion for hours or days. "We're not going to wear him down," Gordon told his supervisors. "He's going to wear us down."

Back at headquarters, police found a duffel bag the man had left behind in the parking lot. Since he'd claimed to have C4, police cordoned it off and maneuvered a robot over to it. As the robot's mechanical arm lifted the bag's strap, it exploded. Screws, nails, and shrapnel flew through the air, burning the front of a nearby car. The guy wasn't kidding.

When word of the pipe bomb reached the SWAT team back at the Jack in the Box, they began debating options for taking him out. One was to put an explosive device on a robot, drive it under the van, and blow it up. They decided instead to position snipers, armed with powerful .50-caliber rifles, the kind soldiers used in war. Their bullets could penetrate the van's thick windows. If the man's head popped up, he was done. But so far he'd stayed crouched out of view.

In three hours of talking, Gordon developed little rapport. But he'd begun to feel a sort of affection for the man. His name was James, and like many of the people Gordon negotiated with, he'd wrecked his life beyond repair. Classic pissed-off white guy, Gordon thought. Gordon asked him to come out with his hands up. Didn't he want to see his son again?

Gordon's lieutenant was running out of patience. He suggested a different approach. What if they tried to piss the guy off? Maybe they could goad him into detonating his explosives and blowing himself up. They had a sniper take a shot at the van's engine block. "What the fuck are you doing?" James said. "I've got a bomb in here!"

Gordon, switching gears, spoke to James like he'd never before talked to a suspect. "We just shot out your radiator, you stupid motherfucker. You're a fucking pussy. You're too much of a pussy to stick around for your son. Get your fucking ass out of the car, and be a fucking man."

The result was near instantaneous. Instead of getting mad, James turned childlike, hurt and vulnerable.

"I'm not a pussy," he said. "I love my son. I want to be here for him."

I got him, Gordon thought. Finally, they'd connected. *I can save him.*

"Let's end this," Gordon said. "It's time for you to come out."

"All right," James said. "Let me smoke a cigarette and think about it."

Gordon opened his car door. He needed to tell the lieutenant to get the snipers to stand down. He made it five steps before he heard the crack.

Gordon stopped, realizing instantly what had happened. The guy had felt it was safe to sit up. As soon as he'd lifted his head, a sniper pulled the trigger.

Gordon climbed into his Tahoe, leaned the seat back, and closed his eyes. He'd not only failed to save the guy, he'd talked him to his death. That was the sort of day when he heard his mother's voice, repeating one of her favorite lines. *You need to get yourself right with God, because time's winding up.*

* * *

On July 7, 2016, Gordon woke in the back bedroom of his brick home in Forney, a growing suburb twenty miles east of Dallas. He swung his feet off the bed, reached for the remote, and turned on *SportsCenter*.

Sports had always been Gordon's escape, but lately even that arena had become clouded. Politics, morning shows, Facebook—it seemed the whole country was talking about police shootings and the Black Lives Matter movement. Even LeBron had weighed in. He'd been playing for the Miami Heat in 2012 when seventeen-year-old Trayvon Martin had left a gated town house community in Sanford, Florida, to buy Skittles at a 7-Eleven. On his way home, wearing a hoodie, Martin had been shot by a neighborhood watch-man who thought he looked suspicious. LeBron and his teammates posed in hoodies in a photograph shared all over social media, joining in the national chorus of African Americans repeating the refrain "I am Trayvon."

Gordon thought LeBron's opinions were respectful and lacked the vitriol of other athletes and movie stars who, in Gordon's view, had been fanning the flames. *Grey's Anatomy* star Jesse Williams had given a speech at the BET awards, in which he'd said: "We know that police somehow manage to de-escalate, disarm, and not kill white people every day. So what's going to happen is we are going to have equal rights and justice in our own country, or we will restructure their function, and ours." The crowd roared, rising from their seats, and the speech went viral.

Williams's words troubled Gordon. To him, it sounded like a call to arms against cops. His wife's cousin posted a link to the speech on Facebook under the title "Awesomeness!" Gordon couldn't resist engaging. "When people say stuff like that, it makes my job harder and a lot more dangerous," he wrote beneath her post.

Gordon was forty-five years old and felt that tensions between minorities and cops were reaching a level he hadn't seen in twenty years on the force. He knew there were problems with how cops policed poor neighborhoods—he'd experienced them firsthand—but in recent years the conversation had been less about reform and more an all-out assault on the profession. Police had become the bad guys.

Lately, Gordon felt caught between warring camps. At work, he defended black people's gripes with law enforcement, explaining how even he still got pulled over while off duty. To relatives and friends, Gordon was always defending cops, trying to explain the use of force and the dangers of the job. He was too black to be blue, too blue to be black.

Gordon and his wife, Shan, had grown up in run-down apartment complexes where many of their friends had graduated to selling dope on street corners. Nearly every man in their families had served time. When they bought their first house in the neighborhood as newlyweds—he a rookie cop, she a special-education teacher—Gordon parked his patrol car out front and ran three miles every morning through the same streets he'd grown up on; neighbors joked he was the only black man they'd ever seen run without being chased. Shan's brother sold crack out of her grandmother's house next door. Every time Gordon put food on the grill, people showed up hungry. He felt as if everyone expected money, something he called the "black tax." Once you reached a certain economic status, the poor left behind expected you to share, to help pull them forward. Not doing so made you a sellout, an Uncle Tom. If a cousin needed $20 for gas, Gordon would gladly hand it over. But people wanted co-signatures on cars, $3,000 loans. He believed what the comedian Steve Harvey said: "The best thing you can do for poor people is not be one of them."

Gordon and Shan bought a lot in a subdivision called Heather Hollow at Windmill Farms, selecting a floor plan with a castle-like turret, four bedrooms, and a two-car garage. It had beige walls, ten-foot ceilings, and granite countertops. Shan decorated with framed family photographs and her favorite sayings. LIVE WELL, LAUGH OFTEN, LOVE MUCH.

When they first moved in, Gordon kept walking outside, astonished by the quiet. He'd spent most of his life in crowded apartments, with neighbors yelling, bass bumping, guns going off. Heather Hollow was eerily quiet. No stray dogs, no cars on lawns, no duct-taped bumpers. Everywhere Gordon looked, he saw order and discipline. He loved putting a steak on the backyard grill, sipping a Blue Moon, and staring at his grass, which he paid people to mow. With its neatly spaced oaks and elms, Heather Hollow was what he'd grown up dreaming of. While off duty, driving his three kids to sports games and drill team practice on weekends, he stopped carrying his Sig Sauer.

The family still attended church in their hometown of Terrell, about twelve miles east, and visited regularly, but they told few where they lived. They joked they were in hiding from their families. Gordon bought a used white Mercedes and listened to old-school R&B while driving the kids to school. One morning, the kids asked him to turn on Taylor Swift. "Oh, you want to listen to white people music?" he joked. "Well, Daddy," his teenage daughter said, "you didn't raise us to be black."

Gordon didn't like how it sounded, but she was right. He and Shan had purposely chosen a neighborhood that was at least half white. They wanted to raise their children as "culturally neutral," able to exist in either world. It was a tricky place to be. They didn't quite fit in with the white families in Heather Hollow; Gordon sensed his presence made some neighbors uncomfortable, as if his family had stolen a key to their secret world. And they no longer fit in with the people they'd grown up with, who Gordon felt resented his Mercedes and the family's Caribbean cruise vacations.

On this morning, as Gordon rose to shower and shave, Facebook buzzed with news of another fatal police shooting, Philando Castile shot in his Oldsmobile in Minnesota. The phone calls to Gordon started early, as they did every time a new video hit the news. Friends and relatives wanted to know what the hell was going on. Why were cops so intent on killing them?

Gordon stepped inside his walk-in closet to get dressed. Unlike many of his SWAT colleagues, he routinely had his department-issued cargo pants, called BDUs, dry-cleaned. Today he picked out an old pair because he knew he'd be lying in the dirt. His SWAT unit that day was holding its quarterly rifle qualification, a target-shooting exercise. Though his specialty was crisis and hostage nego-tiations, he still had to shoot. He picked up his gear and hurried out of the house, hoping not to be late.

2

The Police Chief

In his sixth-floor office at police headquarters, Chief David Brown clicked through e-mails about the most noteworthy crimes overnight, an armed robbery, a double shooting of two juveniles, a possible gay bashing. But the biggest news was the two police shootings elsewhere that week—one in Louisiana, the other in Minnesota. Both had been captured on cell phone cameras and shared around the world.

The first of the week's shootings had happened that Tuesday outside a Baton Rouge convenience store. A caller told a 911 dispatcher that he'd been threatened by an armed man who was selling CDs in the parking lot. After police arrived, a bystander recorded an officer wrestling the man to the ground. As officers pinned the man on the pavement, one could be heard saying, "He's got a gun, gun!" and, "Bro, if you fucking move, I swear to God." Then three pops, a pause, and three more, as an officer fatally shot the man point-blank. The video traveled across Facebook and Twitter, and the man's name, Alton Sterling, became another rallying cry. "This is what lynchings look like in 2016!" tweeted 49ers quarterback

Colin Kaepernick. The FBI and the U.S. Department of Justice announced civil rights investigations, and the Louisiana governor weighed in: "The video is disturbing, to say the least."

On Wednesday, another video hit, this one recorded by Castile's girlfriend in Minnesota. She broadcasted live on Facebook, "We got pulled over for a busted tail light in the back and the police just . . . they killed my boyfriend." Handcuffed on the sidewalk, her phone still recording, the woman began to cry and pray. "I ask that you cover him, Lord, that you allow him to be still here with us, Lord. Still we need him. I need him." She kept broadcasting from the back of a patrol car, still in handcuffs, as her four-year-old daughter told her, "It's okay, I'm right here with you."

That Thursday morning, Brown received an e-mail from a black editorial writer at the local newspaper, the *Dallas Morning News*. The subject line was in all caps: PHILANDO CASTILE, ALTON STERLING. "To say that I'm frustrated and frightened is an understatement," the e-mail said. "I'm really struggling on what more we can say to our readers, our sons, our daughters on these cases."

Brown began a reply: "I just read and reread the same news . . . don't know if words can do justice to any of this." At fifty-five, the chief had a stern, quiet temperament, maintained a shiny bald head, and wore dark-rimmed Buddy Holly glasses. A black man born in Dallas, Brown grew up on the city's poorer southern side. Dallas feels less like a city than a collection of loosely joined villages and, like big cities across America, is sharply segregated by class and skin color. When demographers created color-coded maps of the city based on race, they were stunning in their clarity—well-off white sections in the north, poor black neighborhoods in the south, Hispanic enclaves in the east and west. Then, in the center of the city, on an island of whiteness, the wealthy Park Cities, two distinct municipalities with their own police forces and elected councils, sharing a school district. One historian described Dallas as "distinctly un-unified." The neighborhood Brown grew up in, South Oak Cliff, was south of the city's muddy Trinity River, long a dividing line between blacks and whites. Many of the city's black residents, 24 percent of the population, still live south of the river, a legacy of Jim Crow–era "Negro districts" carved out of largely undesirable land. At one point in the early '20s, the Ku Klux Klan claimed Dallas as its most active chapter nationwide.

* * *

Brown joined the police department in the early 1980s as a street cop, chasing crack dealers in his own neighborhood. He spent several years as a crime scene investigator when the city's murder rate was off the charts, pointing his camera at scores of mangled bodies, dusting for fingerprints, examining blood spatter. He spent those years covered in the stench of death and learned how to forget it. He spent time as a supervisor on SWAT before becoming a community policing supervisor. In that post, he patrolled a large, low-income housing development on foot and became a convert to the philosophies of community policing, the idea that cops and residents should get to know each other and work together to stop crime. If the system worked, when somebody got shot, residents trusted cops enough to tell them who'd done it. Brown had faced more than his share of tragedy. He'd lost a former partner gunned down on the job in 1988. His younger brother was killed by a drug dealer in Phoenix a few years later. And in 2010, weeks into his tenure as chief, his son, a twenty-seven-year-old with bipolar disorder, killed a cop and another man in a neighboring city before being fatally shot by officers.

During his ascent through the ranks, supervisors praised Brown for his professionalism, steadfastness, and dependability. Brown kept to himself, and when he became a supervisor, he developed a reputation as dictatorial, abrasive, and vindictive. Cross him, and you might find yourself working midnights in a far-flung precinct. He made few close friends at the department. He was seen around town in restaurants eating alone.

As a thirty-three-year veteran who hadn't skipped a step up the chain, Brown understood the department in a way few of his predecessors had. What he understood now, in the summer of 2016, was that his job was in peril. After a dozen years of lows, crime was on the rise. Murders and aggravated assaults were making more headlines, reflecting a national uptick. Response times were the worst in a decade. The Texas governor offered to send troopers to Dallas to help.

To make matters worse, cops were quitting by the hundreds. They'd long put up with lower pay than nearby departments because of a generous pension—after working thirty years, many retired as millionaires. But now, after too many risky real estate investments, the pension was foundering.

A moment that helped define Brown's time as chief was a Ferguson-like incident that happened about two years into his tenure, on a hot July afternoon in 2012. Police had gotten into an unusual number of shootings that year—fifteen by summer—and had killed seven people. One afternoon, officers responded to a 911 call to a drug house on one of the city's poorest blocks, in a neighborhood called Dixon Circle. An officer chased a suspect down an alley, over several fences, and into a horse corral. They fought along the way and kept fighting in the animal pen. The officer, who was white, fired his gun. The suspect, a thirty-one-year-old black man, collapsed in a pile of dirt and manure. The man had been a Robin Hood–like figure in the neighborhood, passing out turkeys at Thanksgiving. Now he lay in the dirt covered in flies, two circles of blood on the back of his white tank top. A rumor quickly circulated that he'd been shot in the back. Crowds grew larger by the hour and police arrived with helmets and riot shields.

Chief Brown pulled back as many officers as he could, to avoid inflaming tensions. Within hours, he told the public what he knew. An eyewitness, an elderly black woman who lived in the neighborhood, said the officer had been fighting for his life. It appeared the officer had shot the suspect in the stomach—not the back. The chief released the names of both the suspect and the officer. He emphasized the officer's actions would be reviewed by a grand jury. With the help of area pastors who urged calm, the chief and his team persuaded neighbors to go back into their homes. He and other city leaders felt as if they'd narrowly escaped a riot.

After Dixon Circle, the chief doubled down on his community policing efforts. He implemented mandatory Taser training, purchased body cameras, and drafted a stricter policy for when officers could chase suspects. He also ordered more record keeping when officers used force so the department could better track trends. He released years of police shooting data on a public website. He required his commanders to attend bias training, and he provided de-escalation training to officers. And he kept putting resources into building relationships with minority communities—midnight basketball with teens, boxing and girl-empowerment clubs, summer internships, a youth choir.

While the strategies endeared Brown to politicians and activists, they were sneered at by many in his rank and file. He fired dozens of cops during his six years as chief, including a popular white female officer who'd shot an unarmed black teenager who was a passenger in a stolen car. From his hospital bed, the teen said he'd been shot after raising his hands to surrender, an account corroborated by an eyewitness. The chief's handling of the matter brought scorn from the Dallas Police Association, whose president complained, "Instead of handcuffing the criminals, we're handcuffing the officers, literally and figuratively." A grand jury indicted the officer for aggravated assault, marking the first time a cop had been criminally charged in an on-duty shooting in Dallas since the 1970s. The officer later pleaded guilty to a reduced misdemeanor of discharging a firearm.

Critics accused Brown of "de-policing" the city, so that officers were afraid to chase suspects or react aggressively. Worse, as far as many veteran officers were concerned, was the chief's strategy of deploying cops for patrol assignments in the city's crime hotspots. The number crunchers at headquarters would figure where offenses were picking up, and Brown would divert detectives and SWAT team members to patrol in hotspots. The efforts improved statistics in the short term, allowing the chief to deliver rosy reports to the City Council. But the drain on investigative resources left more crimes unsolved and hammered morale. Lately it seemed everyone in town was calling for the chief's resignation. Even representatives of the local Black Police Association—longtime, loyal supporters—had abandoned him.

Brown expected July 7 to be another day of triage, figuring out which of the blooming crime hotspots most demanded his dwindling number of troops. But in his office, e-mails about the police shootings elsewhere kept coming. A local television station wanted him to appear on its 5:00 p.m. newscast. Pastors wanted him to speak to congregations. A black supervisor in the city's accounts payable division wanted his advice on what to tell her children.

"I woke up to my wife crying," tweeted Elijah E. Cummings, U.S. representative from Maryland.

"Something is profoundly wrong," Hillary Clinton said on Facebook.

"WE ARE SICK AND TIRED OF THE KILLINGS OF YOUNG MEN AND WOMEN IN OUR COMMUNITIES," Beyoncé wrote in an open letter.

President Obama weighed in from Warsaw: "All of us, as

Americans, should be troubled by these shootings, because these are not isolated incidents."

Chief Brown was troubled. In his response to the newspaper writer's e-mail, he said he'd found the Castile video upsetting. "The girlfriend's praying and the four-year-old's words got to me, I must say," he wrote.

As morning stretched into afternoon, Brown learned about protests planned that night in cities across the country, including Dallas. That complicated his crime-fighting plans. Instead of deploying troops to hotspots, the chief would need to divert at least one hundred officers to the protest. He also needed to decide whether to send SWAT. Anti-cop sentiment was running high, and it would be reasonable to station snipers on rooftops and park armored cars around the perimeter. But SWAT stood out in their heavy black vests, helmets, and M4s. The chief had been no fan of the images from Missouri after Michael Brown's death, where police with tanks and tear gas looked like soldiers.

The chief's intelligence officers, after meeting with protest organizers and monitoring social media, deemed the potential for violence low. SWAT, instead of deploying to the protest, would continue with hotspot duty.

Brown drafted an e-mail to the mayor and city manager, telling them he expected about six hundred protesters in a city park that night. "The black community all over the country is on edge, very angry about recent shootings," he wrote. "We have worked to have great relationships but this is a very sensitive time for police/community relations."

3

The Protester

Shetamia Taylor got up early on July 7. She'd already ironed her yellow blouse and capri pants, preparing for another eight-hour shift at the distribution center of Conn's, a furniture and appliance chain. Her husband, a tow-truck driver, was still asleep. She was scrolling through Facebook when she saw the latest police shooting video, shared by many of her friends. She clicked.

Taylor was thirty-eight, a mother of four boys. She'd grown up in a middle-class suburb in Louisiana, daughter of a high school principal and an elementary school teacher. Hers had been the only black family on the block when David Duke, former grand wizard of the Ku Klux Klan, was running for governor. Racism wasn't something her parents talked about at the dinner table. If it came up, her father, a Vietnam War veteran, would try to lighten the mood with a joke. Be a good person, respect authority, work hard, and you'll be fine, he told his kids.

Taylor mostly believed that. She'd lived for seven years in a small, mostly white town in Minnesota, about two hours southeast of where Castile had been pulled over. She loved the hills and lakes and trees and fresh air, but she did not love being one of the few black people there. Every time she went out to run errands or grocery shop, she felt like she was onstage as people turned their heads to look. She was pulled over repeatedly, several times by the same white officer. She complained to the department, which did nothing as far as she could tell, but she tried not to let it bother her. She got married and moved to Texas in 2008.

She'd followed the news about the police shootings over the past few years and watched all the videos. In many cases, she could pinpoint a reason why that wouldn't happen to her own boys, twelve, fourteen, fifteen, and eighteen. Eric Garner, it seemed to her, had been resisting arrest when New York City police put him in a fatal chokehold. Twelve-year-old Tamir Rice, sad as his death was, had been holding what looked like a real gun. Alton Sterling had been a felon with a firearm. Clearly, there was a problem. She found the footage distressing and didn't think any of them deserved to be killed. But none of those videos challenged her belief that if her boys kept straight they would be fine. She'd had discussions with each of them about how they should behave when interacting with cops. Be polite, and do what they said. Don't invite trouble. Give others, including cops, the benefit of the doubt. "Closed mouth, open mind," she often said. "That gets you a long way in life."

But the Castile video had shaken her. Castile's girlfriend, Diamond Reynolds, was respectful and courteous to the officer, calling him "sir" as her boyfriend sat dying in the driver's seat. It was the officer who seemed out of control, yelling and hollering. This couple had been driving home from the grocery store on a Wednesday night, and now the man was dead. Watching the video, Taylor looked into the woman's eyes and listened to her voice, earnest and composed in such a violent, chaotic situation. The woman, her genuineness, the intimacy of the video, affected Taylor hundreds of miles away, and tears rolled down her cheeks.

Watching it made her feel vulnerable in a way the other police-shooting videos had not. *They really are killing us,* Taylor thought. It made her question whether she and her husband and her boys actually were safe. *Lord, have I done everything I need to do so that these children know how to act when they leave this house?* She felt as if she could no longer sit on her hands. *We have to do something. I have to do something. What?*

She went back to her bedroom to get dressed for work, walking past the yellow capri pants she'd laid out. It didn't feel like a day for yellow. She put on a black shirt, black pants, and black shoes.

She thought about the video as she drove to work. She arrived and greeted three black women whose cubicles adjoined hers. "Have y'all seen that video?" she asked. The women hadn't. "Come here," she said, pulling out her phone. They leaned into the center of the cubicle to watch. One started crying; another shook her head. Their white manager, sitting nearby at his desk, saw what they were doing. "He was a criminal!" he yelled. He thought the women were watching the Alton Sterling video.

"Not today," Taylor yelled back. "I am not in the mood today." Taylor turned back to the women. "We've got to do something," she said. "This is too much."

After lunch, Taylor saw on Facebook that protesters had planned a rally downtown that night. Taylor decided to go and take her boys. One thing Taylor could do, she thought, was teach them that they had a voice and could use it in a productive way. After she got home, she ran upstairs to tell her husband about the protest. "We're gonna go," she told him. "Nah," he said. "It's too hot." She was going anyway. She told her kids to put some Totino's pizza in the oven and get ready to leave.

Her oldest, eighteen-year-old Kavion, had watched the Castile video. She didn't want him to feel bitter or helpless, nor did she want any of her boys to fear or hate cops. They would go to the rally to protest police brutality—not police officers. There was an important difference, she told them. There were good and bad apples on the police force, just like everywhere else. They would go to show their support for Castile's girlfriend and all she was going through. They would speak out against that particular officer's actions and help prod authorities to hold him accountable.

Just after 6:00 p.m., Taylor and her boys climbed into their Dodge Caravan and headed to downtown Dallas.

4

Dallas SWAT

SWAT Senior Cpl. Matt Banes pulled into the firearms training compound, his Tahoe bouncing over the gravel drive. The gun range sat on a couple dozen acres southwest of Dallas, a hilly landscape of mesquite and cedar trees along the banks of Mountain Creek Lake. Above the main pistol range, a hand-painted wooden sign hung over a fresh row of paper targets: IF YOU AIN'T HITTIN, YOU AIN'T WINNIN. Most officers went their whole careers without having to fire their service weapon on duty. If they did have to unholster their weapon and shoot another human being, it often happened in less than two seconds. An eternity could unfold inside the seconds it took to slide off the safety, put a finger on the trigger, and squeeze. Once the sequence had been executed, the officer crossed a complicated line. It might have been self-defense, it might have been justified, but the officer could not escape the fact that he'd killed a human being. It bothered many deep down in ways they didn't often talk about.

Banes, in his fifteen years as a cop, had been in two shootings; he'd killed one suspect and wounded another. As he drove through the barbed-wire gates of the range, he passed a metal-sided armory where range masters handed out earplugs and ammo, then he ascended a small hill to a back parking lot. This part of the range had been claimed by Dallas SWAT. The men over the years had constructed their own training compound from scratch, lugging in cement blocks and two-by-fours. They'd built a rambling house with changeable rooms and hallways where they practiced entry drills. The team had gathered stacks of old doors that they practiced slamming with battering rams and blowing open with explosives. They'd built a sixty-three-foot rappelling tower to practice scaling buildings and dropping out of windows.

Since his time at the academy, Banes had dreamed of joining SWAT. For officers, SWAT was the equivalent of making partner at a law firm, the apex of a policing career. Hundreds tried out for a rare opening, but only a few were chosen. Officers had to be exceptional marksmen and in top physical shape. That was hard enough. More important, they had to demonstrate a tactical mind and the ability to think clearly in moments of extreme stress.

Officers who didn't have the SWAT dream as recruits often acquired it during early years on patrol. A cop would race out to some god-awful scene, where a bad guy was terrorizing his wife or children or neighbors. The cop would watch the SWAT guys roll up in their armored personnel carriers, hanging off the sides with their M4s, muscles flexing beneath their heavy entry vests, hair perfectly fixed as if they'd taken an extra moment with the blow-dryer before heading out to save the world. They'd ride past that cop and silently communicate that they were tougher, quicker, better. So much better, in fact, that the patrol cop barely warranted a glance as they rolled past the plastic perimeter tape and went to handle the problem. A couple of hours later, they'd roll out more smugly, if that was even possible, leaving behind the mess and the paperwork. SWAT had a saying: When citizens got in trouble they called 911. When police got in trouble they called SWAT. The team was the city's last line of defense. No unit on DPD was more respected or reviled. Other cops tended to despise SWAT officers almost as much as they wanted to be them.

But lately, in this era of police protests, SWAT had been feeling particularly maligned and unappreciated. With their big guns and crates of explosives, SWAT teams had become law enforcement's guilty secret. They were the essence of what people no longer wanted on their police forces, beefy men with soldiers' tools. As the pendulum swung toward community policing, the warriors were being left behind. It seemed as if Chief Brown, who'd once been a formidable SWAT sergeant, had turned on them. The team kept shrinking, now down to four squads and forty men. The chief had taken away their weekly training sessions and daily workouts, sending them instead to patrol duty. To men who were invested in their biceps, this was galling. It was also, in their view, dangerous. Fully geared up, their equipment weighed about sixty pounds, carried on their backs and legs, often in searing heat. Being in top physical shape was essential.

It was also true, though, that SWAT was what many imagined it to be, a lagoon of testosterone and toxic masculinity. The officers listened to heavy metal while grunting through their workouts. Some quoted the movie *Dumb and Dumber* endlessly. They traded pictures of naked blondes dancing with AR-15s. They drew pictures of penises on everything—white boards, lockers, helmets. Very elaborate, lifelike ones. SWAT guys had to have enough testosterone to rip down doors, barge into drug houses, and deal with heavy equipment and explosives under threat of violence. Everything they did was physically intense. Everything they handled could hurt them. In moments of calm, that level of testosterone, for some, was difficult to tame.

On this sunny morning at the rifle range, the heat already pulling beads of sweat from his skin, Banes stood outside his marked police Tahoe, gearing up. He put on his helmet, eye protection, gas mask, tactical belt, rifle, and pistol. He was five feet nine, 175 pounds, and clean shaven with a shiny bald head. He was one of the newest officers on the team and did not yet feel as if he'd been fully accepted into the fraternity. Some teammates called him Skeeter because of his East Texas roots and country accent. He was in no rush to join his squad on the firing line. As Banes saw it, these quarterly rifle qualifications were just another dick-measuring contest. *Let's get this shit over with*, he thought.

Despite being a seasoned veteran, he still felt a flutter of nervousness before every rifle qualification. As an undercover narcotics officer, Banes had spent years entering the homes of armed drug dealers while wearing cowboy boots and a T-shirt, a pistol hidden in his waistband. He could do this without hesitation, though a shot or two of Jim Beam never hurt. On narcotics, they'd get together after work to drink beer and see who could belch the loudest. SWAT guys wanted to go to CrossFit and see who could do the most burpees.

Being on a firing line with a group of geared-up SWAT guys tended to mess with Banes's head. Most SWAT officers thrived in competition, rose to it, bloomed in it. Not Banes. He found it difficult to perform with people calling him, drill-sergeant-style, an idiot and a fucking moron. When Banes got stuck in an alpha standoff, which happened weekly if not daily, he tended to yield. Sometimes he felt like he was in a *South Park* episode with a bunch of boys making *hoo hoo* grunting noises and chest bumping like primates. "If it's that important for you to be King Ding-a-Ling," he'd say to himself, "then have at it, asshole."

He walked toward the firing line where he would complete a series of timed drills. He had to achieve 95 percent accuracy to keep a spot on the squad. That wasn't difficult for any of these men; most scored a perfect 100 every time. What they competed over, because everything was a competition, was who could get the most shots inside the x-ring, a 3-inch circle in the center of their paper targets. Also called the "ghost ring," it was barely visible from twenty-five yards, and nearly impossible to make out from farther distances. Every SWAT officer yearned to put all fifty shots inside the x-ring, a feat rarely accomplished. Part of it was their weapon, the M4, which had a relatively short 10.5-inch barrel, good for close-quarters combat but not the most accurate on long-distance shots. Still, some came close. For years the record was held by Misty VanCuren, one of the few women in the team's history, who'd hit forty-two x-rings in a rifle qualification about a decade earlier. The team's current ace, a former U.S. Marine sniper named Garret Hellinger, routinely scored forty-five and held the current record of forty-eight.

Banes was wildly inconsistent. Sometimes he came in among the top shooters, with thirty-eight x-rings, and sometimes he scored among the lowest. Once his sergeant, a supervisor he'd believed to be no more dangerous with a pistol than with a bottle of Windex, had challenged Banes during a qualification, and to his great embarrassment he'd lost. His teammates offered prodigious scorn, some of it quiet—men turning away while shaking their heads—some of it loud. "Fucking Banes needs remedial."

Banes took his spot on the firing line, a flat strip of patchy grass divided into nineteen lanes and ending in a mound of dirt to catch the rounds. Above each lane hung a paper target. The most senior SWAT guys got first pick of position, usually selecting an outer lane, #1 or #19. That decreased their chances of hitting a teammate's target to the left or right, which wasn't hard to do from one hundred yards and resulted in an automatic fail. As one of the newer guys, Banes crammed in the middle. A team leader called out: "Lock and load, shooters make ready."

The words always gave him a small adrenaline dump. He inserted a magazine into his pistol and chambered a round into his rifle, which hung by a sling across his shoulder. He raised the rifle and dialed his optic to the proper setting. He got in a fighting stance, knees slightly bent, shoulders curled forward into his rifle, focusing downrange on his target. In a long-standing tradition, the officer who scored lowest would pick up lunch for his entire squad. Banes hoped it wouldn't be him again. His wife was still annoyed by that $300 charge a few months back at Pappadeaux Seafood.

"Shooters, stand by." The line fell quiet. Rifle stock snug on his shoulder, Banes lifted his M4 into a low ready position and waited for the timer to sound.

BEEP.

Everybody dropped. Banes went to his knees then lay prone, stomach flat on the grass. He took a second to align his spine with his muzzle, hoping to achieve a natural point of aim. He rolled the safety off with his thumb and inhaled half a breath. If he inhaled too much, his chest would rise too high off the ground, throwing off his aim. He fired his first shot. Then another. He tried to keep a smooth cadence, one pull every three seconds. The sound of more than a dozen M4s exploded across the range as rounds hammered the paper targets. Then it was quiet, and Banes exhaled. He lifted himself off the ground, back to the line.

"On safe. Let 'em hang," the team leader said, reminding officers to put their rifles on safety and point their muzzles downward.

It was time for the hundred-yard walk to discover which of Banes's inner warriors had shown up, the ace or the idiot. He often could gauge how he'd done by the feel of the rifle's recoil against his shoulder—*I think I pulled my third round a little low right*—but today he'd felt smooth. Usually his teammates walked downrange casually, relaxed, and making small talk. Banes would speed walk, anxious to see how he'd performed. Now, as he approached his target, studying the small grouping around the bull's-eye, he relaxed. Lunch wouldn't be on him today. He walked back to the fifty-yard line to prepare for the next sequence.

After it was over, Banes stood in the parking lot, taking off his gear. He'd done well—a perfect 100, with thirty-four x-rings. Usually after a qualification, he broke down his rifle and cleaned it, popping out the pins, greasing it down. Today, he didn't have time for a full cleaning, so he snaked out the barrel one time and poured lube over the bolt carrier group. He didn't want it to dry and seize up next time he had to use it.

* * *

After the rifle qualification, Banes went to lunch with the others as they waited for their afternoon assignment. They walked into Dodie's in their gear and sat around a long wooden table. Banes dreaded the moment when the waitress would appear with her notepad. His favorite dish, angel hair pasta with Cajun shrimp and a side of broccoli, was called the My Little Sky. It made the guys snicker every time he ordered.

The teammate most likely to give Banes a hard time was Gerry Huante, considered by many to be SWAT's toughest. At forty-six, he was one of the older guys but could outperform most in their CrossFit workouts. He was six feet and 215 pounds of taut muscle, much of it tattooed with swirling designs depicting good and evil; along his left arm, a dove faced off with a raven. If asked to name their one foxhole pick, most would select Huante. Not because they enjoyed his company, but because he'd give them their best shot at coming out alive. He was a beast physically, a genius tactically. He often was the leader of the entry team, the most dangerous job on SWAT. While he had the skills to be a squad leader, he lacked the temperament. He'd fought nearly every guy on the team and called nearly every sergeant and lieutenant—even a deputy chief or two—a moron, or a fucking moron, to their faces.

Huante took special pleasure in harassing new guys, and lately his focus had been Banes. Huante had appointed himself the arbiter of whether a guy was tough enough to be on SWAT. Teammates did not always approve of Huante's hazing rituals, but they served a purpose. If you could survive Huante, you could be trusted when bullets started flying. Huante was constantly grabbing Banes, pushing him, pulling him into bear hugs. It masqueraded as friendly horseplay but felt to Banes like it had an edge. Usually at some point during lunch, Banes would push back his chair to go to the restroom. Huante would grab his arm, circling his wrist or biceps in a death grip, and he'd sit there smiling, still chewing on his food. Banes knew, as did the rest of SWAT, that what happened next was up to Banes. He could submit and sit back down or he could resist. If he resisted, he and Huante would soon be rolling across the table in their police uniforms, punching each other as a restaurant full of people watched. That was the thing about Huante. He didn't care. He never backed down. So Banes did.

As they waited for lunch, talk turned to the latest police shooting video, this one out of Minnesota, and the protest scheduled for downtown that night. Many of them were fed up with Black Lives Matter. They'd worked late the night before and had come in early for the rifle qualification. They were irritated they might have to spend another night away from their families so people could shout about police. But during lunch, they got word that they wouldn't police the protest and would continue instead with hotspot duty. Then the men started complaining about that. What boneheaded commander had made that decision? Calling off SWAT while hundreds of anti-police protesters swarmed their city? Banes sat quietly and listened to the men complain. *First you bitch because we're going to the protest. Now you bitch because we're not. You miserable sons of bitches are always bitching.*

Banes waited to see if Gordon, their negotiator, would chime in. Gordon was one of two black officers on their squad of ten. The other, a team leader, never talked much about race. But Gordon did.

Gordon watched the videos of every shooting and loved to discuss the details.

Banes liked Gordon, considered him one of his closest friends on the team. Although they came from different worlds—Gordon kid from a poor black neigborhood, Banes a white country boy from East Texas—they found it easy to joke about race. Gordon might greet Banes at lunch by saying, "Hey Banes, how many crosses did y'all burn this weekend?" Banes might reply, "Not as many fried chickens and watermelons as y'all ate." Banes once shined a flashlight on Gordon in a dark restaurant in a mock effort to make sure, considering Gordon's dark skin, that the waitress could see him. Despite the banter, Banes felt as if there were a racial undercurrent that the men couldn't laugh their way out of, a silent suspicion of things unsaid, thoughts held back.

When they discussed the high-profile shootings of recent years, Banes often found himself surprised by Gordon's thoughts, never knowing which side he'd come down on. Sometimes he played the role of defense attorney for the cops, a passionate, staunch champion of the officer. Other times he was the fiercest anti-police prosecutor. Today, it seemed, Gordon was leaning toward the latter. He thought Castile was one of the worst shootings he'd ever seen, he told the others.

Banes didn't like to second-guess other police officers. He'd been down enough dark alleys, stared into enough gun barrels, to know that sometimes you had to make split-second decisions and pray. He thought Black Lives Matter was making an already difficult job even more dangerous. Large swaths of the community seemed to believe that cops like him went to work every day hoping to murder black people. He thought the rhetoric was making police officers scared and soft. Banes had no problem with the images that had come out of Ferguson, the ones where cops looked like soldiers. Cities could use more of that, not less. What happened to the sheriff being in charge? *If you loot stores, then we're going to squash you.* People wanted to strip aggression and violence from policing. They seemed not to understand the darkness that cops encountered every day. The best way to fight evil, Banes believed, was with violence.

He'd grown tired of SWAT callouts, drunk men barricaded inside their houses with shotguns, husbands and wives attacking each other with knives, crazy people off their meds. Night after night his cell would ring, and he'd leave his wife and sons and drive across the city through the dark. He began to feel as if he were getting summoned to help the same person over and over. The same sorry actor on a different stage. Banes found himself losing patience. Everyone faces struggle—death and divorce and custody battles and financial problems and Mother Nature. He wanted to shout inside these houses: *Can't you just handle your life and be a fucking man?*

Over time, Banes stopped rushing out for calls. He'd turn on the coffeepot first. He'd drive over to a bridge where a man was threatening to jump, a man who'd gotten him out of bed twice before, and he'd look around at his teammates strapping on their rappelling gear, looking dedicated and serious. All Banes wanted to do was shout up to the guy, "Jump, motherfucker! Jump!"

He'd teach at the police academy and see cadets in their skinny jeans, young men he doubted could drive a manual transmission or change a car tire. These were the men who were becoming police chiefs and administrators, making no-chase policies, no-cuss policies. When were they going to start handing out pink guns? In his early years of policing, Banes felt like they did real police work. If you ran from police and got caught, you might get a few licks. Suspects knew it and didn't complain.

As the presidential election neared, Banes hoped Republicans would retake the White House. He thought Obama had set law enforcement back years by giving credibility to Black Lives Matter, which Banes saw as siding with the criminals over the cops. Obama and his Democrats were all about handouts, lax drug laws, and lighter sentences, Banes believed. Most cops he knew supplemented their paychecks by working extra jobs, directing traffic at schools, providing security at nightclubs, running themselves ragged to provide for their families. It galled Banes, patrolling neighborhoods where, as he saw it, too many able-bodied people sat around watching huge televisions with a million cable channels, collecting food stamps and getting free medical care at the city's charity hospital, their bills footed by taxpayers. Banes was shocked when it appeared Donald Trump might capture the Republican nomination—he considered the New York tycoon too much of a "loudmouth shit talker"—but he did like that Trump appeared pro–law enforcement, pro–border patrol, and pro-military.

Banes paid his lunch tab and climbed into his Tahoe. He headed to hotspot duty, prepared for another shift of sitting beneath oak trees, watching squirrels.

5

The Trauma Surgeon

Dr. Brian Williams kissed his wife and daughter good-bye and walked out of his four-bedroom house into the afternoon light. He climbed into his silver Honda and placed his hospital lanyard, one with his photograph identifying him as a doctor, around his neck. He always did this when he got in the car, whether he was driving to work or not. He'd also listed his status as a military veteran on his driver's license, and he'd bought a U.S. Air Force Academy frame for his rear plate to signal he was a graduate. He deployed these markers like hopeful talismans in case police pulled him over.

Williams was the only black doctor on a team of twelve trauma surgeons at Parkland, a public hospital that served mostly poor, minority patients. It was where President Kennedy was rushed the day he was assassinated. Williams had done this drive a hundred times, but today he was particularly aware of his rituals. He'd watched the two recent police shooting videos and could not shake the image of Castile dying in the Oldsmobile. With the amount of blood on Castile's shirt, Williams knew a bullet must have hit a major blood vessel in his chest, causing his organs to fail one after another. As long as Castile had been awake, he'd been in terrible pain, Williams thought. It was one thing to see such a death in the emergency room, another to see it on Facebook. The video felt so intrusive, so voyeuristic. *This guy is dying a miserable death, and it's being broadcast live.*

Williams had been watching these kinds of videos since Rodney King in 1991, but now they happened more regularly and seemed to play endlessly. Williams didn't talk much about race, even with his closest friends. He had a résumé of accolades—an honors degree in aeronautical engineering, a prestigious surgical residency at Harvard—and he'd been successful in part by not calling attention to his skin color. He'd been "code switching" long before he knew there was a name for it, trying to leave his blackness behind when he entered the hospital, so that his colleagues—mostly white—could find no fault with his speech, mannerisms, or viewpoints. But the videos were bringing back for Williams memories of all the times his skin color had mattered.

He'd grown up on military bases across the world, from Albuquerque to Okinawa to Honolulu, as his father served in the U.S. Air Force. The bases were diverse and integrated; his parents' friends were a mix of racial and ethnic backgrounds. But there were incidents, a few of which would never leave him. When Williams was about five years old, he approached a white child on a playground. The boy's mother ushered him away as Williams looked on, confused. His own mother tried to explain: *She doesn't want him to play with you because you're black.* A few years later, on another base in another city, Williams tried to join a pickup baseball game at a neighborhood park. One of the boys looked at him and shook his head. "We're not letting any niggers on the team today," he said. Williams realized early on that his skin color meant something, although it took him years to understand what.

Williams excelled in school and earned a spot at the Air Force

Academy. In basic training he learned to shoot an M16, how to march, how to run five miles while singing songs with fellow cadets. Studying aeronautical engineering required learning math that made calculus look like child's play. He graduated with military honors in 1991 and spent the next six years in the air force, running classified missions as a test flight engineer on F-16 fighters. It was during this time, in his twenties, that he had the first of several encounters with police.

While driving to visit his sister, he was stopped one night in rural Alabama for speeding. Blue lights flashed, and he pulled over on a dark road. He waited for what felt like an eternity, then saw another police car arrive as backup. Williams sat with his hands at ten and two o'clock on the steering wheel as his heart thumped. Nothing happened, but the encounter left him rattled, mostly because he'd been terrified he might get hurt. For his white friends, not getting a ticket during a traffic stop was a win. For Williams, if he only got a ticket, he was thrilled. Another time, while driving back to base in Florida, Williams was pulled over for running a red light. In civilian clothes, he kept his hands on the wheel, no sudden movements. The cop asked him to step out of his car, then directed him to stand spread-eagle, hands on his hood, while he ran his license and registration. Williams did as he was told, and again nothing happened, but it was humiliating to stand like that on the side of the road. He wondered if the cop would have demanded the same of a white man.

At twenty-eight, Williams entered medical school at the University of South Florida. During his first cadaver dissection, holding a 10-blade scalpel and tracing a line down the torso, he'd been awed by the beautiful complexity of a human beneath the skin. He was among about eight minorities in his class of one hundred twenty in 1997. Few professors or doctors looked like him. A couple of times, when he entered hospital rooms with trainees, patients told the group that they did not want Williams involved in their treatment or exams. They never said it was because he was black, but as the only minority it seemed the obvious reason. He'd excuse himself, humiliated but feeling patients' wishes should be respected. One time a white female resident spoke up. "Absolutely not," she told the patient. "This is a teaching hospital, and he is a student, and he gets to stay."

He did his residency at Harvard, then spent two years as a fellow at Emory University in Atlanta. He lost track of the number of times black patients or their families told him he was the first black doctor they'd ever seen. Some grabbed his hand, got teary, and told him they were proud. Those moments made up for other unpleasant ones. Once, when he walked into a hospital room wearing a white coat, a patient's wife took one look at him and said, "His tray's over there," having assumed he was there to clean up.

Williams moved to Dallas in 2010 to become an assistant professor of surgery at UT Southwestern Medical Center and a trauma surgeon at Parkland Memorial Hospital. He and his wife moved into a high-rise apartment in a trendy and mostly white area. One day Williams stood outside with snowboarding gear, waiting for a ride to the airport. A patrol car pulled into the parking lot. He didn't give it much thought until he realized two officers were walking toward him strategically, as if expecting him to run.

The officers approached. "What are you doing here?"

"I live here," Williams said.

"You live here?"

"Yes," Williams said.

"Can I see some identification?"

Williams slowly took out his wallet. One officer went back to the squad car to run his license, while the other stood watch behind him. After a few minutes, the first officer returned and told him to have a good day. Later, when Williams told his wife, who is white, what had happened, she was angry. She asked why he'd shown his license. "Because I didn't want to get shot," he said.

In the days that followed, Williams, too, became angry. He described the incident to a doctor friend who also served as a reserve police officer. The friend looked up the report and told Williams someone had called 911 to report a "bald black man acting suspiciously."

Williams stayed focused on his work, believing the sight of a black man in a surgeon's coat was at least some contribution toward leveling the racial landscape. Trauma was one of the most high-stress and fast-paced fields of medicine. On a single shift, Williams might remove a gallbladder, amputate a leg, treat a gunshot victim, clamp an aorta. He worked in the Golden Hour, the critical sixty minutes after a traumatic injury. His adversary was the Flat Line, the sound of endings, the sound of failure. His favorite challenge was gunshot cases, which required detective work. He had to figure out the bullet's path, what organs and blood vessels and tissues had been damaged, prioritize injuries, and quickly repair them. He had to keep his cool at 3:00 a.m. while his adrenaline pumped and machines beeped and he was elbow-deep in a patient's abdomen, directing a team of six to eight.

Williams was respected at the hospital because of his hands but also because of his temperament. He'd felt that to succeed as a black doctor, or in any predominantly white field, he had to be professional always. There was no room for error. This meant never showing any hint of anger or aggression. His white male colleagues could get away with outbursts—in some cases it lent to their mystique. But Williams knew that would brand him as an angry black man, and quite possibly get him fired. Successful females, he believed, also followed this rule. He also never invoked race, one of the quickest ways to make white colleagues uncomfortable. Sometimes doctors called him "Brian" while calling everyone else "Doctor." Sometimes he didn't get invited to weekly golf games or leadership meetings. He suspected his skin color factored in, but he never raised the concern. Race was best handled as an unspoken elephant. Any uppityness, any mistake, would stoke some colleagues' suspicions that he wasn't as smart or talented as they were. That had consequences beyond his own career, he thought, because the black race often was viewed as a collective. It wouldn't be just Dr. Brian Williams messing up; it would be black people.

In recent years, as Williams watched the controversial videos—Eric Garner, Alton Sterling, Philando Castile—he was surprised by how much they frustrated and angered him. He'd worked hard to compartmentalize his life, but found he related deeply to those men outside convenience stores and on roadsides. Even he, a surgeon at one of the country's busiest trauma centers, could on any road, outside any home, be reduced to a "black man acting suspiciously." A menace. A threat.

Williams had spent years telling himself that he didn't have anything to complain about. Hadn't progress been made? Wasn't his life dramatically better than those of his parents and grandparents? Wasn't there a black president? Wasn't it true what Martin Luther King Jr. had said: "The arc of the moral universe is long, but it bends toward justice." But now, watching all those videos, that arc seemed endless. He felt a growing guilt about his silence. He'd always gone out of his way to mentor young black doctors, but there was more he could have done.

That Thursday afternoon, Williams walked into the hospital carrying an overnight bag. He wasn't supposed to be working; he'd agreed to cover a colleague's shift. He took a moment to unpack his things in a room with a small bed, then headed down to the trauma department. As he slipped into an elevator, the images of Castile bleeding out in his car still played through his mind.

6

Wonder Woman

Officer Misty McBride told colleagues she was headed out for dinner break. She planned to walk a couple of blocks for Thai food. McBride was tired and hungry, looking forward to the end of a typical shift. She'd responded to a 7-Eleven, where a woman was coming off something, maybe crack, and causing a scene. Then to a city plaza where someone had passed out high on a park bench. Now, as she thought about dinner, protesters were gathering not far away.

McBride worked for Dallas Area Rapid Transit, the city's public transit system. With whistles clipped to their uniforms, DART officers mostly dealt with lost travelers and the city's homeless. They rarely unholstered their Glocks. No DART officer had been killed in the line of duty since the agency's police force was founded in 1989. In the hierarchy of prestige among local police agencies, DART ranked toward the bottom. But its officers relished their underdog status and took their training seriously. In addition to preparing for Code Purples—train versus pedestrian—they practiced for active shooters and took part in Homeland Security terrorism drills. Today, McBride had picked up her ten-year-old daughter, Hunter, from cooking camp and met her parents for lunch. She was a single mother, and her parents watched her daughter while she worked, usually from 1:00 to 9:00 p.m.

At six feet one and 250 pounds, McBride could hold her own on the streets. The regulars called her Officer Mac. She had long brown hair that she wrapped in a tight bun. She wore a Wonder Woman patch on the front of her ballistic vest. McBride had wanted to be a cop since she was a girl, spending mornings with her grandfather watching reruns of *CHiPs*, imagining herself patrolling the California highway with the show's motorcycle cops. One female character, blue-eyed officer Bonnie Clark, tackled suspects, drove fast, and could handle the cheesy passes from the guys in her unit. When McBride grew up, she wanted to be like her.

She was assigned to a special team of officers tasked with patrolling the Triangle, a hub of the city's public transportation system. Thousands passed through every day on buses and trains. Many gathered in a small square called Rosa Parks Plaza. The square was anchored by a life-size bronze statue of Parks, sitting on a bus seat with her pocketbook in her lap, just as she had on the day she refused to give up her seat and move to the back of a Montgomery, Alabama, bus. Behind her, water cascaded down a thirteen-foot stone wall inscribed with a quote from Martin Luther King Jr.: "Until justice rolls down like waters and righteousness like a mighty stream." When the city announced the plaza's construction in 2008, it billed the quarter acre as a "tranquil place for downtown workers and residents to have lunch." In the years afterward it had become instead a gathering spot for the city's homeless. The base of Parks's statue smelled of urine and was covered with green patina and pigeon droppings.

Dallas has long viewed itself as a can-do city, a city with swagger, brash and overflowing with attitude, built on wheat and cotton and oil, the birthplace of Neiman Marcus and home of America's Team. But downtown began to empty in the 1960s as Eisenhower's federal highway system plowed through poor neighborhoods and created a concrete noose around the business district. A decade later, a judge ordered forced busing of students in an effort to desegregate Dallas's schools. Middle-class whites fled to the growing suburbs, and many businesses followed. Then the savings and loan crash of the 1980s hit hard and office vacancies skyrocketed. In 2001, the city was struggling to revitalize its core when it received a bruising rejection from a relocating Boeing, one of the world's largest aerospace companies, which picked Chicago instead of Dallas for its headquarters. Boeing's brass did not mince words. They admitted to preferring Chicago's vibrancy, green space, and public transportation. Downtown Dallas was dead, they said, and had no culture.

With no navigable river, no harbor, no mountains, Dallas still dreamed of becoming a "world-class" city. Local philanthropists helped city officials build a $110 million five-acre deck park atop a sunken freeway running along the northern edge of downtown, and a soaring white cable-stay bridge on the southern end that spanned the narrow Trinity River. But some realities could not be wished away. Homeless people still thronged its downtown streets, haranguing passersby, and it often fell to DART officers to handle them.

McBride and a dozen other officers had been handpicked by DART's chief to patrol downtown. It took a special kind of officer to work here, someone outgoing and comfortable talking with all kinds of people, all day long. One of the agency's unofficial mottos was "Not everyone needs to go to jail." Officers were encouraged to find creative solutions, directing people to shelters or helping them find meals.

Now, as McBride headed to dinner, a fellow DART cop named Brent Thompson tossed her the keys to his patrol car, suggesting she drive the couple of blocks to a restaurant.

"I'm not that much of a fat ass that I can't walk," she called back.

Thompson laughed, then insisted. He had four daughters, and he was protective of the team's female officers. Also, with so many people arriving for the protest, it felt unusually busy downtown. "Take my damn car," he told her.

After dinner, she returned and went looking for Thompson. She found him in a small office that served as a break room. McBride tossed the car keys back to Thompson, who was talking on the phone.

"Is that Emily?" McBride asked. Thompson nodded. Divorced from his first wife, Thompson had recently married a DART colleague, Officer Emily Crawford. Both were well liked at the agency. They planned to honeymoon in New Orleans in a couple of weeks.

"Hi Emily!" McBride yelled. "I love you!"

McBride told Thompson she needed a ride to headquarters after their shift. He nodded, and she went back outside. She headed along Lamar Street, planning to stand guard until the protest ended.

7

Hotspot Duty

SWAT negotiator Larry Gordon backed his Tahoe beneath an oak tree north of downtown. It was early evening, still hot, and he didn't plan to do much for the next couple of hours at his assigned hotspot. Through his windshield, he watched traffic moving along Greenville Avenue, a bustling two-lane road of restaurants and apartments.

Gordon understood his assignment as twofold. Park his marked police Tahoe somewhere visible, his presence suggesting to criminals that they reconsider their evening plans. And stop anyone who looked suspicious, maybe write a few tickets. That part Gordon wasn't going to do. *Sorry Sarge, nothing going on tonight.* If he stopped cars, he knew what he'd find: people with suspended licenses and warrants for unpaid traffic tickets. People like his mother and cousins and friends. To Gordon, writing those tickets was harassment, the very reason so many minorities hated cops.

Instead, Gordon passed the time on the phone with his niece. She'd called after watching the Castile video, which had her so upset she was crying. She couldn't understand why cops were so intent on killing black people. What would it mean for her son when he got older? How could Gordon stand being a cop?

Gordon told his niece he, too, found the video disturbing. When a police officer did something wrong, Gordon thought other cops should speak up. He thought they should join hands and shout, "Fire him!" That might restore some of their credibility.

But to Gordon, the Castile shooting was an outlier. He'd watched every police video that had outraged the public in recent years. He thought a couple of them were indefensible, including Walter Scott ("You can't shoot a running man in the back") and Sandra Bland ("You can't talk to people like that—you have to be professional"). But on balance he thought most of the officers' actions were justified. The narrative unfolding on the evening news—that police were murdering black men arbitrarily—was false. He recited to his niece numbers he'd memorized for training sessions he gave across the country.

"You know we shoot a lot more white people than black people, right?"

"That can't be true," his niece said.

"In 2015, about two hundred fifty black males were shot by police," he said. "Guess how many white guys they shot? About five hundred. By far, we shoot more white people."

Gordon's point wasn't that skin color played no role in the odds of getting shot during an encounter with police; he knew it did. It was just that officers did a dangerous job, and sometimes they had to protect themselves with force, no matter what somebody's color was.

He had gotten his numbers from the *Washington Post*, which along with other groups had been trying to get a clear picture of what was happening. No government agency kept detailed national data on police shootings. This frustrated academics, who warned that the emotional debate was unfolding in a statistical vacuum.

It had taken social scientists and lawyers years to prove discrimination in mortgage lending and wages; measuring bias in policing remained in its early stages.

To prove bias—that people are treated differently because of skin color—experts needed to isolate race from factors like poverty and crime rates. They didn't have the level of detail they needed. But the broad picture showed this: of the roughly one thousand people killed by cops in the United States each year, more than a quarter were black—though black people made up just 13 percent of the population. When it came to unarmed men getting killed by police, the racial disparity was even greater. An unarmed black man was about four times more likely to be killed by cops than an unarmed white man, according to the *Post*.

But experts did not yet agree on why. There were two main theories, generally described as a bias theory and a threat theory. The first said cops were more likely to shoot a black man because of racial bias, either overt or implicit. Prejudice, ingrained in the fabric of the country, primed officers to see dark skin as both lesser in value and more threatening, making black citizens a target for police killings and abuse. Under this theory, all else being equal, cops will use more force against blacks than whites. The second theory blamed the racial disparity in shootings on the fact that black men were more likely to live in poorer, crime-ridden areas, where cops were more active and on higher alert.

Gordon thought both theories were true. Blame history, blame racism, blame whatever, but a lot of mayhem came out of poor black communities, Gordon believed. "You know why police are in poor black neighborhoods?" he told friends. "Because black folks are out selling dope and shooting each other." The squeaky wheel got the oil. Black people, he said, needed to do more to call out crime in their communities.

Gordon, like most cops, was irritated by the growing number of anti-police activists, the "Hands Up, Don't Shoot" crowd. To him, it seemed like black lives mattered only when they were ended by white cops. Where were the activists when a black child got caught in the crossfire between two drug dealers? What about the black grandmother who lived with bars on her windows, scared a crack-head would break in, rough her up, and steal her television? When she called 911, it was Gordon and his teammates who showed up to help. To Gordon, it seemed like police were among the few who really cared about what was happening in black communities.

Gordon knew all the explanations for crime in poor black neighborhoods. Rich people had gated suburbs to disappear into. Poor people had their corners. They were overpoliced, endlessly harassed. After enslaving an entire population for centuries, the country had pushed black people into crowded housing projects on swampy land, given them failing schools, denied them jobs. What did everybody expect to happen? Gordon also knew the arguments about the inherent unfairness of the criminal justice system, so unforgiving when it came to blacks using drugs, so lax when it came to prosecuting black-on-black crime. Gordon believed all of it was undeniably, outrageously unfair. But what was Gordon supposed to do with that? What was any officer supposed to do? When there was a problem, their job was to handle it.

As Gordon talked with his niece, he could hear the fear in her voice. She truly feared a white cop might one day murder her son. Gordon told her what he told his own three kids: "Your skin color will not get you killed. Your mouth will get you killed." No matter which cop stopped you—even if he was a white, racist hillbilly from some two-bit Texas town—Gordon could almost guarantee that as long as you were respectful you would not get hurt. "Be as cordial as you can," he told his teenage son. "Your goal should be to look great on video." If there's a problem, if you've been wronged, there were complaints to file and, if it came to it, lawyers.

"You can't have court in the streets," Gordon liked to say. If he got into trouble, he was going to call for help, and fifty of his armed buddies were going to show up. That, you might not survive, he said. To Gordon, that was the common denominator of most police shootings of recent years. Many suspects had resisted officers and refused to comply. To him, it was evidence of a world increasingly skeptical of authority. The same thing happened to his wife, a schoolteacher, when she called parents about a student misbehaving. They argued with her, suggesting the problem was not with their kid but with her. It drove Gordon nuts. What happened to police officers and teachers being respected?

Gordon kept talking with his niece, listening to the chatter on the police radio as protesters kept arriving downtown.

8

The Foxtrots

At 6:30 p.m., the Dallas Police Department activated its command post. Supervisors gathered near city hall, talking into their radios, getting updates, situating their teams. Commanders stationed officers strategically across downtown, some riding bicycles or on foot, others parked in patrol cars beside highway ramps and intersections. Protests and rallies were routine in Dallas, and officers knew the drill: bring water, be friendly, and wait. By 7:00 p.m., most of the department's one hundred assigned officers were in position.

Handling protests often fell to response teams from substations across the city. Tonight, positioned on one edge of downtown would be the Foxtrots, a team that worked out of Southwest Division. Their supervisor, Sgt. Ivan Gunter, arrived and stepped out of his patrol car.

Gunter was a forty-seven-year-old black man with the look of a miniature action figure; the muscles of his arms and chest bulged out of proportion to his five-foot-seven frame. Born in Dallas, he'd joined the police department twenty-five years earlier, after abandoning a master's degree in sociology. He was friendly and easy to get along with, and he treated his officers more like colleagues than subordinates. He'd helped handpick the unit, a mix of whites and Hispanics who worked out together, ate together, and kept up with one another's family troubles, girlfriend issues, and Starbucks preferences.

The Foxtrots backed one another up on dangerous calls—shootings, stabbings, car jackings, and armed robberies. Rather than working regular beats, they handled special assignments in their district. They had special training in surveilling suspects and tracking down fugitives, and acted like a junior SWAT team, responsible for their own seventy-five square miles. The department didn't allow units to have their own logos, but the Foxtrots created one anyway, a growling fox with a lightning bolt shooting across the background. Gunter had it made into a patch, which the teammates wore on their ballistic vests.

The Foxtrots parked near the city's former municipal building, a five-story stone edifice on the east side of downtown. With its classical symmetry and Corinthian columns, the hundred-year-old building had played a defining role in the city's history. Jack Ruby had shot Lee Harvey Oswald in the building's basement, a moment etched in the nation's memory by a Pulitzer Prize–winning photograph that showed Ruby with his gun drawn and Oswald with his mouth open in shock, two days after he assassinated Kennedy.

As Gunter stood outside his car, one of his most experienced officers, Lorne Ahrens, approached. Fellow officers knew Ahrens for his guile and ability to get suspects to talk. He was six feet five, weighed almost four hundred pounds, and could rip burglar bars off a house with his bare hands. Friends called him "Meat" and loved summoning him as backup. But those who knew him well considered him a softy. They'd seen him roll around with his children, eight and ten years old.

Tonight Ahrens, who was white, was partnered with Michael

Krol, another large white officer of about 340 pounds. Colleagues liked to watch and laugh as the pair climbed into their patrol car and it sagged under their weight. Krol was the only member of the team who liked working traffic accidents. While others loathed the paperwork, Krol enjoyed the meticulous task of figuring out who had collided with whom, at what speeds and angles.

Ahrens seemed uncharacteristically concerned, Gunter thought as he chatted with him. The Foxtrots had worked many protests, and Gunter knew Ahrens was bored by them. Now Ahrens wanted to know if the men could wear their heavy vests. Something about the assignment had him worried. The department provided officers with thin Kevlar vests, which could stop or at least slow the average handgun bullet. But many cops, like Ahrens, spent $300 to $400 of their own money to buy vests with plates that could protect them from the faster bullets of assault rifles. The vests were heavier and hotter, but Ahrens and his teammates liked the protection.

Gunter shrugged. "Good idea," he said. "Let me check."

Gunter radioed the command post. A couple of minutes later a response came back. No vests. Commanders didn't want officers to appear threatening to the crowd.

Gunter was frustrated. He didn't like telling his officers they couldn't wear protective gear, especially experienced cops like Ahrens. Yet Gunter also understood where his commanders were coming from. They were sensitive to appearing too militaristic before an anti-police crowd. He tended to respect the department's chain of command, trusting they would make the right decisions. But he knew Ahrens would be angry. Gunter wasn't surprised when Ahrens, hearing the news, shook his head in disgust.

Across the intersection, a homeless man approached another Foxtrot, Patrick Zamarripa. The thirty-two-year-old was a military veteran who'd done tours in Iraq. He had dark hair and was wearing the fluorescent yellow uniform of a bicycle cop. With a happy-go-lucky personality, Zamarripa was one of the easiest cops to supervise, responding to any of Gunter's requests with "Yes, sir!" He had a knack for getting into foot chases. At least once a week, the Foxtrots heard him call out breathlessly over the police radio, "I've got a runner!" Zamarripa was a die-hard Texas Rangers fan, and tonight his girlfriend, Kristy, was texting him from the stands as she watched the game with their two-year-old daughter.

The homeless man waved his arms to get Zamarripa's attention. Someone had stolen his potato chips, the man explained. Zamarripa walked him to the 7-Eleven and stopped at the snacks aisle. The man looked at him, then picked out a bag. "Want two bags?" Zamarripa asked. "Just one," the man said. Zamarripa paid for the chips. As they walked back, the man thanked Zamarripa repeatedly, then asked if he could stay near him so no one would take his chips. Zamarripa nodded. The man sat down on a curb and ripped open the bag.

Zamarripa and the other officers passed the time chatting. They listened to their radios as commanders updated the crowd size at Belo Garden, a couple of blocks away. By 7:45 p.m. the crowd had swelled to around seven hundred.

9

The Protest

Shetamia Taylor and her four kids walked into Belo Garden around 7:00 p.m. The park, part of a master plan to remake the city's core, had been built a few years earlier atop what had been a parking lot. Its landscaping was meant to evoke a blackland prairie, with dozens of native grasses and trees, blooming mounds of black-eyed Susans and Texas asters.

Taylor took in the scene. Alongside the waving prairie grass stood hundreds of people, a crowd that was mostly black but included dozens of whites. There were young mothers holding babies, grandmothers, toddlers perched on fathers' shoulders, college students waving posters. Police officers in shorts and sunglasses cruised by on bicycles, hopping off to pose for selfies with the crowd. This was the America that Taylor wanted to be part of, people from different places gathering in a pretty spot, talking about how they wanted things to change.

A black man wearing a ball cap stood atop a grassy berm and shouted to the crowd. "At the end of the day, we, as the people, have to be fed up and say, 'Enough is enough.'" He slapped the back of one hand into his other palm for emphasis, and the crowd joined him in his chant. "Enough is enough! Enough is enough!" The event had been organized by Dallas pastors and activists who in the weeks after Michael Brown's death in Ferguson had formed a small group called the Next Generation Action Network. They held regular protests, usually attended by a dozen or so, rather than the hundreds who, sparked by the videos of Sterling and Castile, had driven downtown on this evening.

"Listen, we have to make a decision," the man in the ball cap continued. "Black, white, brown, tall, skinny, short, it doesn't matter. One injustice one place is an injustice in every place." The crowd clapped and cheered as the man raised his voice. "And we've got to come together, as a people, and declare that 'I'm not tolerating this anymore.'"

It had been a day of protests across the country. Demonstrators in Washington, D.C., locked arms and marched from the White House to Capitol Hill. Hundreds gathered outside the Metropolitan Museum of Art in New York City, standing on the steps with their hands raised, so many that they shut down parts of Fifth Avenue. In St. Paul, demonstrators chanted outside the governor's mansion. In Oakland, California, marchers spilled onto a highway and stopped traffic; one man climbed on top of an 18-wheeler and raised his fist in the air. Close-up shots of marchers, many enraged or in tears, led the evening's national news broadcasts.

At the park in Dallas, the crowd began an impromptu march along Main Street. This was a surprise to the police, who'd been told by organizers that there would only be speeches. Hundreds spilled into the narrow avenue, lined with office towers, some in work clothes, others wearing flip-flops and jeans. Many had their fists in the air as they chanted "Black lives matter" and "Whose streets? Our streets!" They held signs: WHO DO YOU CALL WHEN THE MURDERER WEARS A BADGE? and AM I NEXT? One man in an

SUV, stopped in traffic, rolled down his window and chanted with the crowd, fist-bumping marchers as they walked by. Most were friendly toward the cops who kept watch, but a few groups angrily chanted, "Oink Oink, bang bang," and "Pigs in a blanket, fry 'em like bacon."

As Taylor and her sons walked, she felt as if they were learning something important. Her youngest, twelve-year-old Jermar, looked over and grinned. "Mom, is this what Grandma and Grandpa used to do when they marched?" She nodded. "Yes."

* * *

As protesters marched, commanders quickly redeployed teams to block streets along the route and stop traffic. They sent the Foxtrots leapfrogging from intersection to intersection. The protesters walked several blocks down Commerce Street, turned around, and headed back along Main Street. At about 8:40 p.m., as the protest began to wind down, the Foxtrots were dispatched to their final post, the intersection of Main and Lamar streets. They parked around a nine-story, cream-colored building that formerly held a Sanger Brothers department store but now housed the county's community college, called El Centro. A couple dozen students and teachers were on the upper floors of the building. College security officers had locked the street-facing doors to keep protesters out.

On the street, Gunter stood in the fading twilight. He heard the marchers coming closer, walking a final couple of blocks, their voices carrying on the wind. He couldn't make out precisely what they were saying, but he could feel the emotion in their chants. As a black man, he sympathized with the movement; he'd had his own run-ins with police as a boy. The crowd came into view, marching past him on Main. He'd been prepared for animosity, but these protesters were friendly. They were far more laid back than Occupy Dallas, the anti-corporate group that had been frustrating city officials for months. Gunter waved at fathers, mothers, and children, posed for a couple of selfies. A young couple who passed thanked him for being there. Behind him, about ten feet away, Ahrens watched Gunter interact with the crowd. "You're just Officer Fucking Friendly tonight, aren't you?" Ahrens called out in mock annoyance.

Gunter grinned and rolled his eyes, then looked at his watch. It was about 8:50 p.m.

"Almost done," he called back.

The protesters had begun trailing off toward their cars, their chants fading into the backdrop of the city's sounds, the dinging of DART train bells, the hum of distant interstate traffic. Gunter listened to the chatter of police supervisors coordinating intersection closures by radio.

"CRH 60 to Lima 302."

"Go ahead."

"Yes sir, are you on Commerce yet, or are you still on Main?"

"No sir . . . I believe it is Foxtrot 720 that still has the intersection of Griffin and Main blocked off. Would you like for him to open it?"

"Yeah, if you're already past him, go ahead and let him open that."

Gunter expected to hear commanders release the Foxtrots from the corner any minute.

* * *

No one paid much attention to the black SUV driving erratically through downtown, although its path would later be meticulously tracked by authorities using surveillance camera footage. One DART bus driver took note of it. He'd stopped to let off a passenger when he saw the SUV barrel through an intersection and a red light. It veered onto Lamar Street and stopped in front of the community college. The driver parked in the street and flipped on his hazard lights.

Behind the wheel sat twenty-five-year-old Micah Johnson. He was five feet six, with brown eyes and a black mustache and beard. He'd brought a cache of firearms: two pistols, a Frasier .25 caliber and a Glock 9 mm; and three rifles, a Saiga .545 mm, a Zastava M70, and a .22 mm. He had hundreds of rounds of ammunition. He brought a tan Condor ballistic vest equipped with plates strong enough to shield him from the police's pistols and M4 carbines.

Johnson got out of the car a few feet away from the Foxtrots, closest to Officers Ahrens and Krol. Most of the team had their backs turned. They were focused on the marchers crossing the street on the other side of them. Johnson lingered on the street for about ten minutes, watching.

During that time, a passerby mistook him for a cop. "Good day sir, officer," he said.

Johnson looked at the man. "I'm not no fucking cop," he snapped.

10

Ambush

At 8:58 p.m., the first gunshot echoed across Lamar Street. Sergeant Gunter, standing in a crosswalk, looked around. He heard another crack, then several more.

Behind him, Officer Krol screamed and grabbed his back as pieces of his body camera flew into the air. He collapsed. Ahrens, standing beside Krol, realized what was happening. He looked at a group of protesters on the corner and shouted for them to run. Then he, too, collapsed.

"Get down, get down!" Gunter yelled, as more gunfire boomed louder and closer to him. He dropped behind his patrol car. It was taking fire, bullets pinging off the metal frame. His unit was caught in the street with nowhere to hide. Gunter recognized the sound of a semiautomatic assault rifle. The thin Kevlar vests beneath their shirts would not protect them, and they didn't have time to get their heavy vests from the cars.

The police radio erupted with shouts.

"Shots fired, shots fired, shots fired," one officer said over the radio, and then he screamed.

"Shots fired!" another officer said.

"Stop him, stop him!" another said.

"We've got an officer hit!" another said.

Gunter saw Zamarripa, in his fluorescent uniform, running toward his fallen teammates Ahrens and Krol. As Zamarripa neared Gunter's patrol car, he staggered and fell to the ground. Gunter scrambled over and dragged him behind the car. Gunter pressed the button on his radio, his voice steady despite the growing chaos. "We got shots fired. Clear this area!"

Officers summoned Air One, the police helicopter, asking for intel from above. The pilot maneuvered closer, but he couldn't see anything. "I can't get to it. It's at the base of the skyscraper."

A breathless officer broke in: "We got two down!"

Another corrected him. "Three down! We got three down!"

* * *

A few feet away from Gunter another Foxtrot, twenty-eight-year-old Jorge Barrientos, ran for cover toward a patrol car, as bullets hit the ground next to him. A chunk of his radio, attached to his belt, flew into the air. *Someone's aiming at me*, Barrientos thought. Just before he ducked behind the car, he felt something slam into his chest. It stung, then the feeling faded. Barrientos coughed into his hand, looking for blood. He didn't see any. Then he looked down and saw a piece of his left index finger dangling from skin. He and his partner crouched behind the car. "Stay down!" Barrientos screamed. A piece of a tire blew off, striking his partner in the face and pitching him backward.

During a break in the gunfire, Barrientos looked out into the street and saw Krol lying motionless on the pavement. He saw Ahrens struggling, trying to apply a tourniquet to his own leg. Then he saw his sergeant crouched over Zamarripa. He crawled over to help. "Grab my med kit," Gunter yelled. It was in the back of his patrol car. Barrientos raised his head, but he felt the disturbed air of bullets whizzing by and sank back down. He couldn't reach the kit without exposing himself.

* * *

Gunter tugged on Zamarripa's bloody shirt, revealing an entry wound in his right upper chest. Trained in combat medicine, Gunter feared his officer had a sucking chest wound, one that might fill his thorax with air and cause his lungs to collapse. He needed to plug the hole. "What do you have?" Gunter asked Barrientos. Barrientos reached into his pocket and pulled out a pack of Marlboro Lights. Gunter grabbed them, slid off the clear plastic wrapper, and placed it over Zamarripa's wound, pushing down.

Zamarripa flinched. *Good*, Gunter thought. *He's with me.*

"I'm sorry, bro, I know it hurts," Gunter told him. "You'll make it. Just stay with me."

Gunter grabbed his officer's hand. Zamarripa squeezed back.

* * *

Another Foxtrot, Ivan Saldana, forty-four, was directing traffic in the middle of the intersection when the shooting started. He raced toward the fallen officers, hiding behind a patrol car along the way. He saw sparks as bullets struck the pavement around him. It seemed like the shots were coming from an elevated position. There were so many that he assumed several shooters were perched somewhere above. Saldana got on his stomach and peered beneath the car. From this vantage point, he could see Ahrens, lying on his belly, struggling to raise himself, as if doing a push-up. Then he saw the big man shake his head and go back down. It looked as if Ahrens was trying to move closer so he could help his partner, Krol. Saldana yelled at him from beneath the car. "Don't get up! He's still shooting!" Saldana felt heat in his right thigh; he'd been hit by a bullet fragment.

* * *

Protester Shetamia Taylor had been standing at a crosswalk with her four sons, waiting for the light to turn, when the gunfire started.

Taylor looked out into the intersection and spotted the most massive cop she'd ever seen. It was Ahrens. He was white with a shiny bald head, his giant, muscled frame punching through his blue uniform. She was staring at him when she heard the sound, a pop like a firecracker. *Who is setting off fireworks a few days after July Fourth?* Then she heard it again, a loud, sharp boom. The big white cop looked Taylor in the eye and shouted, "He's got a gun. Run!" She stared at the massive officer as he winced, then crumpled down on the pavement.

Everyone ran from the open street. Taylor's oldest, eighteen-year-old Kavion, grabbed his little brother, twelve-year-old Jermar, and yanked him into a doorway, where they crouched. Fourteen-year-old Jajuan sprinted forward alone, disappearing into the crowd. Taylor felt a flash of pain in the back of her leg, as if someone had pushed a needle through her calf to her shin. She grabbed her fifteen-year-old son, Andrew, and they tumbled onto the street, between a car and a curb. Bullets pounded the pavement as she tried to cover her son.

In a moment, a police officer appeared by her head, asking if she was okay. Another appeared at her side, checking on her son. A line of officers appeared along a brick wall, guns raised. These officers, the same ones the crowd had just been protesting, were circling them.

"Is anybody hit?" an officer asked.

"No," Taylor's son said. He was crying and shaking. Taylor knew she'd been shot, but she was afraid to say anything, fearing her son would become hysterical and draw the gunman's attention. The officer looked at her and asked more sternly. "Is anybody hit?"

"Yes sir," she admitted now. "I'm hit in the leg." Her leg throbbed, but all she could think about was her boys, scattered out there without her.

Beneath her, Andrew was alternating between holding his breath and screaming. Taylor heard him say to the police officers: "Get my mom out of here! Please, help my mom!"

One officer, wearing a red shirt and a ball cap, knelt beside them, talking in a soft Texas drawl. "You're okay," he said, gently patting her. As gunfire continued around them, Taylor had never been more terrified. But the officer seemed calm and in control. She found herself relaxing at the sound of his voice, as he spoke to her son. "Nothing else is going to happen to your mom," he told Andrew. "We're here." Her son kept poking up his head to look around, and she'd pull him back down.

* * *

The officer with the drawl, Greg Weatherford, had been standing a block away when he heard the shots. He was assigned to work the protest as an undercover, to keep an eye out for troublemakers. A forty-eight-year-old white man, he'd tried to blend into the crowd wearing a ball cap, a big dip of tobacco in his mouth. Weatherford had enjoyed catching the eyes of every uniformed officer he knew, raising his fist into the air and shouting, "Fuck the police!"

When the gunfire erupted, he ran toward the sound and spotted a black woman splayed out on the pavement with a screaming teenage boy, surrounded by officers. He knelt beside Taylor and her son as bullets sliced through the air, sparking off the pavement and clinking off the car's frame. The woman was bleeding from a gunshot wound to her leg. "Someone get me a tourniquet!" an officer yelled. As the officer wrapped it around her leg, she moaned, and Weatherford told her, "You're gonna be all right, babe," he said.

As he crouched, Weatherford could feel the rounds snapping by his head. "We're sitting ducks right here," he said to the other officer. They needed to move the woman and son. At some point, he figured, the gunman would have to reload. That's when they'd make their move and put the woman into a patrol car.

Weatherford looked out into the chaos. A couple hundred yards away, he saw a gunman laying down fire around a pillar. He considered pulling out his gun but thought it was too far a shot for his pistol. Also, there were cops everywhere.

Then he heard the snap of a pistol, followed by the crack of a rifle. Cops, somewhere, were shooting back. "Who's returning fire over there?" Weatherford asked, wondering which cops had emerged from cover to begin an offensive push.

* * *

After the gunman took aim at the Foxtrots, hitting nearly every officer on the team with bullets or shrapnel, he turned and headed in the other direction toward the DART train and bus station. The block was filled with transit cops.

DART officer McBride was standing near the transfer center, looking forward to her shift ending, when she heard the first booms. She looked over at another officer. "Firecrackers?" she asked. Then they heard it again.

"Oh shit," she said. "That's gunfire."

They took off running toward the sound, across train tracks, through an intersection. While running, McBride felt a pain in her left arm. It flew up on its own, flopped down, then burned, as if someone were holding a lighter to it. Her glasses flew off, and the world became foggy and overbright. She felt like she was standing exposed in the center of a lit football field. She tried to raise her arm, but it wouldn't move. The sound of gunfire, so loud moments earlier, had faded, as if she were listening to the world from under water. She flung herself on the ground and started crawling. Ahead, she saw the statue of Rosa Parks. She lugged her body toward it, hoping to use it as cover. *Rosa is going to save my ass*, she thought.

As she crawled, she saw the fuzzy outline of two huge legs running toward her. It was an officer she patrolled with. She felt her weight collapsing into the officer's frame as he guided her out of the street toward a brick wall.

"Get my tourniquet," she told him. She'd taken a first-aid class months earlier, learning how to apply a tourniquet to herself or another officer if shot in the field. As they worked on her arm, another officer flagged down a patrol car. McBride climbed into the front passenger seat, and a female officer she'd just had dinner with got in to drive. They sped toward Baylor hospital with lights and sirens. When they slowed for the first red light, the officer driving flung her arm out, the way mothers do to protect children riding in the front seat, knocking McBride's wounded arm. She howled in pain.

* * *

Brent Thompson, the newly married DART officer who'd gotten his patrol car back from McBride after her dinner, was driving near the community college when the first shots rang out. A forty-three-year-old former U.S. Marine, Thompson reacted quickly. He caught sight of the shooter slinking between thick concrete pillars that lined the front of the college building. He got out of his car, unholstered his pistol, and ran in that direction. What happened next was recorded by a bystander on a hotel balcony above.

Thompson hid behind a pillar about fifteen feet away from the shooter, leaned around, and fired. He surprised the gunman, who flinched, then fired back. The men ducked and bobbed, playing a life-or-death game of hide-and-seek around the pillars. As Thompson slipped behind one of the pillars, he lost sight of the shooter. In seconds, the shooter discovered Thompson's blind spot and snuck up from behind. As Thompson leaned around the pillar, searching for his target, the gunman appeared at his back and fired. Thompson collapsed on his side, his pistol dropping, his Oakleys flying off. The gunman stood over Thompson and fired a dozen more shots into his body.

* * *

Officer Gretchen Rocha found herself across the intersection near the college, ducking behind the engine block of a patrol car when the first shots were fired. A twenty-three-year-old trainee, she'd been on the street for three weeks and was assigned to the Foxtrots. She was newly married with an eleven-month-old. Amid the unfolding chaos, she had little idea what to do. She heard her trainer's voice in her head: *Just keep moving.*

Rocha saw the fallen officers Ahrens and Krol lying in the street. Patrol cars screeched toward them as bullets flew all around. When officers began dragging the wounded men toward the cars, she ran to help. She put her gun back in the holster and helped heave Krol into the back of a patrol car. Then she noticed the driver's seat was empty. She jumped in. Another officer climbed into the back and started CPR. He asked if she knew how to get to the hospital. "No," she confessed. He shouted directions while pumping on Krol's chest.

Rocha pressed the gas, jumping a curb as they sped away. Gripping the steering wheel, she noticed a throbbing in her right arm. She looked down and saw a growing circle of blood. She, too, had been hit, in the arm and leg. She pressed harder on the gas, watching the speedometer climb to 118 mph.

11

The Offensive

Henry Edwards, a twenty-seven-year-old rookie officer, had been sitting in his patrol car a couple of blocks from the college when he heard the shots-fired call on the radio. He always kept his rifle close, locked muzzle-up beside the driver's seat. He grabbed it, racked back the bolt, and chambered a round. "Let's go!" he shouted to his partner.

Edwards had been a police officer for about two years, working in one of the city's toughest policing divisions. He had dark brown eyes, a boyish smile, and, at five feet five, was one of the shortest officers on the force. He easily could have passed for a local high school student. Decades earlier, Edwards's short stature would have kept him from being a cop. But courts in the 1970s had ruled height requirements to be discriminatory.

Edwards drove along Main, pointing his AR-15 out of the driver's-side window, scanning the street. He was one of the only officers in the area with a rifle in his hands. The police department had a limited stock of beat-up Rock River AR-15 rifles, but the waiting list was long. If an officer bought his own, he could jump the line and immediately enroll in rifle school. Edwards had spent

$1,700 on a custom Colt. It was a splurge for a rookie, but what Edwards lacked in brawn he made up for with firearm skills.

Edwards had grown up in Long Beach, California, the son of a kindergarten teacher and an Army veteran who sold generators. As a kid he'd been obsessed with Nerf guns and G.I. Joe. For his fifth birthday, he'd asked for weapons. "What do you mean, weapons?" his mother asked. "Guns, knives, rockets, and bazookas," he replied. Edwards spent hours reading a 416-page encyclopedia, *Military Small Arms of the 20th Century*, and could recite obscure facts about combat handguns, fighter jets, and tanks. He asked his parents for shooting lessons in middle school. It was early 2000, a couple of years after Columbine, and his schoolteacher mother wasn't thrilled. Still, she drove her minivan thirty miles east every week to the closest skeet shooting range. She worked on lesson plans in the car while Edwards learned to aim a shotgun and track clay pigeons across the sky.

In college, Edwards worked part-time at a gun shop, shooting every rifle and pistol he could get his hands on, learning how to fieldstrip weapons and put them back together. He began collecting AK-47s. He'd buy them on small-arms Web forums in disassembled kits, fascinated by how the Stalin-era weapon had been modified by so many countries—Bulgaria, Poland, Russia—each making a unique version. Edwards purchased a later variation of the gun, an AK-74, a lighter model that used a bullet known for its devastating effects on soft tissue.

A knowledge of AKs was helpful to any officer patrolling a large American city. It was the world's most ubiquitous weapon, the anchor of modern warfare. AKs were light, extremely durable, and simple to operate, and they transformed even the most poorly trained soldier into a formidable adversary. Bury it in snow, sink it in a bog, coat it in desert sand, and chances are it would still fire. Saddam Hussein plated his in gold. Castro engraved them as gifts.

Lionized in rap songs and gangster films, AKs were the weapon of choice for drug dealers across the globe.

Now, as Edwards and his partner drove past the JFK Memorial, a giant cube-shaped cenotaph with its interior open to the sky, they saw hundreds of people sprinting into the street. It reminded Edwards of a scene from a Godzilla movie. The smell of gun smoke wafted into the patrol car's open windows. He and his partner pulled up near the community college, where the road was blocked by police cars. They got out and ran, joining other officers along the side of the building. It was about 9:00 p.m., a couple of minutes after the first shots were fired. Dozens of police sirens wailed out of sync. It was so loud the officers could barely hear each other. Then came the repeated, echoing crack of a semiautomatic rifle. Edwards knew no cop would be dumping rounds like that downtown. It had to be the bad guy.

"Where is he?" Edwards yelled to his partner.

Edwards took a knee by the exterior of the college, trying to get low and small. He looked out into the street and saw two fallen men on the pavement. One lay facedown, the other faceup. Both were still, and pools of their blood stained the asphalt. Edwards first thought they were civilians, then noticed their blue uniforms. *Wait, are those cops?* It was Krol and Ahrens. As Edwards took in the scene, the gunfire grew louder. *He's right there,* Edwards thought. He poked his head around a corner of the building, looking down a long corridor of pillars lining its facade. About fifty yards away, he saw a man's head dart from behind a pillar, training his eyes back at Edwards and swinging a long gun toward him. The men had caught sight of each other at the same moment. Edwards had never before shot at a suspect, but he felt no hesitation. He squeezed his trigger, firing two quick shots.

The man ducked back behind the pillar. Edwards wasn't sure if he'd hit him, so he stayed put, waiting. Time seemed to slow as Edwards looked through his sight and studied what he saw.

The gunman emerged again, a silhouette in the dim light. He walked directly into Edwards's sights. The man did not appear antsy or amped up, Edwards noted, but perfectly calm. Serene even. *He's just fucking walking*, Edwards thought. The man looked back at Edwards, then turned in the other direction.

Edwards positioned the red dot of his scope squarely on the gunman's back. *Here it comes, motherfucker.* He squeezed. As the bullet left, he felt the same sensation as when he hit a tennis ball just right, like he'd nailed the sweet spot. He'd barely felt any recoil. He thought he'd hit the man squarely in the back. Edwards raised his head slightly and shouted to his partner, "I got him!"

He puzzled over what he saw next. The gunman was still moving. It wouldn't occur to Edwards until later that the man was wearing body armor. Edwards got back on his sights and laid into him, pounding out another six rounds. It made a huge sound across downtown.

Edwards thought he might have hit the gunman's arm and his magazine clip. He saw puffs of dust as other rounds hit the pillar. Later, while watching Edwards's body camera footage, people would marvel at his performance under fire: "This kid is not even breathing hard." As the gunman retreated from the open street, Edwards shouted to his partner, "Fuck, let's go!" He and his partner advanced slowly, pausing for cover behind pillar after pillar. As they pursued the gunman, Edwards noticed a spent magazine and a couple of bullets on the ground. He paused to study them and recognized them as those of an AK-74.

* * *

City police officers are trained to move quickly when there's an active shooter. The protocol stemmed from Columbine, where the first cops on the scene waited for SWAT to arrive and gear up, as the shooters killed twelve students and one teacher. Since then, departments have taught officers to immediately push toward the threat. Most active shooter situations are over within fifteen minutes, and shooters often kill themselves when confronted. Officers are taught that, even if their partner is bleeding out on the sidewalk, they should say a prayer and keep moving. On that night, Edwards did what he'd been taught.

Edwards's partner, Jake Deloof, found it impossible to run past fellow officers as they lay bleeding in the street. He broke away from Edwards and was among the first to reach Krol and Ahrens.

He crouched and put his hand on Krol's back. The officer was facedown as he shook him. "Hey, hey!" he said. No response. He moved to Ahrens. "Where are you hit?" Deloof asked him. The officer's eyes were closed, but he responded by patting his chest and moaning. Deloof started cutting the fallen man's shirt off, and another officer, Debbie Taylor, who knew Ahrens well, leaned over him. "Stay with me, Lorne. Stay with me," she said. Deloof gave her some gauze, and they began stuffing it inside a bullet wound in his chest. "We got you, Lorne," Taylor said. "We got you!"

* * *

Another DART officer, Bob Craig, had reacted quickly to the gunfire. At sixty-three, he was one of the oldest officers on the street. People called him Old Man Craig. He'd come to policing late in life, after twenty years in the restaurant business. He and two other DART officers were about a block from the college, near a McDonald's, when they heard the shots. The three men sprinted toward the sound, running into a parking lot packed with cars.

Craig trailed behind his younger colleagues, yelling for pedestrians to get down. His partner made it to the edge of the parking lot first. When Craig got there, he found his partner leaned over the trunk of a car with his Glock trained on the pillars lining the front of the college. Craig followed his partner's gaze across the street, but he didn't see the gunman yet. Just orange bursts of muzzle flash from behind a pillar. "Is that him?" Craig asked his partner. "Just shoot!" his partner said. Craig caught glimpses of the man—a half-moon of his head, a sliver of shoulder—as he and his partner fired, drawing the gunman's attention. They ducked behind the car as the gunman took aim at another DART officer a few feet ahead of them and out in the open. The officer jumped left and right as bullets corkscrewed off the ground around him like fireworks. Finally, he flung himself behind a car.

Then the gunman laid into the car Craig was crouched behind. It sounded like someone was on the other side of the car, pounding it with a hammer. He felt he was being physically touched by the sound, like thunderclaps inside his chest. He and his partner popped up again, still exchanging fire with the gunman. Craig saw the gunman spin and fall to the ground behind the pillar. "He's hit!" Craig shouted. But then the gunman appeared again in a full sprint toward the college's side entrance. Craig and his partner kept firing as the gunman ran.

* * *

A police officer for the community college, John Abbott, had been standing just inside the building when the gunfire started. Dozens of students and teachers were in classrooms. Abbott and a couple of other officers ran to the college's side entrance, enclosed by two sets of glass doors. They approached the doors just as bullets shattered them. The glass fell like sleet.

"Fuck!" Abbott shouted, slipping on broken glass. He retreated a few steps and called out, "Anybody hit?" Rifle fire continued outside as Abbott shouted, "Get down, get back!" He ducked behind a wall, then began walking back toward the doors, pointing his handgun as he advanced toward the gunfire. "Goddammit, where's it coming from?" he shouted, using his hand to push the remaining glass out of the door so he could see. He spotted a black SUV parked beside the college, its hazard lights flashing. As another ten or eleven shots rang out, he shouted back to a colleague, "Get the fucking rifles!" An officer sprinted for the AR-15s they kept locked in an equipment room.

In a moment, there was a lull in the gunfire, and Abbott saw patrol cars speed into the street to rescue the wounded. Abbott rushed outside, too, and he saw a bleeding officer on the sidewalk.

Abbott had been a Navy corpsman and a DART officer before joining the college security team. He rushed over to the fallen officer, who was covered in blood. "Goddammit!" Abbott said. He pressed the button on his radio. "519, we have an officer down at Elm and Lamar. Officer down, officer down. Give me EMS, *now!*"

He bent down and cradled the officer's head and neck, his fingers feeling for a pulse. Studying the man's face, he realized it was Brent Thompson. The men had worked together years earlier.

"Clear his throat out," Abbott yelled.

He tried to open Thompson's shirt, and a DPD officer pulled out a knife and sliced through it. They saw Thompson was not wearing any protective gear.

"God, where's your fucking vest, man! Goddammit!" one of the officers screamed at Thompson. Another said, "He's hit in the head. He's dead."

"We're not calling this!" Abbott shouted. "This is my friend. Let's go!"

They lifted Thompson's arms and legs and carried him to a patrol car. As they shut the door, Abbott screamed at the driver, "Go, go, go!"

Abbott looked around the street, darker now, wondering where the shooter had gone. He hit the button on his radio. "519, is he in the building?"

He stood there waiting for the response, then learned the shooter had gotten inside the college. He shouted to the officers nearby: "He's in the building! He's in the building!"

12

Code 100

SWAT team member Danny Canete was sitting in a police Tahoe, talking with his mom on the phone. He was on hotspot duty about two miles from downtown. Canete's two best friends, his teammates Ryan Scott and Brandon Berie, were sitting in the front seat of a nearby Tahoe, watching a CIA thriller, *Spy Game*, on a cell phone. They'd all been working since morning and planned to burn clock until their shift ended at 11:00 p.m.

The men, always together, were known on SWAT as the Three Amigos. They joked that Canete was the brains, and the other two were the muscle. At five feet seven, Canete was the smallest and had been trained in classical piano before becoming a cop. Scott was a former Marine and National Guardsman who'd served tours in Iraq and Afghanistan; they called him Rhino because of his lumbering way, laid back until it was time to charge. The third, Berie, was young and handsome, one of the team's few bachelors. With his dark brown eyes and rippling biceps, they called him Biebs, after teen heartthrob Justin Bieber.

Canete was midsentence with his mom when he heard the

dispatcher say, "Officer down." He told his mother he had to go, threw the phone on the floorboard, and peeled out of the parking lot. Scott and Berie sped behind him with their lights and sirens blaring. Minutes later, they arrived and parked off Elm Street, just beside the college, without realizing they'd landed right in the hot zone.

As Canete got out of his Tahoe he heard gunfire. He saw dozens of patrol officers taking cover in the streets and parking lots, hunched behind cars. *Shit, this is still going on*, he thought.

He ran to the back of the Tahoe, lifted the tailgate, and punched in a code to unlock his gun drawer. As he grabbed his M4, Scott ran by, already wearing his plate carrier and carrying his rifle. Canete slammed the tailgate and followed. His own vest was on the front passenger seat, but he didn't stop to grab it. His competitive adrenaline was thumping; he didn't want Scott to beat him to the shooter. The men jumped over a waist-high iron fence into a parking lot, joining a dozen cops taking cover. Berie tried to load a magazine into his rifle, fumbling for a second and making a racket. A patrol officer, an overweight veteran nicknamed Big Ross, looked over. "It's okay," he said. "You got this." Berie grinned.

The officers scanned the street, trying to take in what was happening. They saw hundreds of screaming civilians and cops, yelling for help, trying to point out where they thought the shooting was coming from. As the Amigos took cover behind a car, Scott noticed an officer pointing at the college, signaling that the gunman had gone inside. Without warning, Scott charged in that direction. The other two Amigos hadn't seen the officer's gesture, and they watched Scott in confusion. *Holy hell*, Canete thought. *What's he doing?* Scott bolted across the open street with no cover, his M4 pushed forward. "Watch for crossfire!" Canete shouted. With so many cops pointing pistols, Canete was worried about friendly fire. But Canete and Berie followed their teammate, sprinting across the street just steps behind him. As the three SWAT officers ran, a couple patrol officers jumped up and followed.

The officers approached a side entrance of the college. They could see that the dark glass doors had been shot out, with jagged shards left dangling. "I got you! I got the door!" Canete yelled at Scott, who already had his rifle trained on it. Canete stepped forward and grabbed the handle, looked over at Scott to make sure he was ready, and swung open the door. Seeing no sign of the gunman, they entered a large atrium. People were yelling and scattering. Frightened students were hiding in corners. The atrium split into a maze of hallways and rooms, a tactical nightmare. Canete noticed a college police officer pointing a pistol at a stairwell door. He could tell the guy was on alert, ready to shoot. "What do you have?" Canete asked him.

"He's in there," the officer replied. Though Canete didn't realize it, the officer had just run into the stairwell and been greeted by a barrage of bullets from above.

Just then, Canete was approached by a short, rookie officer he recognized, holding a rifle. It was Henry Edwards. Canete knew patrol officers weren't supposed to carry rifles at protests, so he was impressed that Edwards had one in his hands already.

"The shooter, he has an AK-74!" Edwards said.

How the hell does he know that? Canete thought.

Berie called Canete over to a small glass window in the door to the stairwell. Inside, there was a red smear of blood on the concrete floor. Berie and Canete looked at each other. Should they go ahead? Or wait for backup?

Canete pressed the button on his radio, wanting to alert other officers that they'd found a blood trail. So many officers were talking he couldn't cut in. "Break, break, break," he said, hoping officers would pause, but they didn't.

"Wanna follow the blood?" Berie asked. Canete and Scott both nodded. "We have no choice," Scott said. They knew the gunman might find more victims upstairs.

Canete looked around. "All right, you, you," he said, grabbing Edwards and another patrol officer, a man named Joe Lopez. "Let's go."

Canete pressed the silver bar on the door and it squeaked open. Berie went in first, stepping forward and pointing his M4. He raised it toward the tower of stairs. "Shit," he said. SWAT officers hated stairwells, labyrinths that offered no cover, perfect places to be ambushed. The officers would have a hard time seeing threats above, and if shots hammered down there was nowhere to hide. Berie stepped forward as the others fanned out around him, each pointing a rifle or pistol in a different direction.

"Slow," Scott said to Berie up front.

"Take long, all the way up," Canete called back to Edwards, wanting the rookie to train his rifle toward the top of the stairs as high as he could see, in case someone leaned over the railing to fire down at them.

They climbed the first flight of stairs and arrived at a small landing. Along the stairs, the officers saw droplets of blood. They saw more blood on the hand railing, as if the shooter had leaned over to look down and see if anyone was following. The shooter had also left red smears on the wall. They paused, studying the stains. It looked as if the shooter had traced a message in red, the letters "R" and "B."

They kept ascending until they reached the door to the second floor. Its silver handle was covered in blood. Through the door's small window, Berie spotted a mark of blood on a wall. This was the floor.

"Here's the deal," Canete whispered, locking eyes with the patrol officers. "The only way we're going to catch this guy is if we can sneak up on him. Turn your radios off. Don't say a fucking word. This is for real. There's no cavalry coming behind us. We are the fucking cavalry."

Canete swung open the door. Berie stepped out first, and the others fell into a diamond formation, each with his gun pointed in a different direction. Compared to the chaos of the lobby, the second floor was eerily quiet. An air conditioner hummed. The sirens outside sounded far away.

Berie signaled to the blood mark on the wall. It was at the beginning of a forty-yard hallway. The men moved along the corridor silently, listening for any sound that might give away the gunman's location. They saw only closed doors. Canete wondered what was behind them. More students? The shooter? He stretched out his arm and tried the door handle to the first room. It was locked. He scanned the hallway but saw no more blood. Somehow the shooter had stopped his bleeding.

The men decided to push forward down another corridor. "Let's flank him," Scott said. They crept along the hallway, moving past framed student artwork and black leather benches. It felt like they were walking into an ambush. There were too many hallways, too many doors, too many places to hide.

As they neared a corner, there was a reflection of movement on a wall of windows overlooking the street outside. Scott raised his rifle and whispered, "I've got contact." The reflection froze. "Police. Let me see your hands," Scott called out. In the hallway were two young women—apparently students—holding on to each other as they walked, weeping and terrified. Canete motioned to them to come to him. "Where is he? Did you see him?" he whispered, putting his hand on one woman's shoulder to try to calm her.

At that moment, the men heard the rapid bursts of a semiautomatic rifle from deeper inside the building. Canete pushed the women toward the stairwell, and the officers moved toward the gunfire. *Who is he shooting now?* Canete thought.

* * *

Down on the street, during a lull in the gunfire, officers had emerged from cover to usher protesters off the streets and away from downtown. One of those was Sgt. Mike Smith, a twenty-eight-year veteran who'd been patrolling downtown for five years. He stood outside a 7-Eleven, warning pedestrians to leave the area, when again came the sound of an assault rifle. The glass windows of the convenience store shattered, and Smith fell to the ground, his keys clanging noisily on the pavement. Other officers ducked behind patrol cars, their ears ringing. This time, several had seen exactly where the shots were coming from, a second-story window of the college. Once again, the calls went out over the police radio: "Shots fired!" "Officer down!" Officers heaved Smith off the pavement and rushed him down the street, looking for help.

Veteran paramedic Daniel Diaz heard the shots from the passenger seat of an ambulance riding along Main Street. He shouted for his intern to take cover in the back. "Get the fuck under the stretcher!" he yelled. As Diaz rolled up his window, his partner looked over. "You know those aren't bulletproof, right?" he said. Diaz shouted back, "It's better than nothing!"

Paramedics had been instructed not to enter the hot zone, but Diaz and his partner did anyway, and they came upon the group of officers with Smith. Diaz jumped out. He saw blood soaking the front of Smith's uniform shirt. He told Smith to lie down on the stretcher, but Smith refused. "I'm fine," he kept saying. Diaz had worked in some of the toughest areas of southern Dallas for two decades and knew how to deal with uncooperative patients. "Lay down, man, you're good," he said sternly. Smith did.

A couple of cops piled into the ambulance, lining a bench along one side. That left little room for Diaz to maneuver. He climbed on top of Smith, straddling him. His partner took off Smith's shirt and found gunshot wounds to his chest and right shoulder. Another paramedic drove them toward Parkland Memorial Hospital.

"Where are you from, man?" Diaz asked, trying to make small talk as he slipped on a blood pressure cuff. Smith said he lived in Carrollton. "Yeah?" Diaz asked. "I used to live in Carrollton." They kept talking, Smith mentioning his two daughters. He said his wife, Heidi, taught school at Mary Immaculate.

"Oh, you're Catholic?" Diaz asked. "Me, too. I used to go to church there, but it's too modern for me."

Smith laughed.

"I like the old-school Latin Mass," Diaz said.

While they talked, Diaz inserted an IV and monitored Smith's vitals. He couldn't figure out how Smith was talking so well, given his dropping blood pressure and slowing heart rate. Diaz reminded himself, *Treat the patient, not the machine.*

As they neared the hospital, Smith struggled to breathe. Diaz grabbed his tools, preparing to do an emergency procedure. He shouted for his partner to help. But Smith looked him in the eye. "Stop," he said. "Take my boots off."

Diaz paused. It sounded like Smith was giving up. "You're going to be okay," Diaz said, and kept working.

"Please," Smith said. "Please take my boots off."

Diaz looked down at Smith's boots, the laces gnarled in knots. He grabbed his pocket knife, cut the laces, and slipped off the shoes.

Smith smiled. "That feels really good."

* * *

Sitting in his Tahoe on hotspot duty, talking by phone with his niece, negotiator Larry Gordon had been listening to the police radio the way all cops do, hearing and not hearing the stream of chatter. Cops hone their radio voices into controlled monotony, never wanting to sound flustered or afraid. One of the most embarrassing things that can happen to an officer is to be told by a dispatcher to calm down.

Just after sunset, Gordon's radio erupted with sounds unlike any he'd heard in two decades on the force. What was coming out of his radio was so unbelievable he thought it must be a prank. Men and women were screaming and shouting and cursing, many of their voices cut off midsentence as other officers broke in. Gordon pushed a button on his console to activate his lights and sirens, turned his wheel, and pressed hard on the gas. As Gordon drove, a voice he recognized broke through over the radio. It was Willie Ford, an officer he'd trained while working narcotics. Ford was a former U.S. Army paratrooper who did not easily rattle. Now he was shouting, sounding distraught as he summoned the police helicopter. "Air One, Air One!" he screamed. "Lamar and Main!"

Gordon could not imagine a scenario that would prompt Ford to break radio etiquette and shout like that. He pulled off the road, climbed out of his Tahoe, and lifted the tailgate to retrieve his heavy ballistic vest. He'd taken it apart that morning for the rifle qualification, slipping out the plates so he could lie more comfortably on the grass, a trick that provided a slight advantage. *Shit!* he thought. Now he shoved the plates back in. He grabbed his M4 and slung it over his shoulder, cinching the strap tight. He knew precious seconds were ticking by, but he'd once heard an Arkansas game and fish officer give a talk about how he'd taken a moment to pull out his M4 while driving up on two men who'd killed two cops. If he hadn't done that, the officer said, he'd have been killed, too. Instead, he shot the bad guys. Over the radio, commanders instructed SWAT to meet at police headquarters. Gordon sped in that direction, but as he pulled into the parking lot, he heard a couple of SWAT teammates describing their pursuit of a gunman through the college. He peeled out of headquarters and drove several blocks, pulling up at the same time as Huante and their squad leader, Kelvin Johnigan, nicknamed "Pup." They climbed out of their cars and Gordon locked eyes with Huante, noting his teammate's uncharacteristic look of concern.

They all knew, without saying, that Huante would take the lead. While it was comforting to fall in line behind Huante, it was also unsettling. Huante was their best protector and the one most likely to lead them right into the storm. He was so fierce, Gordon imagined that he'd lost his fear of death. Gordon had not lost his. It was all he felt, and it coursed through his body with every heartbeat. They walked beneath tall buildings, every dark window a menace, every doorway a threat. Gordon was grateful that their squad leader, Pup, was there. He was one of the few men who could keep Huante in check.

Huante led the men alongside the wall of a brick parking garage, toward the college. By this time, about twenty minutes after the first shots, the streets were eerily empty. Sirens wailed from patrol cars parked haphazardly about, their doors left ajar. The men jogged across an intersection, passing small dark pools along the concrete. Gordon glanced down at one and instantly regretted it, realizing he was looking at brain matter and blood. His heart pounded faster. As the men approached the shattered glass doors of the college, Pup turned to Gordon. "You don't have to go up," he said. "You can stay down here and set up a command post." Gordon looked at Pup. Was he joking? Gordon would never live that down. He shook his head. "I'm going," he said. Pup grinned. They stepped into the airy atrium of the college, and Gordon wondered if they'd make it back out.

* * *

Chief Brown was at home, just about to take off his uniform, when his cell phone rang. It was his second in command, David Pughes.

"Hello, uh, Chief?" Pughes said. He sounded out of breath.

"What is it?" the chief asked.

"We've got shots fired and three officers down," he said.

"How many shooters are there?" he asked.

"We don't know yet," Pughes said. "There are reports of several."

"And what is the condition of the officers?" the chief asked.

"They're low sick," Pughes said, using police slang for really bad off.

The chief hurried back to his car and drove to Dallas City Hall, listening to his commanders over the radio. Brown walked into a specially fortified emergency command center in its basement. The space had white walls, rows of tables and laptops, large televisions, and wall-mounted city maps. It had backup power generators and was built to withstand hurricane-force winds. The center had seen an unusual amount of activity in recent years: a man shooting up police headquarters, a local man and his nurse contracting Ebola.

After terse greetings to several officials, the chief told an assistant to summon a dispatch team, so he could listen to 911 calls in real time. His public information officers were gathered around a desk, monitoring Facebook and Twitter. He told them to put the feeds on a large screen. The best information was coming from citizens posting cell phone videos. Reporters were broadcasting live, and their breathless coverage played on the televisions. Area politicos and law enforcement officials arrived one after the other: the mayor, the county judge, several commanders with the Texas Rangers. FBI officials also showed up and took over a small conference room in back. If evidence indicated terrorism, the FBI could take control at any moment, whether local officials liked it or not. The agency's regional head seemed content to wait and see how it played out. The room became noisy as people shouted back and forth. Many eyes were on the chief, pacing in his steady, unflappable way, talking on his cell phone, periodically walking up front to relay an update.

In his six years as police chief, Chief Brown had not lost a single officer in the line of duty. Now he got word that three officers were dead, two more were fighting for their lives, and at least another half dozen were injured. Some of those were his officers, and others worked for DART.

The chief's initial assessment, given the amount of gunfire, was that the city was under coordinated attack from multiple gunmen, likely in elevated sniper positions across downtown. He ordered his SWAT commanders to search parking garages and high-rises. He also ordered officers to search for a group of men who'd shown up at the protest in camouflage, carrying AR-15s. Because Texas is an open-carry state, this was legal. Now the chief wondered if they'd carried out the attack.

Commanders issued a Code 100, a rarely issued alert informing officers that they faced a deadly threat. If they encountered the suspect, they needed to be ready to shoot on sight.

13

The Firefight

The Three Amigos—Canete, Berie, and Scott—and the two patrol cops, Lopez and the rookie Edwards, headed toward the gunshots on the college's second floor. They fell into what they called a heavy head formation, putting as many officers as possible in front so they could shoot forward without hitting each other. Canete noticed a strange smell, tinny and unfamiliar. The shooter's blood? He could tell from the other men's body language that they were thinking the same thing. *He's close.*

Scott, a former Marine, began tactical breathing, a loud, whooshing inhale and exhale to lower his heart rate. Every instinct was telling them to turn around. No matter how much a cop trained, it was still hard to run toward a gunfight. Scott was trying to prepare himself. *You're about to get shot. It's gonna hurt. But it's not an excuse to bail. No matter what happens, stay in the fight.*

The men advanced down the hallway, thirty yards that felt like thirty miles, together in one fluid movement, feeling as if they were part of a machine that was driving itself. The hallway widened into a space almost like a traffic circle. It had three exits—two that led into hallways and one into a stairwell.

Berie pushed forward, covering the stairwell. The two others broke right, each taking a hallway. From where Canete stood, he caught a slight shadow of movement. "Contact," he said quietly.

The other Amigos stayed locked in their positions as Canete pressed his head against the wall, looking down the hallway. He knew the shadow might be a student or teacher. Then he saw a tuft of dark hair and a form that appeared pressed against the wall, slinking away from the officers. Canete watched the figure leap across the hallway into a small alcove. He saw a rifle, a plate carrier, a right arm soaked with blood, and cargo pants. Canete raised his M4 and steadied for a shot, but the figure disappeared. The guy's movements were confident and tactical. He was not their typical street criminal.

"Plate carrier!" Canete said in a harsh whisper.

"Kill that motherfucker," Scott whispered in reply.

"Take the shot, take the shot!" patrol officer Lopez said.

Canete could no longer see the suspect. *Son of a bitch*, Canete thought. *He's going back the other way.* He thought about the officers they'd left guarding the hallways and classrooms. Would the shooter sneak up on them? Canete stayed focused on the corner, the rifle pressed into his cheek, ready to shoot.

Then came a voice from down the hall, low and taunting. "Black power, motherfuckers."

Who is he talking to? Canete thought. Then he realized, *Oh, us.*

Edwards, the rookie, standing just behind Canete, said, "Get him, Danny!"

The gunman was shouting now. "Black supremacy! Black liberation!"

Then the gunman snapped around the corner. Half his face

appeared but lower this time. He'd dropped into a crouch, a move Canete understood was intended to throw them off. The black barrel of the gunman's rifle was pointed directly at him.

In one fluid motion of muscle memory, Canete clicked off the safety with his thumb, glided his index finger into the trigger well, and squeezed.

* * *

Canete's path to the police department had been unusual. He'd grown up in South Dakota, where his father was an accountant. His mother, a nurse, homeschooled Canete and his two sisters until high school. The kids ran out the daylight chasing chickens, climbing barn silos, exploring the granary and hog house. When Canete got bored, he'd practice piano. He started off taking lessons from ranchers' wives, learning watered-down versions of Bach and Beethoven. He spent hours at the old upright in the family's living room, progressing to Rachmaninoff and Debussy. He began competing in regional competitions. When he was about ten, he heard Chopin's "Military Polonaise" for the first time. It was bombastic and dramatic, with endless trills up and down the keyboard. *If I can learn to play that*, Canete thought, *I can learn to do anything*. He wasn't blessed with long fingers, and as he strained to reach the notes, the muscles of his forearms burned. Over months of practice, he built up enough stamina to play the grueling piece. He played it at a regional youth competition and took home second place.

Canete earned a full piano scholarship to Colorado State, where he spent his nights alone in practice rooms. He'd sit for four and five hours at a time, without a drink of water or a bite of food, and play the same notes again and again. The effort was as much mental as physical. Preparation was the only way to succeed at competitions, to withstand the strain of sitting under the stage lights and facing the silence of large audiences. Nerves could make a pianist's hands shake and sweat. Some competitors took beta-blockers to calm themselves, but Canete researched what was happening with his body and learned to talk himself through it. *My heart rate is going up. Blood flow is increasing. Here comes the adrenaline.* The more he understood his physiological response, the better he could control it. He'd breathe deeply and travel to a quiet corner of his mind. He learned that repeatedly visualizing a performance in the days before a competition helped inoculate him against the stress. He'd open the music in a quiet room and visualize himself reaching for every note and chord of a fourteen-page piece. Preparation dictated mind-set, which dictated performance.

Through piano, Canete learned lessons that would define his approach to work and life. It shaped how he viewed the world and everyone in it. Nothing was too hard, everything was doable, so long as you were willing to work for hours or days or even years. He learned that any overwhelming task could be broken down into smaller pieces, first notes, then measures, then lines.

During the school years, Canete's focus was music. During the summers, he switched to rock climbing. He would disappear for weeks into the Black Hills, living out of his brown Honda Accord, exploring trails and camping under the stars. He loved lacing up his shoes, the smell of the air, beginning the ascent, being on the rock. He found that, like piano, climbing required a combination of mental and physical toughness. He loved being three hundred feet in the air, holding on to the mountain by his fingertips and toes. He had to forget about everything except what he was doing at that moment. Even with ropes, you could break bones by falling and crashing into the rock face. In moments of fear, he found his senses sharpened and heightened. Colors glowed bright and beautiful. He became aware of every move his body made. He'd never experimented with drugs, but he imagined they created the same thrilling intensity.

Canete's friends and relatives called him an adrenaline junkie, but Canete didn't see it that way. The flood of stress hormones was as uncomfortable to him as anyone. The allure of placing himself in the way of danger was in learning how to override the stress, being able to perform in spite of it.

After college, after crisscrossing the country for music auditions, playing at Lincoln Center and too many weddings, he enrolled to get a master's at the University of North Texas at Denton. But by then, his drive toward a life in music was fading. He hadn't been able to secure a coveted spot in a symphony orchestra; hundreds showed up for every audition. At twenty-five, to the shock of his parents and friends, he left the master's program and moved to Dallas to become a cop.

* * *

The thing that surprised Canete most about the police academy was how little training it required to get a badge and a gun. He'd spent years perfecting a single piece of music. Here, instructors would teach life-or-death concepts in an hour, do one exercise, then move on. Canete, ever the overachiever, read every book in Barnes & Noble about shooting and spent hours in the woods aiming at Coke cans. After initially lagging in daily runs, trailing recruits who'd returned from military tours, he showed up at the track every morning before class, and he got faster. After eight months at the academy, he took home two second-place awards, one in fitness and one in shooting.

He spent five years on patrol before he began trying out for SWAT. That it took him two years and four tries to make it wasn't for lack of skills, but because his cockiness sometimes grated on people. It's not that his confidence was misplaced; he was great at everything he did. It was just that he knew it. With his big words, book knowledge, and college degree, some officers found him hard to take. Canete knew he could be off-putting. He'd once confided in his mom, "There's a fine line between confidence and arrogance, and I don't always know where that line is." He finally made it onto SWAT because other officers could not deny his tactical mind and abilities.

That's when he started reading about Japanese samurai, maybe the fiercest and most honor-bound warrior class in history. They valued both fighting and the arts. The best samurais knew how to take out a dozen enemies with a sword and write perfect calligraphy. They lived by a code of honor, what they called Bushido, or "the way of the warrior": to take the right action for the right reason at the right moment. They viewed among the highest achievements the ability to remain calm when faced with mortal danger.

In this era of police shootings and Black Lives Matter, many people believed police officers should be less warrior, more guardian. Canete thought that wasn't exactly true. The world needed its warriors. Just well-trained ones.

* * *

While large segments of communities saw the police shootings of recent years as moral failures, fueled by racial animus, SWAT officers tended to view them as examples of cops who hadn't been taught how to manage fear. To SWAT, which had the luxury of relentlessly training for high-stakes scenarios, the viral videos showed officers who hadn't traveled enough dark hallways. They hadn't been taught to wait that extra tick, the time needed to accurately process potential threats. SWAT saw men and women succumbing to a basic human reflex: *See threat, stop threat.* They saw adrenaline causing tragic errors in judgment.

The shooting of twelve-year-old Tamir Rice stood out. It was a cold morning in 2014 in Cleveland, Ohio, with snow blanketing the grass. Tamir was walking aimlessly along a sidewalk outside a recreation center. He was big for his age, five feet seven and 195 pounds. He held an Airsoft pellet gun, a lifelike replica of a Colt, purchased at Walmart. The guns, which shoot pellets, usually have orange tips, marking them as toys. Tamir had borrowed one from a friend, who'd taken it apart and been unable to refasten the tip.

A security camera captured images of Tamir wandering along the sidewalk, at times raising the gun as if he were about to shoot. A man sitting in the park called 911, telling a dispatcher about "a guy in here with a pistol." He described the person as black, wearing a camouflage hat and a gray jacket. The caller was calm and told the dispatcher it was "probably a juvenile" and the gun was "probably fake."

Tamir kept walking. He picked up a handful of snow and tossed it into the air. He walked to a gazebo and sat at a picnic table. Then he got up, walked around some more, pointing the gun, then sat back down. He placed his head on his arms and sat still for a couple of minutes. A marked Cleveland police car sped toward him, drove over a curb, and parked in the grass. Tamir got up and walked toward it. The two officers inside hadn't been told the suspect might be a juvenile. They thought they could be dealing with an active shooter outside a rec center filled with kids. They jumped out of the car with pistols drawn. One of them, a twenty-six-year-old rookie, fired two shots. It was over in less than two seconds. Tamir died the next day. An Ohio grand jury declined to indict the officers in his death, which a prosecutor described as a "perfect storm of human error."

Many SWAT officers who watched the video felt terrible for Tamir, but they also felt bad for the cops. They understood why the officers had unholstered their guns. But they also saw poor training. Why had the officers driven straight up to someone they believed might be an active shooter? If they'd allowed proper distance and cover, they would have had more time. Many police shootings happened in minutes. As an incident stretched on, it became increasingly less likely an officer would shoot. Time could be an officer's biggest ally.

There was another video out of Minnesota, of an officer standing on the side of a four-lane highway during a traffic stop. That officer, Jeronimo Yanez, was talking politely to a driver when a car sped by, nearly hitting him. "Oh shit!" he screamed. "Fucking A!" He ran to his car and gave chase.

"I literally almost just got hit by a car," Yanez said over the police radio. After a two-minute chase, the driver pulled over and got out with his hands up. Yanez and another officer cuffed him. Then Yanez, in his late twenties, sat back down in his patrol car, breathing hard. Another officer noted his amped-up state. "You're all right, dude," the officer said. "Take a minute."

"I'm sorry, man," Yanez said. "I just fucking flipped out."

"Don't worry about it," the cop said. "Stuff happens."

Yanez kept breathing hard. The camera recorded his deep breaths, in and out, which continued for thirteen minutes. His body clearly had trouble processing the adrenaline and stress.

The incident was of little consequence, and the dash cam video probably never would have surfaced. Except that eight months later Yanez again found occasion to draw his gun. This time he pulled the trigger and killed Philando Castile.

* * *

On the second floor of the college, seeing the barrel of the gunman's rifle pointed at him from less than forty feet away, Canete's training and instincts took over. As he and the gunman let loose on each other, the sound of their high-powered rifles exploded across the hallway. Every shot sounded like a grenade. Canete had been in two prior shootings, and in each one he had experienced "auditory exclusion"—like his brain had turned off his ears. But that wasn't happening now. The sound was almost overwhelming. Canete, who'd left his plate-carrier vest in the car, was wearing only his thin patrol Kevlar vest, which he knew wouldn't protect him from the gunman's high-caliber rounds.

He shot through the wall, aiming where he imagined the man's neck and head to be, releasing about five rounds. At the same time, the gunman's return fire shattered a glass panel near Canete's head, and shards flew. Bullets ripped through the walls and ricocheted off metal door frames, sending sparks into the air. Sheetrock disintegrated, clouding the hallway with dust and sending debris into Canete's eyes. Canete flinched and jerked off to the side, rolling out of the line of fire.

The other two Amigos, Scott and Berie, thought Canete had been hit. They immediately took his place, leaning out in a high-low position, each searching for a shot. Both men had a fraction of a second to make their own high-stakes decisions—shoot or don't shoot.

* * *

They'd arrived at a fateful moment most cops never have to face. Pull the trigger, and you might be a hero. Or you might choose wrong and kill an innocent person—and in the same motion disgrace yourself, maybe lose your career, maybe even wind up in prison. Or you might wait a second too long and get yourself killed.

Beginning in police academy, cops are trained in scenarios designed to help them make split-second decisions on whether to pull the trigger. They enter a pretend home, searching for a bad guy, and come upon a suspect with both hands up. Many cops, early in their training, shoot the surrendering suspect.

As Scott and Berie searched for a shot, they knew they had to stop the gunman. But they also knew they were responsible for the consequences of every bullet that left their firearms. They hadn't cleared the building, and they didn't know where those bullets would stop. There might be college students on the other side of the gunman, or cops running to help. The two SWAT officers, facing the same threat from the same vantage point, came to opposite decisions.

Scott's military background played into his calculation. He'd been rocketed and mortared in Iraq, where soldiers were taught to respond to aggression with overwhelming force. They were taught that once they engaged, the fight should be fast and brutal. Now, Scott decided lethal force was justified. He couldn't see the shooter, but the bullets that just came from that direction provided plenty of evidence he was there. Scott slid off his safety and unloaded. He felt as if he could not pull the trigger fast enough. Down the hallway, the shooter did the same. Both men were unleashing the kind of suppressive fire deployed in war zones. It wasn't exactly "spray and pray," but Scott emptied about twenty-six rounds, nearly a full magazine.

Berie, standing just behind Scott and over him, was focused on his sights, waiting for a shot. He'd never been to war; he'd been schooled in the rules of engagement of city policing. Officers were taught to never, ever fire unless they had a clear view of their target. Berie couldn't see anything in the dusty, smoky hallway. He kept looking, waiting for the target to present.

Quickly, Scott ran out of ammo and pulled back, as did Berie. They had the shooter pinned down, but considering their own weak position, that was of little comfort. The men were breathing hard. Gun smoke had set off the building's fire alarm, and a robotic voice was blaring, "Attention, an emergency has been reported. . . . Do not use the elevators."

Canete, who had not been hit, looked behind them down the hallway, hoping to see officers arriving to back them up. But the corridor was empty. He wondered what the hell they should do next.

14

Baylor Hospital

Detective Cesar Soto was working overtime, helping his narcotics squad break down a large indoor marijuana-growing operation. He'd just walked into the property room when he heard there was an active shooter downtown. He paused, listening for details. Then he heard injured officers were being transported to Baylor University Medical Center, right nearby. He climbed into his Ford F150 and sped that way.

When he pulled into the ambulance bay, it looked like business as usual, people coming and going from the emergency room. Soto stepped out of his truck and began waving people out of the area. Then he heard the sirens approaching. He saw a patrol car come flying around the corner into the parking lot, clanking on its rims, sparks flying and smoke pouring from underneath the hood. Soto stood there, amazed at the sight. As the car lurched to a stop, he saw it was riddled with bullet holes. *Jesus.*

Soto ran to the rear passenger door and yanked it open. A DART officer was slumped forward in the seat. Soto grabbed his shoulder and pulled him back. The officer had a gaping head wound.

Soto and a couple of other officers laid the wounded man on the ground as someone went to find a stretcher. From behind him, Soto heard a scream. He looked over his shoulder and saw a bystander, an older woman, looking at the officer, her hands covering her mouth as she kept screaming. Officers did chest compressions until a gurney arrived.

Another patrol car careened into the parking lot and came to a stop, and Soto heard someone pounding on the glass in the back, apparently stuck inside. Soto opened the passenger door and a huge officer fell partially out. The officer who'd been pounding the glass was straddled across his chest, working on his wounds. Soto immediately recognized the giant wounded officer as Lorne Ahrens, whom he'd worked with at Southwest. Soto and other officers slid Ahrens to the ground and looked him over. Soto was relieved to see little blood. But Ahrens's head was rocking back and forth. "I can't breathe," he said. "I can't breathe." Another gurney arrived, and the men struggled to heave Ahrens onto it. Soto looked him in the eye. "Just try to relax," he said.

By the time they got Ahrens inside, Soto looked back and saw his partner helping a tall female DART officer with a wounded arm through the door. Then another car came wheeling in. Soto opened its passenger door, and there lay a middle-aged black woman accompanied by a frantic teenage boy. Soto helped get her into the hospital, then stood in the ambulance bay in a daze.

Soto was a former Marine. He thought he'd seen just about everything as a city cop. He'd fished a dead child out of a pond. He'd seen people burned to death in car accidents. He'd seen people do awful things to one another. But seeing this mortally wounded officer, the thought kept returning: *I can't believe a man did that to another man.*

Soon, someone approached a pool of blood and brain matter left behind on the pavement, and gently placed a towel over it, out of respect. That wounded man had been doing his job like any of them, and now pieces of him lay on the ground.

* * *

In a trauma room, DART officer McBride lay in a bed as nurses inserted an IV and hooked her up to tubes and machines. She recognized a nurse she'd met a night or two earlier while dropping off someone who'd passed out from snorting bath salts. As the nurse worked, pain shot through McBride's arm. "Dammit," she yelled, then let out a moan and turned to her partner. "Call my mom," she said. "I don't want her to hear about this on the news." Her partner began removing her boots and pants and protective vest with its Wonder Woman patch. McBride had already handed over her Glock. Now she told her partner to get the second small gun strapped to the back of her ankle. A doctor came in, a white surgical mask hanging from his neck. He picked up a pair of scissors and leaned down to cut her shirt and undershirt. When McBride realized what he was doing, she looked up at him. "Don't cut my bra," she said.

Her partner looked over and rolled her eyes. "Misty, seriously!"

"I love this bra!"

The doctor, tall with a curly mustache, smiled as he bent down and snipped it in the front.

"You asshole," she said. He laughed.

A male nurse went to work taking off her tourniquet.

"How'd we do on the tourniquet?" she asked him.

"Honestly?" he said. "It looks like shit."

The doctor examined her wounds. A bullet had pierced her left arm, ripping through her triceps and shattering the bone. The doctor and nurses rolled her over, and she screamed in pain. They found two bullet wounds, one entry and one exit, in her abdomen.

They slipped an oxygen mask over her face as they worked. The room fell quiet, and McBride saw a Dallas police sergeant pacing outside her room, talking on the phone. She listened to his conversation and heard the words, "DART has a twenty-seven."

Twenty-seven was code for dead.

McBride struggled to take off her oxygen mask and rise from the bed. Which of her colleagues had been killed? She flailed, trying to rise, as nurses came to hold her down.

* * *

The wounded protester, Taylor, felt arms reaching into the car to pull her out. As they rolled her into the hospital on a gurney, her son walked beside her, still crying. "Andrew—I'm right here. I'm okay," she kept telling him. She needed him to calm down so he could help find his brothers.

A nurse rolled Taylor into a private room. The television showed news of the shooting, and a reporter noted the number of dead officers was rising. Taylor prayed her boys were okay.

She called her husband. "Don't freak out," she told him. "I've been shot. I'm at the hospital. And I need you to find the kids."

A long pause, then he said, "What?"

"I lost the kids!"

"What do you mean, you lost them?"

She tried to explain, then repeated, "Go find them. Do not come to this hospital until you have them."

About an hour later, Andrew appeared in the doorway. She realized for the first time that her son was covered in her blood, from his socks to his T-shirt. "Mom, they found them. They're all okay," Andrew said. Jajuan was with another mother who'd taken him to her apartment. There, he'd broadcast live from Snapchat. A cousin in Minnesota saw it, then called relatives in Dallas.

Taylor cried out from her hospital bed. "Thank you, Jesus!" she said. "My babies are okay!"

She noticed her shout drew the attention of two police officers, standing outside her door. They looked at her; both were crying. A few moments later, she heard one say to the other, "He didn't make it." The officers hugged and wept, and Taylor felt flooded with guilt. She'd cried out in celebration that her children were alive, but that officer was not.

15

Target Identification

SWAT team members arrived downtown from all directions and tried to find their teammates. When Banes stepped out of his marked SUV a couple of blocks from the college, he felt as if he'd been dropped into a giant, real-life shoot-don't-shoot drill. There were cops everywhere, civilians everywhere.

The drills had bedeviled Banes when he first joined SWAT. He'd shot a couple of mock innocents, part of the reason teammates started calling him Skeeter. During one training session, Banes rounded a corner and came upon a target in a fighting stance with a dark object in his hand. He fired. Teammates turned on the lights, and Banes realized the object was a cell phone. Huante, who'd been training him that day, was disgusted. "Who picked this fucking idiot?" During another session, trainers put a paper bad guy at the end of a hallway, with a nice big view of the muzzle. Easy. Banes rounded a corner, spotted his target, and, boom, bad guy dead. Then the trainers had Banes run the scenario again. Same bad guy at the end of the hallway. Banes fired. This time, Huante yelled at him, "You stupid motherfucker." Banes studied the target, realizing his teammates had covered up the rifle muzzle with a piece of ripped paper, making the person unarmed. "Target identification, you fucking idiot," Huante said. "Target identification."

One of the team's veterans liked to say, "I don't care how good you shoot. I don't care how fast you run. I want to know if you can see." Starting out, when most cops entered a dangerous space, their eyes narrowed as if looking through a straw. Stress caused tunnel vision. Not fully taking in a scene led officers to make deadly miscalculations. Many senior SWAT guys believed former athletes, particularly basketball players, were best at absorbing scenes quickly. During the fast-paced game, players had to read the whole court, know where everyone was moving, where the ball was going next. Many SWAT guys thought it took two to three years to fully train their eyes. Their exercises were as much about seeing as shooting straight. Over time, Banes had trained his eyes to work like a camera, capturing a still shot and sending it to his brain for quick processing.

As he advanced past an office tower next to the college, he tried to accept information from his full field of vision, searching for anyone whose body language suggested aggression. He entered the college, hurried through its atrium, and stepped into the stairwell, following the gunman's blood trail. He felt like a bull's-eye as he moved quietly up one stair, then another. He heard a blast of gunfire, close, but far enough away that he knew he wasn't in imminent danger. Then above him, a stairwell door swung open, and two figures sprang out. Banes snapped his M4 into firing position. He waited a split second and focused on the midsections and the hands, looking for weapons. In one of the figure's hands, he spotted a small black object. He focused on it and realized it was a cell phone. His view widened, and he saw the phone was held by one of two young women, scared and crying. He lowered his gun. As they ran past, he felt flooded with gratitude for Huante's shaming and all those drills, and he began scanning for the next target.

Banes stepped onto the second floor and saw Canete come wheeling around a corner, eyes wild. "Follow me!" he said.

They ran down the hallway, joining the other guys. Banes was shocked by the scene, dozens of spent rounds and chunks of Sheetrock scattered across the carpet. This was not a SWAT call; it was a war zone. The fire alarm was so loud he could barely hear. "Shut the fuck up!" Banes yelled at the ceiling. "Goddamn."

He decided to load bonded rounds into his rifle, bullets that could penetrate doors and walls. The sound of Banes loading a new magazine and slapping his rifle bolt forward filled the hallway. Hearing it, the gunman called out a phrase, something that sounded like "Abedi Mahoya!"

Banes turned to his colleagues. "Who is that talking?"

"That's him," Berie replied.

Then the gunman unloaded, firing down the hallway toward them. They stayed pressed against a wall. The other guys had become acclimated to the sound. But even for Banes, a veteran cop who'd been shooting guns since high school, a semiautomatic rifle blasting away in the enclosed space was startling. He pulled back from the corner and reflexively ducked, then felt embarrassed by his reaction. The hallway fell quiet again, and he steadied himself.

"No surrender!" the gunman yelled, before firing again.

Banes took his turn as lead, replacing Berie, and mounted his rifle against the wall. He looked through his optic, waiting for a shot.

Seconds ticked by as the cops debated what to do. "Anybody got a banger?" someone whispered. Banes had several small canisters called flash bangs on his vest. He could pull the pin on one, toss it, and it would explode with blinding light and thunderous sound. Its pressure wave would blow out windows. The distraction could give them time to run down the hallway and kill the gunman. Banes thought about it. Flash bangs were good for disorienting the average bad guy, but this gunman appeared well prepared. *He's a real deal badass*, Banes thought. The second the canister hit the ground, the guy would probably start shooting again. "You guys sure you want to bring the heat?" Banes said. It was a miracle no one had been hit; how many more bullets could they dodge? They decided against it.

The gunman was shouting again, "Black power! Black power!"

"He's psyching himself up," patrol officer Lopez said to the men.

Banes stayed focused on the corner as Canete and Berie took turns crouching beside him.

"I am energy," the man shouted. "Therefore, I cannot be destroyed. Die, white devils! Black supremacy! Black liberation!"

Berie called out down the hallway. "What's your name?"

"X!" came the reply.

"Huh?" Berie called back, confused.

"X! I am he who cannot be named, who will not be enslaved," the gunman shouted.

Canete spoke up. "Hey X, what's going on with you, buddy? What's going on? Why are you so upset?"

"I'm really tired of hearing these goddamn sirens," the gunman yelled.

"Yeah, we're working on the sirens," Canete said. "X, I need you to put that gun DOWN and come on out here."

"Why would I do that?" he said.

"Well, I know you're prepared for this. Obviously, this isn't going to end well," Canete said. "X, you got the entire police department raining down on you. If it's the fight that you want, well, you got it. So we can end it like this or—"

"Revolution!" the gunman screamed. "Revolution!"

Officer Lopez started talking. "If you come out," he said, "we mean you no harm."

The gunman shouted back. "I don't care about dying."

Lopez continued. "I know you don't, but you care about your

word. You think the media is going to be done with you after they see what happens? But if you go to court, it's going to get dragged out."

X poked out his gun and started firing again. Lopez, startled by the sound, returned fire with his pistol.

Edwards, standing about fifteen feet behind them and around a corner, felt something hit his left arm. The rookie looked down. A round had come through the wall, ricocheted, and nicked his arm, bouncing off. "Rounds through the wall! Rounds through the wall!" he shouted.

No shit, Henry, Canete thought.

Canete wanted the squad to move out of the hallway and into the concrete and cinder-block stairwell. But Banes, still taking lead on the corner, wasn't sure. They wouldn't be able to see the gunman from back there. "Listen to me," Canete told him. "I want you to pull back here to me, now." Banes nodded, deferring to Canete's judgment. He'd hold cover while the officers tried to cross eight feet of open hallway to the stairwell. "Y'all move," he said. "I got this." He stayed focused on the hallway. As the men started moving, the gunman poked his barrel around the corner again to fire.

Banes peered through his optic, positioning the red dot. His hold on the target? Solid. Confidence in his shot placement? High. He squeezed. The first few rounds shot like fireballs out of his M4, freshly oiled after his rifle qualification that morning. Banes no longer heard the sound. His ears seemed to close as his eyesight sharpened. He felt almost like he could see each bullet as it left his rifle. He saw smoke puff out of his muzzle, just as it curled out of his adversary's muzzle down the hallway. The clouds seemed to meet in the middle in a swirl, filling the hallway.

The gunman's rounds ricocheted and sparked everywhere, as if someone were waving sparklers. The shooter's head disappeared, but Banes stayed focused on the corner, fearing the gunman was about to charge. *I'm going to die here*, Banes thought. *I'm about to die.*

16

White Boy Wayne

Fifteen years earlier, when Banes arrived at the police academy, he'd already served in the Coast Guard for four years, chasing Mexican drug runners across the Gulf of Mexico, full throttle in a go-fast boat, armed with an M16. After a few years on the police force, he had applied for narcotics, but a sergeant cautioned the unit against hiring him. Banes, the supervisor had said, was oblivious to danger. Fearless, but not in a good way. He was going to get himself or somebody else killed. Narcotics supervisors hired Banes anyway; fearless was something they prized.

As an undercover, Banes took on the character of White Boy Wayne Matthews, who he might have been in real life if he hadn't been raised by a churchgoing fifth-grade science teacher and a computer programmer. Banes had grown up in the country, in the small town of Greenville, Texas, with three brothers. The Banes boys spent their youth catching and skinning snakes, hunting whitetail deer, reeling in bass, fieldstripping rifles, riding dirt bikes, and getting stitches after boxing matches.

Hundreds gathered at a rally in downtown Dallas on Thursday, July 7, 2016.
Smiley N. Pool/ *Dallas Morning News*

An overhead photograph shows the intersection of Main and Lamar streets moments before the gunman began his attack. Officer Patrick Zamarripa, who was killed, can be seen standing by a patrol car on the lower left. Two of the other slain officers are standing in the crosswalk at top: Senior Cpl. Lorne Ahrens (center) and Officer Michael Krol (right). To the left of them is Foxtrots Sgt. Ivan Gunter. Smiley N. Pool/*Dallas Morning News*

Dallas police lined up along a wall at the corner of Lamar and Main, training their weapons toward the El Centro campus after shots were fired.
Smiley N. Pool/*Dallas Morning News*

Rookie officer Gretchen Rocha ran to help load an injured colleague into a police cruiser during the gunfire. Smiley N. Pool/*Dallas Morning News*

After she was shot in the leg, protester Shetamia Taylor (middle, in a dark shirt) was helped by officers including Greg Weatherford (in the baseball cap). Smiley N. Pool/*Dallas Morning News*

These images, captured by security cameras, show the gunman's path through the community college minutes before he engaged with Dallas SWAT.
Dallas SWAT

Officers followed the gunman's trail of blood up a staircase inside the community college.
Dallas SWAT

Larry Gordon, forty-five, was the lead negotiator who spent hours talking to the gunman.

Smiley N. Pool/*Dallas Morning News*

Larry Gordon and his wife, Shan, who is a schoolteacher. Larry Gordon

Early in his negotiating career, Larry Gordon talked a young woman off the ledge of a Dallas skyscraper.

Photograph provided by Larry Gordon

The Three Amigos, from left: Senior
Corporals Ryan Scott, thirty-nine,
Danny Canete, thirty-four, and
Brandon Berie, thirty-one.
Smiley N. Pool/*Dallas Morning News*

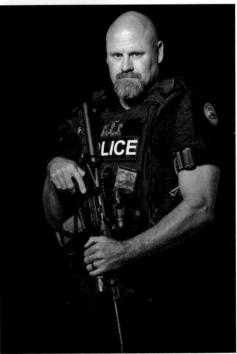

Senior Cpl. Matt Banes, forty-one.
Smiley N. Pool/*Dallas Morning News*

Senior Cpl. Gerry Huante, forty-six.
Smiley N. Pool/*Dallas Morning News*

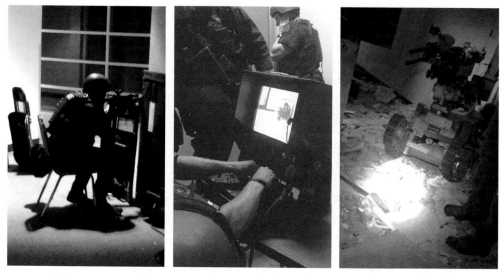

[left] Hours into the standoff, SWAT officer Danny Canete kept watch behind a ballistic shield, holding cover for negotiator Larry Gordon and other SWAT officers. Dallas SWAT

[center] SWAT officer Jeremy Borchardt remotely guided the robot, armed with C4, into the gunman's hideout. As soon as the machine rounded a final corner, the gunman could be seen from its camera. Dallas SWAT

[right] The robot, an eight-hundred-pound Remotec Andros Mark V-A1, remained upright after the blast. Dallas SWAT

SWAT officers peered around a corner after the explosion, trying to figure out whether the gunman was dead. Dallas SWAT

Just before 4:00 a.m., negotiator Larry Gordon (far left) and members of Dallas SWAT sat in the El Centro lobby, watching Mayor Mike Rawlings and Police Chief David Brown give a news briefing. Dallas SWAT

Dallas mayor Mike Rawlings stood with Dallas police chief David Brown (left, with sunglasses) as officers saluted the flag-draped casket of Officer Michael Krol. Tom Fox/*Dallas Morning News*

President Barack Obama joined hands with Dallas mayor Mike Rawlings and other dignitaries during an interfaith memorial service.
Smiley N. Pool/*Dallas Morning News*

Magnus Ahrens, eight, son of fallen Dallas police officer Lorne Ahrens, dropped flowers inside his father's grave in Dallas on July 13, 2016.

Rose Baca/*Dallas Morning News*

Dr. Brian Williams, the trauma surgeon who treated three of the fallen officers at Parkland hospital.

Dallas Morning News

Shetamia Taylor taught her sons Jajuan Washington, fifteen, and Kavion Washington to prepare their Thanksgiving meal at her Garland home on November 23, 2016, a few months after the shooting.

Nathan Hunsinger/*Dallas Morning News*

Narcotics was one of the most dangerous and difficult assignments on the police force. Officers had to scrub off their good-guy personas and fit into the worlds of suspects. Playing a convincing role could be a matter of life or death. Officers had to do things they would never do, say things they would never say. The best undercover personas contained half-truths about who an officer was. White Boy Wayne was an East Texas hillbilly, a heavy-drinking outlaw who loved cheap whiskey, rode Harleys, and wore do-rags. Banes loved slipping into crack houses and cultivating hookers as informants. He loved the audaciousness of leaning out of his car window and yelling out, "Come over here and show me them titties." He loved walking up as a white redneck to the blackest dope house in southern Dallas and asking, "What's up, motherfuckers?" His philosophy as an undercover was to be so outrageous, so obnoxious, that the street creatures would tell him to calm down. He was so over-the-top that he couldn't possibly be a cop. Banes enjoyed days drinking Jim Beam, poured so strong it burned his nose, sitting at strip clubs investigating coke dealers. He grew a brown scraggly beard, about ten inches long, which his wife tenderly braided into three strands.

It was hard to be Wayne in the suburbs, though. He'd return home to his wife and three boys in a tidy four-bedroom, and neighbors would avert their eyes. So would his kids' principal at the elementary school's Meet the Teacher night. Banes didn't tell people he was an undercover, because he could never be sure his and Wayne's worlds wouldn't collide. His family often met his parents at an Italian restaurant where they were regulars. Sometimes his mom didn't like the way other diners looked at her son. She was a devout Baptist who wore pearls, baked casseroles, sang soprano in the church choir, and never cussed. She'd pass a table and whisper-shout to strangers, "My son's an undercover policeman. He doesn't usually look this way—it's his job." Banes smiled politely but reminded his mother that it wasn't a good idea to tell people.

One day a rookie detective on the narcotics unit asked for Banes's help on a drug buy. At first Banes said no. He was deep into a case against a crack operation fronting as a car wash. And it was an unwritten rule not to ask another undercover to do your dirty work. But the officer persisted, and Banes finally agreed. His assignment was simple, something he'd done many times. He'd buy some crack to help build a case against the dealer.

Banes walked up to a brick apartment complex one afternoon. His cover team, three other officers, waited around the corner. The front door was cracked so he invited himself in. An older black man, in his fifties, looked surprised to see him.

"Oh, hey man," Banes said. "I'm looking for Sweet Pea. She usually comes over here and handles my business for me."

"What are you trying to get?"

"A solid fifty."

"I can do that."

The man stood up and put on his shoes. Banes gave him $50, and the man walked toward the door. "Where you going?" Banes asked.

"To get your shit," the man said, and then left.

A basic rule on narcotics is never let your money walk. Sometimes dealers disappeared and never returned. Banes looked around the apartment, saw enough stuff worth $50, and figured the man wouldn't leave him there if he didn't plan on coming back.

Banes had a cell phone in his pocket. He was on an open line with his cover team so they could hear what was happening. He spoke aloud: "Black guy, tan slacks, fedora, walking through the parking lot." They'd see where the guy went and hit the stash house later. But they lost him in a breezeway. A few minutes later, fedora guy came back with the crack, and Banes left. Mission accomplished.

The rookie detective asked Banes to return a couple of days later. He wanted the stash house. They went back together; same fedora guy, same routine. While they waited for him to return, Banes videoed the apartment, recording the layout for when they returned with a search warrant. Fifteen minutes passed, then twenty. This was taking too long. Banes, looking out the kitchen window, saw a burgundy Honda pull up. A huge guy covered in tattoos walked toward the apartment.

"We got a bad motherfucker about to walk up in here," Banes said to his partner. They sat down on the couch.

The door opened and the guy, surprised to see them, pulled out a pistol. "Who the fuck are you?"

"Sorry, man," Banes said, standing to leave.

The man pushed him down on the couch. "Sit down. Y'all better not be no punk-ass police."

"Man, I been up in here a couple times, I ain't ever seen you," Banes said. "I was just trying to get a fifty."

A couple of other guys arrived. They talked quietly with the pistol guy for a moment, then looked at the rookie Hispanic detective with Banes. "Give me every motherfucking thing you got," pistol guy said. The detective looked confused. "No speaka English," he said.

About that time, fedora guy came back with the fifty. Pistol guy, not happy he'd let strangers in, threw him on the couch and started choking him.

Banes debated whether to pull his gun. He probably could shoot pistol guy in the back. He looked over at his partner, who knew what he was thinking, and shook his head.

Banes rose. "All right, seems like y'all have a family affair. We're going to get out of here."

The man rose and racked the slide on his pistol with a loud clack. Now there was meat in the gun. "You ain't going nowhere. Give me your wallet."

Banes handed it over. He wondered where the cover team was. He expected a brick to fly through the window any second, and he was ready for it. He'd learn later that his phone had died, and they had no idea what was going on.

As the man went through his wallet, looking for evidence that Banes was a cop, he tried to stay calm, but his anxiety was becoming unmanageable. Someone, he thought, was about to get shot. And he didn't want it to be him. He looked around the roach-infested, urine-stained apartment. *I'm going to die on the floor of this place*, he thought. He thought about his wife and sons and, for the first time, regretted his career choice. *I have sacrificed my life for fifty dollars' worth of crack.*

He watched the man, making a plan to pull his handgun. If he died today, he wanted to at least take pistol guy with him.

After examining the wallet, pistol guy set it down and looked over at Banes. He studied the driver's license photo of Wayne Matthews, then wrote down his address. "If you are not who you say you are," he said, "I will come find you. I will kill your wife after I've fucked her. Get out."

Banes moved toward the door. On the way, he reached back slyly and grabbed his wallet. He stepped into the daylight. The air had never smelled so fresh. As he walked along the sidewalk, cussing at the rookie detective for getting him into that mess, he felt his hands trembling, the adrenaline wearing off.

They walked around the corner, looking for their cover team, when the burgundy Honda peeled around the corner. *This ain't over*, Banes thought.

Banes felt a flood of panic and fear. Three people were in the car—two men and a female driver. Pistol guy stepped out and walked toward him. "You think you're a slick motherfucker, don't you?"

Then something strange happened. Banes felt his heart rate

slow as a warmth traveled through his body. He felt weirdly, unexpectedly calm. Almost as if a force had dropped a protective cloak over him. It was as close as he'd ever come to having a spiritual experience. He suddenly felt as if he were on the range. *Shooters, watch your target.* He spread his feet. When the man reached toward his waistband, Banes did the same. He raised his gun. Time unraveled in slow motion. Banes, looking through his sights, noticed they appeared as big as a basketball. Squeezing the trigger, he watched the man, whose arm was bent as he grabbed for his gun. He saw the man's shirt twitch beneath his armpit. Banes might have grinned then. *Double lung and heart shot.* The man spun around and collapsed on the pavement.

Then the calm evaporated, as quickly as it had come. Banes looked at pistol guy, bleeding on the street. He wasn't moving, and for some weird reason that made Banes angry. *Get up and fight, bitch!* He wasn't expecting to feel this much rage. It felt so big he didn't think he'd ever be able to reel it back in. People came out of their apartments. Banes ordered the female driver out of the car and onto the ground. Still, she reached into her purse. "Are you fucking stupid?" Banes screamed at her. "Get your hands where I can see them!" She looked back at him calmly, saying in a Texas drawl, "Baby, you ain't gotta kill everybody."

In that moment, Banes realized that's what he kind of wanted to do. Kill everybody. Just drop every person standing there watching him. Finally, his cover team wheeled around the corner.

The incident was later deemed a "good shoot," but sometimes Banes would lie in bed at night seeing images of the pistol guy's bedroom. He'd walked around the upstairs tactically, as a detective, as he'd done many times. He would never have thought about the home again if he hadn't killed the guy. Now those images were impressed on his mind, the man's toothbrush and toothpaste laid out neatly beside the sink. The tidiness of the man's closet. How he didn't have a bed frame, just a mattress on the floor and a sleeping bag. Banes had seen parts of that man's life that probably some of his close friends hadn't.

That man was a hardened gangster, Banes thought. But he also was just a man. With a toothbrush and shoes. A man who probably hadn't had a science teacher mom and computer programmer dad. Banes didn't regret what he'd done. But he couldn't shake a dark, anxious feeling.

Less than a year later, Banes was involved in another shooting. He and other narcotics detectives approached a wood-frame house to serve a search warrant. A suspect inside fired a pistol, hitting one officer in the leg. Banes and the others returned fire. Banes ducked behind a barbecue smoker while his teammates took cover behind an old couch on the curb. The uninjured suspect got away. Afterward, Banes felt like he'd been pulling the arm on a slot machine. Eventually his number would come up. Eventually he was going to prove that sergeant right and get himself killed.

He'd had plenty of dealings with SWAT over the years. During his time as an undercover, he'd gone to their briefing room dozens of times ahead of drug raids, which SWAT sometimes handled. Once Banes, with his long beard and ratty pants, had stood in front of a white board, explaining the layout of a stash house. He'd offhandedly mentioned that there were a couple of junked cars in the backyard. A SWAT officer with a big dip in his mouth raised his hand. "Do you have the VIN numbers for those vehicles?" Banes thought, and managed not to say, *No, as a matter of fact, while I was risking my life to make a drug buy from these huge-ass, penitentiary-bred dope dealers, I did not skip past the pit bulls in the backyard, open the doors of the junked cars, and collect the VINs.* Banes saw it as less a real question than another SWAT power play, a way to emphasize that he, lowly narcotics guy, was asking them, the mighty SWAT guys, for a favor. They wanted to make it clear that, if they were about to risk their lives so he could rack up another dope collar, he'd better get those VIN numbers next time, and for that matter anything else they wanted. Banes left every SWAT briefing thinking, *What a bunch of dickheads.* And yet he couldn't shake the appeal of becoming one of them. Facing the dragon with a dozen heavily armed buddies sounded a whole lot better than what he'd been doing.

He heard about an opening on SWAT and put in his application. Along with a couple dozen other hopefuls, Banes joined the weeklong tryout. He was one of the older recruits—thirty-eight, up against officers a decade younger. He lagged behind on the one-and-a-half-mile run but came in first on the three-hundred-meter sprint. He was not a tactical wizard or the most impressive physically, but he was a solid cop who'd handled himself in two shootings.

At the end of the week, the recruits sweated through push-ups in the summer sun. When they were finished, Banes walked toward his car. One of the squad leaders, Pup, called out to him, "Nah Banes, we ain't done yet." Banes turned around. That's when he saw Huante walking toward him, a hunting knife in his hand. He was coming right at him, looking at him with those crazy brown Huante eyes. *What the hell?* Banes was too tired for another tousling match with Huante.

Huante stepped up to him, reached over, and grabbed his beard.

"If you're going to be on SWAT, this motherfucker has to come off right now," Huante said. He sliced off his braid and shook it in the air. With that, Banes was the newest member of Dallas SWAT.

* * *

On the second floor of the college, Banes realized someone was yelling at him.

"Get out of there!" It was Canete. Banes bolted toward the stairwell and crouched low, breathing hard. He looked at the wall where he'd just been standing, scorched black by his muzzle blasts and filled with bullet holes. "Jesus, are those rounds?" he asked. Canete nodded. Banes leaned back against a wall, thinking about what had just happened. He hadn't gotten the gunman. He prayed he hadn't hit anyone else. Then he started laughing, as he tended to at the worst, most inappropriate moments. He saw the other guys look at him. *What the hell is wrong with you?*

As the men stood in the stairwell, someone suggested they get the gunman talking again. Banes spoke up, his East Texas accent echoing through the stairwell.

"What's the point in dying today, X? You still got a lot to say. All your actions tonight are going to require an explanation. Tell us what you want."

The gunman called back, "Y'all are gonna have to kill my ass, and I'm going to do my best to kill you."

"Roger, that," Banes said. "X, I hate to break it to you, but you sound very narrow-minded right now. Dude, are you a cop?"

"Fuck no!" the man yelled. "I'm trying to kill as many of y'all white pigs as I can. How many did I get?"

Banes thought about a large bloodstain and a pair of Oakleys he'd run past on the sidewalk, and he wondered how many cops had gone down. "What kind of gun are you shooting, man?" Banes asked.

The gunman answered, "An AK-74."

"You mean AK-47?"

"No, AK-*74*," the gunman said.

The answer gave Banes a chill. This guy knew his weapons, and he wanted to make sure Banes gave his choice due respect. He hadn't gone into a pawnshop and just picked something up. He'd made choices that only an experienced shooter could appreciate.

Banes had shot plenty of AKs. He knew the AK-74 used a bullet with a hollow cavity inside the nose, which makes it prone to rotating—or "yawing"—when hitting a target. If it yaws while inside a human body, it creates a wider swath of damage. It was a devastating round that could penetrate body armor.

"Want some water?" Banes asked.

"I'm good," the gunman said. "I've got my CamelBak."

Banes knew the shooter had been injured, but he seemed calm and sharp. Like he was playing paintball. Banes heard the gunman reloading again; he'd done so at least twice. He was well trained, his tactics solid and graceful. He was using wide angles and concealment, moving like a professional. Like them. *Who is this guy?* Banes wondered. *Was he working alone? Was he funded by a terrorist group?*

The gunman was close enough that Banes could hear him breathing. When he took a drink of water, Banes heard him swallow. As Banes contemplated his adversary, some glass from a shattered window fell to the floor, breaking the silence. The gunman must have thought officers had been coming for him, because a moment later he started laughing. "Man, I thought you guys were getting sneaky and coming through the window back here," he said. Banes couldn't help it; he laughed, too.

He's actually kind of funny, Banes thought. *Probably somebody I could have a beer with.* Banes thought about his wife and three sons. *Why am I here? This is the most ridiculous thing I've ever been a part of.* Men who might have gotten along in different circumstances, trying to kill each other in a narrow hallway. *For what?*

Banes caught a whiff of marijuana. "X, you firing up a little weed over there, man?"

"Not anymore," the gunman called out.

Banes tried to keep the gunman talking. "You just shot up the whole city of Dallas. That's it. That's all your story is."

"No it's not," X replied.

"I'm telling you, unless you got a better explanation that you can share with us, it's called being a coward."

Banes continued: "X, what's your real name? It's not like we're not going to know what your real name is, one way or another."

"That name is just my slave name," X replied.

"Your slave name?" Banes said, incredulous. "X, you're ate up, you're ate up, man."

Banes continued. "X, why don't we get you some water, get you a doctor, and move on with this?"

"I can't. I can't go back. There's no stopping this," X said.

"Evidently, the only person you got to talk to is me," Banes said. "I don't know if I'm going to relay your message necessarily very clearly—"

"Fuck that. FUCK THAT!" the gunman yelled.

Banes waited a minute, then called back, "X, you calmed down now? I think that weed's making you paranoid."

17

Code Yellow

At Parkland hospital, Dr. Williams had been handling typical evening arrivals, a car crash, a gallbladder surgery. He was about to do an appendectomy at around 9:00 p.m. when his pager buzzed. *Multiple gunshot victims.* Williams hurried into the trauma bay as nurses rolled in a severely wounded Dallas police officer. The man lay unconscious on a stretcher, parts of his uniform cut off, covered in blood.

Williams always put on a gown, booties, and a face mask to protect himself from blood-borne pathogens. He stressed to trainees that it was never okay to skip this. But now, he broke his own rule. There wasn't time. It was clear the officer was dying. Every second would count.

He usually stood back and directed his team, but tonight Williams snapped on rubber gloves and joined the group of a dozen nurses and residents beneath saucer-size lights. Machines beeped as they slipped a blood pressure cuff onto the officer's arm and inserted an IV. As Williams took his place beside the patient's chest, he sensed a heightened intensity among his team. Police officers and firefighters were in and out of the trauma center regularly; many were friends with the hospital staff. Williams knew what his teammates were thinking: *He's one of ours.*

Williams focused on the officer's chest and abdomen as residents and nurses worked on his arms and legs. As he worked, he began to lose hope. Assault rifle wounds differ drastically from those caused by handguns. Inside the human body, a handgun bullet carves a wound path roughly the size of its diameter. If it doesn't hit an essential organ, and if the victim doesn't bleed out on the way to the hospital, the chances of survival are good. Wounds from assault rifles, however, tend to be devastating. Their bullets travel roughly three times faster than those fired by a handgun. They rip through the body with more energy, shattering bones, shredding organs, and leaving gaping holes. The exit wound can be as big as an orange. A Florida doctor who treated patients in the Parkland school shooting compared an assault rifle bullet's path to a cigarette boat speeding through a narrow canal. The shooter does not have to be accurate. The wounds are often so devastating that, even if doctors reach a victim immediately, the odds of survival are slim.

After several minutes of trying to revive the officer, Dr. Williams looked up. "Can anyone think of anything else?" he asked. He scanned his teammates, peering at him over their masks. No one could. "We can't do anything more," he said. Williams peeled off his gloves, tossed them on the floor, and looked at the clock on the wall, calling out the officer's time of death, shortly after 9:00 p.m.

Hospital officials, expecting multiple casualties, declared a Code Yellow. They summoned extra staff, checked units of blood, and lined up teams in the hallway, each with a stretcher. Hospital police officers retrieved AR-15 rifles and stood guard; no one was getting into the ER without a badge. Cop cars wheeled up outside the ER, unloading more officers.

Williams rushed across the trauma department to Room 8. He

stepped through a group of residents and began working on the second officer to arrive. His injuries were similar to those of the first. Williams again made frantic attempts to revive the officer, but he quickly saw the man stood no chance. After a couple of minutes, Williams again pulled off his gloves and called out time of death. He stepped over to an industrial sink and turned on the water, watching the officer's blood spiral down the drain.

About that time, paramedics rolled in a third officer, who'd been brought in by ambulance, his boots off. This one was conscious and talking. Williams looked him in the eye and put a hand on his shoulder as the men spoke.

At first his injuries looked less severe, but as Williams examined his chest, it became clear he'd lost a lot of blood and needed immediate surgery. Williams sent him to an operating room with another surgeon who'd arrived to help.

Stepping into the hallway, Williams saw that the trauma unit had filled with dozens of uniformed officers. Some stood guard, holding rifles. Others talked quietly in small groups. Some wept; all waited for word. Williams rode the elevator upstairs several times to check on the third officer. He watched through glass as the other surgeon worked.

18

Words or Weapons

Having decided against remaining downstairs to set up a command post, negotiator Gordon followed Huante and Pup along the trail of blood, up the stairwell to the college's second floor. Their radio reception was spotty, and they didn't know exactly where the other SWAT guys were. As they advanced through the maze of classrooms and hallways, Gordon caught sight of an officer sitting behind a Coke machine with his arms around his knees. Gordon jerked to a stop, fearing the officer had been shot. The man looked up, and Gordon recognized him from his police academy class. The officer had a look of terror in his eyes. Gordon felt a wave of understanding, then revulsion. *Come on, man. Get up!*

Down a long hallway they finally spotted a couple of teammates, Canete and Banes, standing just outside a stairwell door. They had their rifles pointed to the side, their bodies tense. Whatever they were facing, Gordon thought, was fearsome. Gordon heard Banes calling out to someone he couldn't see. *Who are they talking to?* Gordon wondered. *The shooter?*

As Gordon married up with his teammates, he was still in

hunter mode, his thumb beside the safety of his M4, ready to slide it off and pull the trigger at any moment. As negotiator, he knew he would need to start talking, but he was having a hard time switching gears. Whatever was on the other side of the wall had left the remnants of an officer's head on the street below. That called for kill mode, not talk mode. The other guys looked at Gordon, waiting for him to engage. His reptile brain wanted only to aim his gun. His thinking mind needed to figure out what to say. He'd been talking armed men out of hiding for years, but never from this close, never with only a flimsy curtain of Sheetrock separating him from a bad guy's rifle barrel. Gordon took his place on the corner, his M4 raised, and forced his mind into negotiator mode.

* * *

The tension Gordon felt, between using words or weapons, has been a long-standing one for cops. Law enforcement started exploring the idea of talking, of trying to coax suspects out peacefully, only after traditional methods of force and firepower failed.

The Attica prison riot was one of several disastrous episodes during the 1970s that prompted police to search for new techniques. At the end of a hot summer in 1971, a group of inmates took control of the prison, holding dozens of Attica employees hostage. After four days of negotiations, state troopers and corrections officers stormed in with shotguns. They retook control, but in the process killed twenty-nine inmates and ten hostages.

A month later, a three-hundred-pound real estate agent dragged his screaming young wife aboard a passenger plane in Nashville, holding two pilots at gunpoint and demanding they fly to the Bahamas. When the plane stopped to refuel in Jacksonville, Florida, a group of FBI agents waited on the tarmac. The pilot, twenty-nine-year-old Brent Downs, who had a pregnant wife and a toddler at home, radioed the control tower, asking for a fuel truck and warning authorities to stay away from the plane. From the tower, an agent responded: "This is the FBI. There will be no fuel. Repeat. There will be no fuel."

The pilot: "Uh, look, I don't think this fellow's kiddin'—I wish you'd get the fuel truck out here."

The FBI: "There will be no fuel. I repeat. There will be no fuel."

The pilot: "You are endangering lives by doing this, and uh, we have no other choice but to go along, and uh, uh, for the sake of some lives we request some fuel out here, please."

Instead of negotiating with the hijacker, agents tried to shoot out two tires and an engine. They heard the sound of muffled shots and watched the pilot slump in his seat. The hijacker also fatally shot his wife and himself. The FBI received intense criticism of its handling of the case. The pilot's widow sued, leading to a landmark court ruling in which the judges said that a reasonable attempt at negotiations must be made prior to tactical intervention. The lead agent had turned a successful "waiting game" into a tragic "shooting match," the court ruled.

Attica and Jacksonville demonstrated the limits of raw power. The episodes helped prompt the New York Police Department and the FBI to launch crisis negotiating teams. They set off into the touchy-feely realm of pop psychology, exploring communication and empathy and trust. The motto of the NYPD's team, still one of the largest in the world, is "Talk to me." Early proponents believed salesmen might make the best negotiators, men skilled at cajoling and manipulating. But people, especially those in crisis, tend to sense when they are being conned. The best negotiators turned out to be the ones who were the most genuine, the ones who could be quiet and listen. Over time, the field developed listening as an active, assertive maneuver. Tactical listening. Listening as a martial art.

This softer approach was not embraced by many officers. In his memoir, *Stalling for Time*, former FBI negotiator Gary Noesner recalled the progress his team made in the 1993 standoff at the Branch Davidians' compound outside of Waco, Texas, where cult figure David Koresh had convinced his followers that he was the messiah. Negotiators coaxed out thirty-five of Koresh's followers over seven weeks. It wasn't fast enough for FBI commanders and the agency's tactical team, who wanted to take the compound by force. While negotiators worked, tactical commanders would flex their muscles, driving armored vehicles onto the property, circling the area with bright lights, and blasting bizarre recordings, such as the howls of dying rabbits. Finally, tired of waiting, the tactical team pumped tear gas into the compound and drove tanks through its walls. The Davidians set the compound on fire. The remains of seventy-five men, women, and children were found in the ruins.

The case tarnished the reputation of the FBI for years and, perhaps more than any other incident, swung the pendulum further toward negotiations. When Noesner taught young negotiators, he warned them that managing force-prone colleagues would be one of their biggest challenges, sometimes more difficult than dealing with the hostage takers and barricaded subjects.

The longest-serving commander of the NYPD's Hostage Negotiation Team, Jack Cambria, said in 2015 that he chose officers for his squad only if they had experienced their own life traumas, pain, and loss. In the testosterone-fueled world of law enforcement, these tended to be the sort of officers who could buy into another negotiator axiom: "Bring them to the table, not to their knees."

* * *

That philosophy came naturally to Gordon. He'd grown up in run-down apartment complexes in a small town just east of Dallas. As a boy, he would lie in bed in his upstairs room, holding his football like a prayer. He tacked an empty pack of his mother's Kool Menthols to the ceiling above his bed and he'd toss the ball at the green package, practicing his release.

The kids in Gordon's neighborhood learned to hate cops early. Mostly white, the officers cruised through the apartment complex, arresting dope dealers. They'd pile out of vans with balaclavas masking their faces. People called them the "Jump Out Boys." They treated the black kids like trash—"Get out of here or I'll throw your ass in jail." Most kids ran, but Gordon sometimes lingered, in awe. He felt something like reverence watching their choreography of force and power. They were the only ones who confronted the neighborhood's violent drug dealers. They bullied the bullies.

Ghosts hovered everywhere in the complex. The spot where a neighbor had killed a cop. The place where a classmate accidentally shot a young girl, Trina, in the face. The stairwell where a dealer pointed a silver revolver at Gordon. Looking back, Gordon thought of that moment as his first crisis negotiation. He was about fifteen years old, sitting with his friend, who'd stolen weed money from a dealer. The dealer pointed the biggest gun Gordon had ever seen at their faces. His instinct was to run up the stairs, but he worried the amped-up dealer would shoot him in the back. So Gordon started talking. *How much money does he owe you? If you shoot him, you won't get your money back.* He told the dealer he'd help his friend come up with the money. After a while, the dealer calmed down, nodding as he put his gun back in his pants.

Growing up, Gordon learned how complicated and contradictory people could be. How everyone, if you got to know them well enough, defied classification into neat and tidy boxes. Good guys and bad guys, for instance. Almost everyone he knew growing up was both. That was his first lesson: everyone has good in them, and everyone has bad in them. People were not one thing *or* the other, but one thing *and* the other. Gordon came to see everything that happened in the hood, and eventually everywhere beyond, as not black and white but deeply gray.

One of his neighbors, a woman named Virginia, may have been the first person who truly surprised him. She was one of the meanest in the complex, raising a houseful of kids alone, always outside with a Budweiser in one hand and a Kool Menthol in the other. Gordon and his friends spent hours on a patch of grass playing their favorite game, Throw Up Tackle. Someone tossed the ball into the air, and whoever caught it tried to sprint to the goal line before the others flattened him. Virginia was always cursing at them. She had two speeds: mean and meaner. One day, Gordon was sitting on the couch in their apartment when Virginia came over. His mother had her back turned to him and spoke quietly, but Gordon could tell she was crying. His mother mopped hospital floors, cleaned houses, and cooked at a local diner, but struggled to keep the lights and gas on and the fridge stocked all at once. That month she'd run out of food stamps. Gordon watched amazed as Virginia wrapped his mother in a hug and said, "Don't worry, I got you, girl." She spoke with a compassion and tenderness that Gordon had not imagined she possessed. He never looked at Virginia the same after that.

Over time, Gordon had this same type of experience with many he knew. His middle brother, Darryl, was always looking out for him. When Gordon was too embarrassed to spend food stamps at Calvert's, the local convenience store, Darryl brought him the Hostess chocolate cupcakes he loved and pressed ham to make sandwiches. When Gordon got bullied in school, Darryl took up for him. One day when Darryl was about thirteen, he flung his body through the flimsy wall of the apartment complex's laundry room, entered the office, and stole a pile of money orders. Neighbors watched the teen sprint away covered in white Sheetrock dust. Gordon's mother turned her son in, and police took Darryl to juvenile detention. Gordon's mother came home from a visit in tears, telling Gordon they had his brother caged like an animal. When Darryl got older, he'd come into Gordon's room with baggies of white rocks. Darryl would stuff the rocks into one end of a broken-off car antennae, flick a flame from his lighter, and suck through the antennae's other end, which was covered with a Brillo pad to keep him from inhaling in the rock. As stale, musty smoke filled the air, Gordon would watch his brother's face transform. The features he knew so well would become unrecognizable. What Gordon saw scared him; he never tried crack. Darryl was a kind, loving brother. And a crackhead.

While many of Gordon's childhood friends ended up dead or in prison, he escaped through sports. By the time he was in high school, his picture often appeared in the *Terrell Tribune*. There he was, on the baseball diamond pitching a no-hitter, on the basketball court suspended midair, on the football field with the ball spiraling away from his extended arm. Gordon and other boys learned lessons on the athletic fields that their fathers hadn't stuck around to teach. As they sweated beneath their gear during broiling Texas summers, they'd be thirsty and tired and feel as if they had nothing left; they learned how to reach down and find more. They'd complain in the locker room that the refs were making bad calls. "Play harder," the coach told them. "Win anyway."

During his junior year, Gordon dated a freshman girl, Shan, a drill team member who danced in a red pleated skirt during halftime. He and Shan spent Friday nights in the Sonic parking lot, dreaming about the lives they'd create. He'd play professional football for the NFL; she'd get a doctorate and become a school superintendent. They'd build a brick house, drive decent cars, and take ocean-cruise vacations.

Gordon received a partial football scholarship to college but dropped out his junior year after his grades slipped. He gave up on his NFL dreams, moved home, married Shan, and enrolled in the Dallas police academy. He'd later go back to school and finish his degree.

As a rookie, Gordon was assigned to Northeast Dallas, an area with both affluent neighborhoods and pockets of dilapidated apartments. For most cops, the rookie years were a surprising introduction into how poor people often lived—in neighborhoods where people got shot and stabbed, where some existed without working toilets. But all that was mundane to Gordon. What made a bigger impression on him was how rich people lived. His patrol included mansions with meticulously groomed lawns. He'd see kids in white pants headed to Little League games, teenagers driving new BMWs. He felt as if he'd stepped on the set of *Leave It to Beaver*.

After a couple of years on patrol, Gordon joined narcotics as an undercover. With his background, supervisors figured he'd be a natural. But he'd worked so hard to get out of dirty apartments that he struggled to fit back into them. Instead of posing as an addict, he adopted a cover persona as a club bouncer, buying dope for girlfriends. When he served warrants on dope houses, he often didn't arrest the wives or girlfriends, which troubled his superiors. These women were complicit; clearly they knew what was going on. But Gordon didn't see it that way. What good would it do to haul a mother off to jail and send the kids to foster homes? The sanctimony many cops had toward so-called bad guys got on Gordon's nerves. One of his fellow patrol officers ranted endlessly about the dope-selling thugs they arrested. The same guy cheated on his wife nearly every night. Gordon got tired of explaining to white cops that just because someone was selling dope he wasn't necessarily a bad guy.

When Gordon tried out for SWAT, he'd nearly gotten passed over by a white supervisor. One of the few black officers then on

SWAT, Kelvin "Pup" Johnigan, saw it coming. Pup was drinking buddies with the white lieutenant. "If you don't pick Gordon," Pup said he'd told the lieutenant, "it's gonna make me wonder about you." In the end, Gordon made it, but he went into SWAT with a chip on his shoulder, feeling as if the mostly white team hadn't wanted him. New guys on SWAT weren't supposed to have opinions—they were supposed to be quiet and learn. Gordon resisted this unspoken rule, and that seemed to get under the skin of one white officer from Mississippi. "Gordon needs to know his place," the officer told teammates. To Gordon, that sounded an awful lot like what people from Mississippi had been telling black folks for decades.

On one call, Gordon and the officer disagreed about which window they should focus on as they provided cover for the entry team. Afterward, as Gordon tried to explain his reasoning, the officer waved his hand in Gordon's face and walked off. Gordon followed, took off his rifle, and shouted, "Motherfucker, I'll beat your ass." SWAT guys pulled Gordon back. In a briefing after, the officer told him, "Larry, I've never seen you act like that before. You acted like those guys we deal with on the street."

Gordon told him, "I am those guys you deal with on the street. You don't know me or where I come from."

* * *

On the second floor of the college, Gordon crouched against the wall with his M4. His teammates told him the gunman wanted to be called X.

"Hey, X," Gordon called down the hallway. "Can you hear me? I just want to talk to you, X. Can you talk to me? What's going on today, man?"

As Gordon listened, waiting for a response, he saw dozens of brass and steel casings blanketing the carpet. It shocked him, the number of rounds that had been fired inside this college. Bullet holes had punched through the walls, leaving black craters and smears. If the guy started shooting again, Gordon would be one of the first in the line of fire.

The gunman shouted back. "I'm here today because of the injustices of my people."

"Your people?" Gordon asked.

"Yes!" the gunman said. "Black people. African. Children of the sun."

Gordon peeked slowly around the corner. He had an overwhelming desire to see the man's face, how big he was, what he was wearing, how he was standing. Anything that might help Gordon figure out what to say. But the hallway turned, and the gunman hid behind a corner, leaving only the voice. Gordon felt disoriented.

From down the hall, Gordon heard the click of a magazine ejecting from a rifle. Then came a loud snap. He pictured the gunman pushing a new magazine with a couple dozen fresh bullets. Gordon started pacing, moving back and forth, trying not to make himself a target. He felt himself slipping into a role he'd performed hundreds of times, flipping to the script in his mind. He tried to shift away from the tense, tactile sensations of the hallway, into the calmer thinking part of his mind. He hoped to prompt the same shift in the gunman. *Let's everybody catch our breath.* That was always the first goal, to slow things down, let the flood of stress and adrenaline subside. It was an axiom among negotiators: *Time is on our side.* As emotionality went down, rationality went up. One of the early pioneers of hostage negotiating, an NYPD detective with a doctorate in psychology, called it "dynamic inactivity."

"What brings us here today, man? I understand you're upset about your black people dying. But what brings us to this point, with guns involved?"

"I'm going to die today," the man said. "And a few more of you are going to be transitioning with me." Gordon noted the steadiness of the gunman's voice. After a shoot-out with half a dozen cops, he didn't sound the least bit rattled.

"What's transition?" Gordon asked, feeling his own stress level rising.

"We're going to transition from this life to the next."

Gordon peered around the corner again. He was recalibrating his mental image of the gunman. He'd pictured some deep-voiced beast. This guy sounded young and light. Well mannered. Almost dainty. Like Carlton on *The Fresh Prince of Bel-Air*.

"X, I think you have a valid point. But listen to me, X. Can you hear me? I can't hear your point because I'm too worried about getting shot," Gordon said. "So how about you put your weapon down and we talk about it. You have our attention now."

The gunman yelled out: "Why don't you all come back here?"

"Hey X, I'm really getting frustrated when you talk about hurting people. It frustrates me." They kept yelling back and forth, and Gordon continued: "I just want to find out what's going on today, how we can help, how we can solve this situation." Gordon asked the gunman if there were others with him, but the gunman wouldn't answer.

"You say you're going to die here anyway," Gordon pressed. "What's it matter, bro?"

The gunman shouted back, sounding furious. "I'm not your fucking brother! Do not call me bro!"

"Okay, I won't call you bro, I apologize," Gordon said quickly. "You said we're killing your black brothers, right? You know I'm black?"

"What?" X yelled.

"Did you know I'm black?"

The gunman paused. "You don't sound black."

"I'm black, bro, I just went to college," Gordon said.

Then Gordon heard an unexpected sound. The gunman was laughing.

"Touché," the gunman called out.

Okay, Gordon thought. He'd just moved the needle, made a small connection. His shoulders relaxed slightly and, for the first time, he wondered if he might be able to get this gunman out alive. He puzzled over the gunman's name, X. What did it mean? X as in Malcolm X? Or X like in a math equation, representing the unknown?

19

The Mayor

Mayor Mike Rawlings sat inside his home in Preston Hollow, one of the city's most affluent neighborhoods. He and his wife had returned a couple of hours earlier from her mother's funeral in East Texas, in a church off an old country road. The church ladies sent them home with tuna salad, and Rawlings made himself a plate before slipping into his chair, turning on the Rangers game, and immersing himself in the team's pitching troubles.

After 9:00 p.m., his wife walked into the room and said his assistant had been trying to reach him. Rawlings called her, and she told him to turn on the news. He changed the channel and saw reporters broadcasting live from downtown, showing clips of people running and cops taking cover. Rawlings dialed Chief Brown, who told him several officers were being treated for serious injuries. "It's a very fluid scene," Brown said. "I'm still trying to figure out what's going on."

A few minutes later, Rawlings climbed into the back of a black Suburban driven by a member of his security detail and sped toward downtown. His northern Dallas neighborhood was an enclave of estates situated on wide, generous lots laced with hundred-year-old oaks. The city's mostly white elite, including former president George W. Bush and his wife, Laura, lived here. Mark Cuban lived nearby in a $19 million, twenty-one-thousand-square-foot mansion. Oil executives and doctors and lawyers resided behind stone balustrades and wrought-iron security gates, with indoor basketball courts and bowling alleys, swimming pools and seven-car garages. Some commissioned life-size stone statues of their children and built water fountains that rose and fell in synchronized rhythms. One of the city's best-known writers, Ben Fountain, called Dallas the most American city because of its unabashed focus on making money. "The free market is basically a third religion, along with Christianity and football," he said.

The only black and brown faces that many residents of Preston Hollow saw each day were those of the people landscaping their yards or scrubbing their countertops. The late liberal newspaper columnist Molly Ivins wrote, "There is a black Dallas, there is a Chicano Dallas, there is a Vietnamese Dallas, there is a gay Dallas, there is even a funky-Bohemian Dallas. But mostly there is North Dallas. A place so materialistic and so Republican it makes your teeth hurt to contemplate it . . . the disgrace of Dallas today is that it is probably the most segregated city this side of Johannesburg."

It wasn't until 2003 that the first black resident moved into the Park Cities, a couple of miles south. The local newspaper, *Park Cities People*, printed a picture of the home buyer, a successful mortgage broker, and her husband along with an article that began, "Guess who's coming to dinner . . . and staying for a while?" The story, which drew national scorn, at one point referred to the woman as a "girl."

Many of the city's wealthy residents never have reason to venture south across the Trinity River, where minorities live in neighborhoods with too many boarded-up houses, run-down apartments, and vacant lots. Dallas has more corporate headquarters than most other major cities in the United States. It also has the third-highest rate of child poverty.

* * *

Rawlings had grown up neither rich nor poor, raised in a middle-class family. His father was a journalist and his mother a schoolteacher. The family had been so religious that Rawlings didn't see a movie until high school. At Boston College, Rawlings played outside linebacker on the football team and majored in philosophy, studying some of humanity's oldest questions. After his religious upbringing, he was shocked by the heresy of existentialist claims that there was no God, no afterlife, and no higher purpose. He spent hours reading Sartre and Camus, though he knew he'd never adopt their worldview. He'd felt things in church pews and on the sides of mountains that they could not account for.

After graduating magna cum laude, he arrived in Dallas in 1976 in a Volkswagen. He worked at a radio station, then took an entry-level job at an advertising agency. He planned to stay in Dallas only a couple of years, because he found the city bland and boring—"a gallon of white milk," he would say later. But by thirty-six, he'd ascended to CEO of the advertising agency, married, and had two kids. Then he was named chief executive of Pizza Hut. He went on to garner headlines trying to reinvent the brand, exploring whether Pizza Hut could beam its new logo onto the moon with lasers. He settled for plastering it on the side of a rocket. He'd never taken a business class in school, never studied economics or market dynamics, but he found much of the philosophy he'd learned, particularly the musings on reality and perception, relevant to modern marketing. If there was no true reality, as Immanuel Kant assured Rawlings in his college texts, then marketing could endlessly influence our perception of it.

After three decades in business and a stint as Dallas's homeless czar, Rawlings decided to run for mayor. He made the city's racial and economic divide a cornerstone of his campaign. "For too long, Dallas has been about north and south, black and white," he told a crowd at city hall. No more, he pledged. But he addressed the inequity more as a business issue than a moral imperative. The city's southern half was 55 percent of its landmass, big enough to swallow Atlanta, but only 15 percent of its economy. Southern Dallas was a vast frontier of unrealized potential—an investment opportunity. The business of Dallas has always been business, and this was an argument Rawlings knew the city's elite could get behind.

He ran the city in the style of a CEO, hustling behind the scenes to raise millions from colleagues and friends, creating a private equity fund for development in southern Dallas. He told people he hated politics, all the pandering and grandstanding. Then one day about seven months into his tenure, he declined to sign a pledge with other mayors backing same-sex marriage—he insisted pledges were pointless. Before dawn the next morning, his telephone rang. It was his grown son, angry and disappointed with him for not taking a principled stand. The call didn't change Rawlings's mind about pledges, but he did begin to rethink his role. Was it enough to be a businessman mayor?

Rawlings's first appearance on the national stage came early in his tenure, on a cold, rainy November day marking the fiftieth anniversary of John F. Kennedy's assassination. Rawlings thought of the memorial as a priceless opportunity for Dallas to rebrand itself. City leaders before him had spent decades trying to shed the "City of Hate" image garnered by the assassination and events that led up to it. A month before Kennedy's visit in 1963, the ambassador to the United Nations, and a renowned figure on the left, Adlai Stevenson, had been greeted by boos and catcalls while giving a speech at Memorial Auditorium Theater. From a podium, he asked the crowd, "Surely, my dear friend, I don't have to come here from Illinois to teach Texas manners, do I?" Outside the auditorium, protesters circled the ambassador's limousine and sang "Dixie." As he tried to get to his car, one protester, the well-dressed wife of an insurance executive, slammed a wooden placard into his forehead. The woman told reporters afterward she hadn't meant to hit the ambassador, adding there had been a "bunch of colored people" behind her. But the televised scene—which appeared to show her delivering an intentional smack to his head—became a national embarrassment. Although the ambassador publicly downplayed the event, he was worried about Kennedy visiting Dallas. "There was something very ugly and frightening about the atmosphere," he told a White House aide. Several people, including the city's best-known liberal, Stanley Marcus, encouraged the president not to visit.

In the aftermath of Kennedy's death, the scorn of a nation turned toward Dallas. City hall received telegrams by the dozens. "Today, you've killed our president," one said. "What kind of people are you? . . . You can take your stinking city and your stinking state and secede from the union. . . . Dallas, the city that spawns the lunatic fringe of the far right. Dallas, the City of Hate."

Dallas spent half a century trying to overcome that bleak day. Eventually the rise of the Cowboys helped, as did the popular TV show *Dallas*. Rawlings saw the fiftieth anniversary as another chance to spin a new narrative.

The mayor spent months working on his speech, and when the day came, he mostly knew the words by heart. He quoted from one of the city's spiritual leaders, the late Rabbi Levi Olan, who had given a poignant talk a year after Kennedy's death. "Contrary to the impassioned judgment of that horrible moment, the city is not guilty of the crime," the rabbi had said. "But in those awesome days following the assassination, the most powerful searchlight man possesses was focused on this city. Every flaw, every raw spot, every wrinkle, and every uncleanness was put under a microscope and shown to the world. The city of rich palaces and tall towers of commerce were set amidst slums and hovels. As the powerful light shown upon it, the city, it was learned, had been inhospitable to honorable debate."

Rawlings told the crowd that the rabbi's call for the city to seek transformation from its tragedy had been heeded. The people of Dallas had improved its substance, along with its image, Rawlings said. "The man we remember today gave us a gift that will not be squandered. He and our city will forever be linked, in tragedy, yes, but out of that tragedy an opportunity was granted to us, the chance to learn how to face the future when it's the darkest and the most uncertain. How to hold high the torch even when the flame flickers and threatens to go out."

* * *

Now, on the night of July 7, 2016, as his city's police force came under attack, Rawlings realized that he and the city were about to be in the national spotlight again. At about 10:00 p.m., he walked into the emergency operations bunker underneath city hall. Chief Brown and his deputy chiefs were there, along with city council members, fire officials, and emergency managers. Rawlings moved around exchanging grave handshakes and greetings.

In a crisis, the mayor felt strongly that people should lead, follow, or get out of the way. Tonight, Rawlings knew, Chief Brown needed to be in charge. While the two men were not personal friends, they respected each other. Rawlings had been one of the few to stand by Brown in recent months, when others called for his resignation as crime spiked. The mayor had always appreciated Brown's unflappability.

Rawlings knew his job tonight would be to face the public, and he began organizing press conferences for the growing number of reporters downtown. Previous crises had taught him that the public wanted information quickly and regularly. If the city didn't put out the facts, people would make them up, usually creating a more frightening version of reality. Rawlings moved between groups collecting information. At that point, the police believed that at least two snipers, firing from elevated positions, had ambushed the officers below. Eleven officers had been shot. Three were dead. Others had life-threatening injuries.

Rawlings wondered whether the night's bloodshed would stain the city's image again, tarnishing it for the next half century as a cesspool of racial violence. The city's reputation was on the line, and the mayor was eager to frame the narrative. His response needed to be swift, the message clear. The city had done a lot of soul-searching in 1963. Pulling back the curtain had exposed things Dallas wasn't proud of. Rawlings didn't think that was the case now. Under Chief Brown, the city had invested significantly in community policing. The department mirrored its community, with African Americans making up a quarter of the force. The city's racial and geographic divide was still stark, but progress had been made, and that needed to be emphasized.

As city council members began to arrive, desperate to assess the situation, Rawlings found himself drawn to a young black council member, Tiffinni Young, who represented one of the city's poorest districts. "We've got to come together as a city," she said. "This should not be a racial thing."

Rawlings felt himself relax. It was as if the councilwoman had walked up to some invisible line and stepped over it, signaling that she wanted to help hold the city together, not divide it. They turned as Brown approached the front of the room with an update. SWAT, he reported, had at least one shooter cornered on the second floor of El Centro College. Officers were trying to talk to him, but he was swearing and shooting at them. He'd asked his commanders for options on how to end the standoff.

Studying Brown, Rawlings wondered if he was thinking the same things. He hoped the shootings would not lead to riots, turning Dallas into another Ferguson. It would be up to him, a white man from the north, and Brown, a black man from the south, to hold the city together. They headed upstairs to the television cameras.

20

The Master Breacher

SWAT officer Jeremy Borchardt crept through the second floor of the community college, his M4 raised. He was an assistant squad leader and one of the most experienced on SWAT, a former rifle instructor, a rappelling master, and one of the team's lead breachers, authorized to carry a cache of explosives in a locked crate in his Tahoe. As he entered the college, Borchardt listened to the police radio on his vest. He heard SWAT break in between the shouts of patrol officers, alerting the team that they had a shooter pinned down on the second floor. He could hear the stress in their voices. They were somewhere inside this rambling building, and he needed to find them fast.

As one of the team's master breachers, Borchardt's job was to help get SWAT around barriers—a critical part of any operation. Breachers were thinkers and problem solvers. These "lead sled dogs," as supervisors thought of them, had to be able to pick up a trail on any path, lead the way. Whenever the team got an infusion of new guys, supervisors studied them to see who might make good breachers, searching out those with a natural mechanical ability, men who weren't afraid to take risks but also had a high maturity level, creative thinkers who were ice-calm under pressure. They had to be skilled at mechanical tasks—picking locks, running chain saws, "breaking and raking" windows. Breaching required an understanding of how things were put together, in order to take them apart. It was about exploiting weaknesses, finding vulnerabilities.

Borchardt could spend hours roaming the aisles of Home Depot, searching for some tool or fitting to use on a breach. He'd performed more operational breaches than any officer in the history of Dallas SWAT. Although Borchardt used many tools, his passion was explosives. "I could talk for hours," he'd say, "about blowing shit up." The team used explosives sparingly, on a couple dozen calls a year, but that was more than in times past. Borchardt had been drawn to the specialty because of its competing demands of precision and creativity. The act of exploding your way past a barrier was limited only, Borchardt believed, by a breacher's imagination. He'd never excelled at math in school but enjoyed the equations of explosives, calculating room volumes and standoff distances.

Now, as Borchardt rounded a corner, he spotted his teammates pointing rifles in the other direction. He locked eyes with Canete, who looked back at him with a mixture of relief and anger—what had taken him so long? Canete pointed to where the gunman was hunkered down. All Borchardt could see was a small sliver of hallway. *This position is shit*, he thought. If the guy came out shooting, they wouldn't see him until the last moment. It would be a draw at best.

Borchardt looked around and studied the Sheetrock walls, pulverized by bullets. So many rounds had been fired, he couldn't believe no one had gotten hit. It was only a matter of time. Borchardt knew better than any of them the danger of working such unprotected scenes. He'd been shot through a hotel wall early in his career. He had a half-dollar-size bullet hole and a six-inch scar on his leg that testified to what could happen up here. He still had nerve damage, and his toes burned when the weather turned cold.

Borchardt urged the men to pull back farther into the stairwell. While their visibility wouldn't be as good, they'd at least have protection of concrete-block walls. "We're not safe here," Borchardt said. The men looked back, annoyed. *No shit.* Borchardt left to scout out the rest of the second floor, trying to come up with a plan.

* * *

Borchardt was thirty-nine with short blond hair and bright blue eyes. He'd grown up on a pig farm outside a small town in Minnesota, raised on the belief that almost anything could be fixed with baling twine and duct tape. He knew the basics of welding, plumbing, and construction. He got a degree in social work from Abilene Christian University, and he and his wife spent their early twenties as house parents at a ranch for troubled boys. He'd grown up on the good lawmen stories of old westerns and wanted to become a cop. He enrolled in the Dallas police academy in 1999, and his wife took a job at a women's shelter. They were devout Christians who believed in forgiveness and grace.

Crime and criminals had been arm's-length, theoretical constructs to Borchardt. Back in college sociology class, he'd believed that most people turned to crime because of poverty and circumstance, conditions he'd been lucky enough to avoid. The experiences of his first months on the job whittled away at Borchardt's farm-boy outlook. On his first night, he arrived at an apartment where a guy had been playing Russian roulette and lost. As Borchardt stepped around bloody remains of the man's head, he thought, *What did I get myself into?* Like most rookies, he'd been assigned to deep nights, the dark hours between 11:00 p.m. and 7:00 a.m. Cops encountered a certain kind of person at three o'clock in the morning. Very often someone up to no good. It was a time of day when everyone lied about everything, Borchardt learned.

In the crowded urban environs of Dallas, he met men and women who seemed to live by a different set of rules. They'd shoot, kill, maim, whatever it took to get their way. Most people who ended up face-to-face with crime weren't doing what they were supposed to be doing, Borchardt came to believe. In a lot of cases, what happened to them actually was their fault. People did incredibly selfish, stupid, and brutal things. He encountered a level of darkness he hadn't fathomed. He began to understand why, when summoned to the latest drug murder, veteran cops were unmoved. *One less shitbag.*

As a patrol officer in 2006, he'd arrived on the fourth floor of a Radisson Hotel early one morning to help a woman who was being beaten. As he stood outside the hotel room, inserting the key card into its slot, a bullet punched through the wall and spiraled into his thigh. Some cops didn't recall feeling pain when shot, but Borchardt felt as if someone had pushed a red-hot poker through his leg. He saw blood spurting, fountainlike, as he hopped away from the door, yelling, "I've been hit." Other officers dragged him down the hallway, and he passed out. A severed artery is what cops called a three-to four-minute wound. That's about how long it takes to bleed out. In the back of the ambulance, a paramedic sat on top of Borchardt, pressing a knee into his thigh to slow down the flow. After he regained consciousness at the hospital, a trauma surgeon told him they'd pumped ten pints of blood back into his body, which held a total of about twelve.

Borchardt spent six months doing physical therapy, and when he was well enough he went back to the Radisson, found the room on the fourth floor, and stood outside. He ran his hand along the wall, feeling the bullet holes, now covered by wallpaper. Could he continue walking up to doors like that? The visit calmed him.

Maybe it was because he hadn't seen the suspect's face, but the shooting hadn't felt personal. He realized he could accept it for what it was—part of the dangerous job he'd chosen. As soon as the doctor cleared him, Borchardt returned to the streets.

He'd been back for about a month when he joined officers in pursuit of a car possibly involved in a murder case. The Chevrolet Caprice spun out, clipped a curb, and skidded to a stop. The lead patrol officer jumped out and ran toward the car's darkly tinted windows, gun in hand. It was a tactical error; after a chase, officers are supposed to draw their weapon from a distance, staying behind cover. The officer, Mark Nix, rushed to the car and brought his baton down against the passenger's-side window. But the glass held firm. Now Nix put his gun on the ground, grabbed his baton with both hands, and raised it into the air. From inside the car, the suspect fired one shot. The bullet struck Nix in his badge and pieces broke off, hitting him in the face and neck. He dropped his baton, grabbed his face, and collapsed. Borchardt and other officers fired into the car, unloading close to sixty rounds, wounding the shooter but not killing him. One officer ran up and dragged Nix into the back of a patrol car. Borchardt climbed in and pumped on Nix's chest all the way to the hospital. After turning Nix over to nurses and doctors, Borchardt stepped out into the hospital parking lot, where he stood, covered in blood, beside the patrol car. "Fuck, fuck!" he yelled, kicking the car hard enough to leave a dent. Nix was soon pronounced dead. Borchardt was angry for months. At the suspect, but also at Nix, for approaching the car so rashly.

After his second shooting, Borchardt's supervisors told him to pick a desk job. "I'm not a desk guy," he'd said. Police who weren't chasing dope and putting criminals in jail weren't real police, he said. He spent two years as a rifle instructor, then endured an unsuccessful stint on narcotics. Even when he grew a beard and wore dirty clothes, people seemed to know he was a cop. "Five-Oh!"

they'd yell as he climbed out of his car. In 2009, he finally got a spot on SWAT, which had been his dream all along.

During his two decades as a cop, Borchardt's life changed, and not all for the better. His wife spent years on antianxiety medication after his near-death encounters, consumed by the idea that next time he'd get killed, leaving her a widow and their three children fatherless. He never seemed to leave work behind. He always required her to walk on his left, so he could reach for his gun. He taught their kids how to use tourniquets in case a shooter showed up at school. He insisted on picking their seats in church, scouting out pews with tactical advantage. Before a crowded Christmas Eve service, he whispered to her and the kids: "If anything goes down, here's where we're going to meet." His wife rolled her eyes. *Can't we just enjoy the service?* Borchardt watched people coming and going during the sermon, scanning the exits. To him, policing wasn't a job, it was who he was.

Over time, Borchardt began to see himself as a modern version of the western lawman, part of an army that kept society's dark underbelly at bay. He came to believe that without cops standing ready with firearms, the world would devolve into chaos. He believed in the quote often attributed to Winston Churchill: "We sleep soundly in our beds because rough men stand ready in the night to visit violence on those who would do us harm."

* * *

Tonight, before the team could make a plan, their first priority was "hardening" their position, establishing cover so they could work safely. Usually they arrived in two Lenco BearCats, vehicles constructed of steel and bullet-resistant glass that they could work behind. Inside the college, they'd have to get creative. The team carried up ballistic panels, two-by-four-foot sheets of Kevlar that they locked into place to create a makeshift wall. It was only about chest high, so they'd have to duck their heads. They ripped down a panel of lights from the ceiling to darken their position.

They needed to set up a perimeter across the second floor, blocking every possible path the gunman could use for escape. Borchardt's biggest worry was that the guy would slip out and kill more cops or civilians. They'd managed to hem him into an alcove, and if he got loose they'd have to start all over again. Still worried about cops getting hit through the drywall, Borchardt positioned one of the team's small fleet of robots as a sentry in the hallway. Its camera sent live video feed to a handheld monitor, allowing the team to move farther back. If the gunman came out, it would give them an extra second or two of warning.

By about 10:00 p.m., roughly an hour after the first shots were fired, SWAT had the gunman at least somewhat contained. The call began to shift from the chaos of an active shooter situation to something more like a barricaded person call, what SWAT called a BP. These were bread and butter for SWAT; the team handled them nearly every week. The best case for any BP was to coax the suspect out peacefully. Tonight, with the gunman boasting about how many cops he'd already killed, that seemed impossible.

Borchardt and a couple of other officers began walking around the second floor. They had a general protocol for BPs, but they'd never faced a situation like tonight. There's no set manual for any SWAT call; each occupies an unfamiliar scene with unique variables. To figure out what to do, officers flip through a mental Rolodex of previous calls and stories they've heard from other teams, searching for solutions.

One of the first ideas was to toss something into the suspect's hiding spot. The team considered tear gas, which prompted many to surrender. But this call had happened so quickly that many officers didn't have their gas masks. The gunman, on the other hand, might well have brought one, for all they were learning of him. The goal of tear gas was to force a suspect out, and Borchardt didn't think that was necessarily a good idea—he'd likely come out shooting.

Borchardt crept quietly along hallways near the gunman, trying to figure out his exact position as he yelled back and forth with negotiator Gordon. Maybe they could attach an explosive to an adjacent wall and collapse it on top of the guy. Or maybe they could blow a hole in a wall to give a sniper a shot. Borchardt took out a pry tool, trying to open a locked door, but the gunman heard. "What the fuck was that?" he shouted at Gordon. Borchardt stopped; he didn't want to agitate the gunman into shooting again.

One officer suggested shooting the gunman through the wall with the team's powerful .50-caliber rifles, but the team didn't like the idea. They didn't have a good enough sense of the gunman's location to aim with precision. They'd have to "spray and pray," and that seemed irresponsible in a building full of cops; they still weren't certain they'd cleared it of students and teachers.

Borchardt walked through the college library down the hall, studying the building's beams, walls, and doors. Could they use explosives to drop the ceiling on this guy? Blow a hole through the floor? Borchardt shook his head. It would take a giant bomb to collapse the concrete and steel structure.

Borchardt thought about their robots. One had an arm that could hold a 12-gauge shotgun. What if they drove it down the hallway and fired on the gunman? It might work, but the robot moved slowly; there was a good chance the suspect could take it out before it fired.

A couple of months back the ATF had lent them a robot capable of carrying explosives. Borchardt had been using it to put small charges on doors, which was often safer than sending guys to the threshold. Borchardt wondered about equipping a robot with a bigger charge and detonating it near the gunman. That did not require precision; they'd just need to get it close enough.

Borchardt started discussing the idea with his sergeant, Josh Hertel. The men had worked together for years on SWAT. Before being promoted to supervisor, Hertel had been one of the team's best breachers. He seemed interested in the idea, but Borchardt could see the other man's gears spinning on all the potential problems.

Borchardt went back through all the other options they'd considered, explaining why he didn't think they'd work, then circled back to the robot bomb.

"How much explosive would you need?" Hertel asked.

"I'm thinking a pound," Borchardt said.

"What?" Hertel said, as his eyes widened. "No. No fucking way."

They typically used very small amounts—grams, not pounds. It was one thing to slap a charge on someone's front door; another to blow a pound of explosives in a community college downtown. "What the fuck are you talking about?" Hertel said. "We couldn't be anywhere near that thing."

The sergeant spelled out his concerns. The first was overpressure, the air-blast shock wave created during an explosion. If the team was too close to the blast, it could damage ears, injure internal organs, and cause brain injury. Most of the breachers had been hit by hot charges and gotten headaches or concussions. SWAT had detonated a pound of explosives indoors during training, but always in controlled environments, where they could safely retreat. In the confined space of the college, the overpressure would bounce off the floors and walls, multiplying by—well, they didn't know how much. Hertel was also worried about the team pulling too far away from the gunman. If they used a pound, would they have to evacuate the floor?

"We've got him contained now," Hertel said. "We've got to stay on top of him."

What if the device failed and the gunman escaped, killing more people? Hertel asked.

21

"Kill 'Em All"

Gordon's teammates locked ballistic panels in place around him. The barrier provided much more protection than he'd had, but the panels didn't cover his whole body. He'd have to crouch down to avoid getting shot in the head. He still felt exposed and vulnerable. He'd never imagined a scenario that would have him negotiating from thirty feet away with a well-trained, heavily armed gunman who could charge out at any moment.

The arrival of the shields also made Gordon realize their equipment truck must have shown up, and it gave him an idea. He turned to his sergeant and asked quietly, "Can we get the throw phone up here?"

The throw phone was an old-fashioned phone receiver in a hard case. Attached to a long black cord, it could be tossed to a suspect so they could communicate. The phone opened two possibilities. If Gordon could get X to talk, he could move off the hallway, relocating to a classroom around the corner. It also provided another appealing possibility. If SWAT threw the phone just right, in a way that required the gunman to reach out and grab it, they could snipe

"I know you guys may be pissed at me tomorrow, but I've got to think about the safety of everybody else," Hertel said. "One pound—do you have any idea what you're talking about?" He seemed to doubt commanders would go for it.

Borchardt kept pushing. "Look," he said. "We're authorized to use deadly force. That doesn't mean we have to shoot the guy." Their general orders authorized officers to use any weapon available to them in a deadly-force situation. If an officer lost his pistol in a gunfight, he could reach for a rock and shatter a man's head. How was this any different? The bomb plan might not be ideal, but sending any officer down that hallway was sending him to his death.

After more back-and-forth, Borchardt could see he'd persuaded Hertel. But there was no telling whether commanders would approve.

"Y'all start building," Hertel said. He asked the breachers to call a longtime explosives expert they knew and get an opinion on how much to use and how far to pull back.

him and end the standoff. The sergeant called down to the truck for the phone, and Gordon turned back toward the hallway.

"Hey X, did you bring a phone?"

The voice called back calmly. "No," he said. "I didn't want anyone to track me."

"What if we brought you a phone?" Gordon asked.

As Gordon spoke, he could hear the fear in his voice, and he wondered if the gunman could hear it, too. In standoff negotiations tone is everything. He needed to project both authority and warmth. Listening to his own words, the way their pitch lilted upward, Gordon worried he was not succeeding. He could tell he was more stressed out than the gunman.

As Gordon tried to get hold of himself, he was aware of the primal ritual going on inside his body. Scientists had long studied amygdalae, removing them from monkeys and rats, trying to understand the systems that regulate fear, emotion, and memory. When a rat's amygdala was gone, he'd walk straight up to a cat. Much of SWAT's training was focused on managing these threat-processing systems. It was a little like trying to control whether you blinked or how you sneezed, attempting to rewire a well-oiled evolutionary machine.

In their daily lives, SWAT officers dealt with the civilian fears that preoccupy everyone—fear of failure or embarrassment or misfortune. The English language has a couple dozen words to describe varieties of fear—fright, anxiety, alarm, apprehension, terror. But SWAT has to master one particular type that most people encounter only rarely, what scientists call "fear of extinction": the credible threat that one might actually die in the next moment. The vast, elemental, inalterable end. The threat is so instinctively intolerable that all species have developed unconscious tools of resistance. For SWAT, this type of fear was a regular part of their lives, a room they kept returning to. They studied its contours, learned to recognize how their bodies moved in it. *My heart rate is going up. Here comes the adrenaline.* Knowing the mechanics and vocabulary helped, but most SWAT officers believed that the only way to influence the system was to repeatedly practice.

Many believed the alpha male rituals of SWAT served as an invaluable pressure cooker. Being able to perform at a high level while a rabid Huante called them stupid motherfuckers had built enviable levels of stress tolerance in many of them. On SWAT, rarely a week passed where the men didn't find themselves approaching a new door, not knowing what waited on the other side, with their amygdalae telling them to run. They'd learned that fear could gift them biologically with clearer sight, sharper hearing, an intense sense of smell. The trick was to receive these gifts without sacrificing higher-level thinking. They had to use their conscious, thinking minds to keep their lizard brains in check.

Gordon knew his balance was off. He'd thought he might die a half dozen times in his career. Tonight, the fear was more intense than he'd ever experienced. It felt ripe and near. The next barrage of bullets might leave Shan a widow, his kids fatherless. He began a visualization technique that usually helped, imagining the blast of a rifle and a bullet hitting him square in the chest. He pictured a bloody circle widening on his uniform as he reached for a tourniquet in the small medical kit on his vest. He imagined the wound burning and reminded himself, *Don't scream like a little bitch. Take it like a man.* The acceptance of getting hurt usually excised some of the fear, but not tonight. He wasn't just afraid for his own safety, he was afraid he'd say the wrong thing, prompting the gunman to charge out and kill someone else. Gordon took quiet breaths, in and out, but the tactical breathing could not slow his heart or quiet his mind. One thought crowded out the others. He wanted X to simply not exist. How could they kill him and get out of here?

The throw phone arrived. Gordon took a deep breath.

"Hey X," he called out. "They brought me a phone. Can I toss it back there? Aren't you tired of yelling? I'm missing at least half of what you're saying."

A moment passed, then the gunman called back, crisp and clear.

"Uh-uh. I know what y'all are trying to do."

Dammit, Gordon thought.

* * *

He took out his earbuds, silencing the police radio so he could concentrate. He needed to mentally move away from his SWAT colleagues. It was something he'd learned early in his career as a negotiator.

On one of his first callouts, a supervisor had handed Gordon a bullhorn speaker. The team needed him to talk with an armed man who'd barricaded himself inside an apartment. Gordon positioned the bullhorn, called a loud hailer, atop the team's armored car and put on a headset. He'd never used a loud hailer before, and he was nervous. What if he sounded ridiculous? The sergeant gave Gordon the signal, and he cleared his throat. He looked up toward the second-story apartment. His heart was beating fast. *This is gonna be embarrassing.*

"I'm Officer Gordon, from Dallas SWAT," he called out. His voice echoed across the neighborhood and sounded unfamiliar. He tried to deepen his voice. "We need us to come out of the house." *Shit.* He was messing up his pronouns. He tried again. "We need you to come out of the house," he said. He couldn't think of what else to say. He told himself to calm down. *Forget about everybody else. Just have a conversation.* He took a breath and tried again.

"Hey man, I'm with Dallas SWAT, and we're not leaving."

Around him, SWAT officers laughed at his informality. Usually the negotiators sounded like a robot, yelling commands to a house. Gordon found out later he'd been talking to a guy who'd already killed himself, but he'd learned an important lesson. If he was going to succeed as a negotiator, he couldn't be worrying about what the other guys were thinking.

Tonight he tried to focus only on the gunman. *If I'm X, what do I want to hear?* He imagined that he and the gunman were feeling the same thing, both waiting for someone to come around the corner and kill them. Gordon needed to make him feel safe and in control.

"I'm just concerned for our safety. I'm concerned for your safety," he called out. "You have a compelling story, though. You know what's going to happen, X?"

"Say what?"

"You know what's gonna happen if you kill yourself? You know what's gonna happen?"

"What?" X asked.

"The media's gonna tell their own story," Gordon said.

"I don't care. My people will know what I have done."

"But X, we want to know. Can we find out?"

"Goddammit, do you not see the proof?" X said. "Keep fighting, that's what I'm doing. If I was a soldier and I was killing fucking Iraqis, y'all would be praising me as a hero, but now that I've killed y'all, the real terrorists, now what? My mission isn't the same?"

"But is it going to be looked at that way, X?" Gordon asked.

"I don't care, my people know," X said.

"But I'm saying, you're doing this for black people, right?"

"Yes."

"How are black people gonna look at it?" Gordon asked.

"There are many of us who feel the way I do," X said.

"I understand that. I understand that."

Gordon thought about the conversation he'd had with his niece on the phone earlier that night.

The gunman continued. "Malcolm X, Martin Luther King,

Kwame, there's been too many people talking," he said. "Revolution, that's what I want. The talking is over. It's time for revolution, brother. If you are my brother, turn your weapon on those behind you."

Gordon didn't respond.

"You know what? Naw, naw, naw. Play the long game," the gunman said. "Play the long game. Stay on their team. About a year later, a year after, or some shit, kill 'em all. Kill 'em all at the funerals, kill 'em all at the wakes."

* * *

In the stairwell, Banes leaned against the wall, listening to the negotiations. When X told Gordon to turn his weapon on his teammates, Banes felt something like disgust. He looked around and thought the gunman's words seemed to have a physical effect on the men around him. People shifted positions, tensed their shoulders, exchanged glances. It was the second time that night X had asked Gordon to shoot his teammates. In an earlier exchange, Gordon had responded by saying, "I can't do that, X. That would be illegal."

He knew Gordon had a job to do. But he didn't like the answer. Banes knew exactly what he would have said to X. *Eat a dick and die, motherfucker.*

22

Seeing Ghosts

X's exhortation to "play the long game," lying in wait for white colleagues, gave Gordon a chill. He thought of what was probably in his teammates' minds as they listened, though he tried not to. They had little patience with even peaceful protests against police shootings, and in truth neither did he. There had been some egregious police shootings caught on video, such as when a South Carolina officer shot a fleeing Walter Scott in the back. Any officer who tried to defend that—and Gordon had encountered one—was blind. But many of the videos showed officers making reasonable decisions under enormously stressful circumstances, Gordon thought.

Two years earlier, Eric Garner had died after a New York City police officer put him in a chokehold. Some departments had prohibited the hold because it cut off the windpipe and could be lethal. When people watched the video of Garner's death, they saw a group of officers piling onto a black man, accused only of selling cigarettes, as he said "I can't breathe" eleven times. Gordon saw cops doing what they thought necessary to subdue a very large man.

Chokeholds were controversial, yes, but Gordon and most officers who'd been policing for long had found them or similar holds useful when dealing with men as big as Garner. Gordon had used neck holds on domestic violence calls. He and his partner would interview the man and woman separately. If they decided to arrest the guy, Gordon would stand behind him and put his hands on his shoulders. He'd slide his hands down to his elbows, then to his wrists for the handcuffs. If the guy tensed and started to fight, Gordon would swing his arm around the man's throat and squeeze. Within seconds, the guy would pass out, almost always defecating or urinating. He'd wake up, suddenly not so tough. Policing, Gordon thought, looked ugly sometimes.

"Eric Garner got killed because he was running his damn mouth," Gordon told friends. Garner had been standing on a corner, long a trouble spot for cops, and when they showed up he told them, "Every time you see me you want to mess with me. I'm tired of it. This stops today." When a cop tried to cuff him, he said, "Don't touch me." How exactly, Gordon said, did Garner think that was going to end?

Gordon felt the same way about the death of Alton Sterling, shot at close range by a Baton Rouge officer who thought he was reaching for a loaded .38 in his pocket. Sterling had reportedly pointed the gun at someone, who called the cops. When they showed up, he resisted and he had that gun. Gordon had been in those situations before. "When you believe you're going to die, right there, there's nothing like it in the world," he told people. "Some animal part of you starts fighting."

Gordon thought the furor over police shootings was fed mostly by anger over more routine encounters. The problem was cops writing tickets in poor neighborhoods, stopping and frisking decent people, treating blacks like suspects rather than human beings.

In Ferguson, where the aftermath of Michael Brown's death was caught on video, people weren't just mad because of his death, Gordon believed. They were mad because they were overpoliced by a mostly white force.

Brown was an eighteen-year-old high school graduate who wrote song lyrics on scraps of paper, hoping to become a famous rapper. One afternoon, he walked into a convenience store, picked up some cigarillos, and started to leave without paying. When confronted by the store clerk, Brown shoved him. The clerk's daughter called the police, and dispatchers gave a description of Brown over the radio.

A few minutes later, a twenty-eight-year-old white police officer named Darren Wilson was driving near the store in a Tahoe. He saw Brown and his friend walking in the middle of the street. The men got into an altercation, and within two minutes an unarmed Brown was dead. He lay on the road for nearly four hours and hundreds of Ferguson residents gathered, including Brown's mother, who wailed at the sight of "Mike Mike." A rumor spread that Brown had been shot with his hands up. The crowd began to chant, "Hands Up, Don't Shoot." By nightfall, thousands had gathered. Police wore helmets and carried rifles and brought police dogs.

Forensic evidence ultimately proved inconclusive. The bullet that hit Brown in the head had a downward trajectory, which could bolster either side's narrative: Brown could have been charging at the officer, head down, or Brown could have been collapsing, in surrender. Word of his death spread quickly across the country as activists took to Facebook and Twitter. When reporters arrived in town and asked residents for their names, many responded, "Mike Brown."

A subsequent U.S. Department of Justice report painted a stark, distressing portrait of the small town. In 1990, Ferguson, with about twenty-one thousand residents, had been mostly white. By

2010, it was 70 percent black. Of fifty-four sworn officers on the police department, four were African American. The city's municipal judge, court clerk, prosecuting attorney, and all assistant court clerks were white. The town relied heavily on tickets to fund its operations. Officers competed over who could issue the most citations during a stop, and they reached numbers as high as fourteen. The fines were overwhelmingly levied against the town's African Americans.

Investigators found multiple cases like this one. A black woman parked her car illegally. She received two citations and a $151 fine, plus fees. The woman, who'd been homeless off and on, struggled to pay. In the years that followed, she was charged with seven failure-to-appear offenses. With each one, the court issued an arrest warrant and more fines. The woman was arrested twice, spent six days in jail, and paid $550—all stemming from the one time she'd illegally parked. She twice tried to make smaller payments of $25 and $50 but the court rejected them. Seven years after the original fine of $151, having already paid $550, the woman still owed the town $541.

Many residents complained about a police lieutenant who forced them to show identification for no reason and then, if they had no warrants, yelled for them to "get the hell out of my face." One afternoon in 2012, an officer stopped a twenty-year-old black man for dancing in the middle of a street and, after the man responded with profanities, arrested him for "Manner of Walking in Roadway." Investigators found that officers had Tased a woman after she refused to remove her bracelets. They had commanded a police dog to attack a teen who was hiding in an abandoned house while skipping school. But officers policed whites differently. In one case, officers had responded to a bar fight where forty to fifty whites were throwing bottles, glasses, and chairs. One subject, the officer noted, "had his ear bitten off." No arrests were made.

Investigators also reviewed the e-mails of town employees. One in November 2008 quipped that President Obama would not be president for long because "what black man holds a steady job for four years." Another e-mail depicted Obama as a chimpanzee. Another circulated this racist joke: "An African American woman in New Orleans was admitted to the hospital for a pregnancy termination. Two weeks later she received a check for $5,000. She phoned the hospital to ask who it was from. The hospital said, 'Crime Stoppers.'"

Ferguson officials routinely insisted that the town's surplus of tickets written to blacks showed that they lacked "personal responsibility." Yet they made traffic fines disappear for friends. In one instance, a court clerk received a request from a friend to "fix a parking ticket" for the friend's coworker's wife. "It's gone, baby," the clerk replied.

Months after Michael Brown was killed, thousands waited outside the town's courthouse to see if the police officer would be charged in Brown's death. The prosecuting attorney announced that he would not. Brown's mother put her head in her hands and wept. His stepfather screamed to the crowd: "Burn this bitch down!" Residents hurled bricks at police officers, looted stores, and torched cars. Ferguson police rolled through in armored tanks, shooting tear gas at the crowd.

The Department of Justice report drew an extraordinary portrait of racial oppression in one American small town. But no one could hold the illusion that Ferguson was in a class of its own. There were plenty of Fergusons, Gordon knew, large and small and, to varying degrees of egregiousness, across the country.

Gordon, too, was guilty of things, as was almost every cop he knew. They'd all done things that, if caught on video, might have gone viral. While working the streets, he'd dealt with young men who stood around on corners like they owned the block and the neighborhood. *You think you're tough?* Gordon would find himself thinking. *Let's see how tough.* More than once, he'd acted on such impulses. He looked back on some moments with guilt and regret. He hadn't shot Castile or anyone else, but he'd contributed to the problem. "You play fucked-up games, you win fucked-up prizes," he told younger cops. "We reap what we sow."

* * *

Gordon kept tossing out questions, trying to find a hook. He needed to catch on something that would interest the gunman, launch them into a back-and-forth.

"What do you do for a living, X, if you don't mind me asking?"

"I've been training for this."

"Do you get paid for it?" Gordon asked.

"Not money," X replied.

"Not money?"

"Just spiritual rewards," X said

"Sometimes that's the best type of reward."

"Yep."

"What have you done for money? You say you're an intelligent guy. You sound like it."

"Yeah, I know I am."

"You go to school?" Gordon asked.

"Nope."

"You didn't go to college? You sound like you did. You sound like a very intelligent dude."

"I know. You gonna keep kissing my ass or shoot me? Come on, now," X said.

The comment caught Gordon off guard and deflated him. X wasn't interested in bullshitting, nor was he receptive to flattery.

This was unusual in Gordon's experience. Most people's favorite subject was themselves, and Gordon often connected by asking people open-ended questions, then sitting back and listening.

"Did I lose you?" he called out.

"Naw, I'm here."

"Okay."

"I'm just waiting for y'all to come around this corner," X said.

"You had me worried there for a second," Gordon said.

"I ain't playing games," the gunman said, then he shouted, "Black Power!" The change in volume startled Gordon, and his finger slid to the safety on his M4. Most suspects, hiding in their houses or attics, were afraid of SWAT, but X was taunting them, inviting confrontation.

Gordon felt the tension building in his neck and shoulders, already burdened by his heavy gear. His usual tactics weren't working. Behind his fear, Gordon felt another emotion, something like embarrassment. It was the same feeling he'd sometimes had as a rookie entering ill-kept homes of poor black people. He'd take in a scene through the eyes of white officers, wondering what judgments they were making about those people—and about him. Gordon had spent lots of time trying to convince his colleagues that black people had legitimate gripes with police. Now, he couldn't help but hear X's ranting about black power through his teammates' perspective.

"What's your family going to say about this?" Gordon asked.

"Don't worry about that. You're trying to soften me up, huh?"

"No, not at all. You're very resolved about what you're doing. I'm just curious what your family is going to think about it."

"My family?" X said.

"Uh-huh."

"We had a talk. We don't really believe in death," X said.

"Your family don't really believe in it?" Gordon asked.

"Well, they're Christians, they believe in the afterlife."

"Uh-huh."

"They'll see me again, and I will see them again."

"You don't mind me asking, are you Christian?" Gordon asked.

"Hell naw," X said.

"You subscribe to any religion?"

"I'm awake," X said.

"Say it again? I didn't hear you."

"I'm not brainwashed, brother. I'm awake."

"I got you," Gordon said.

"What about you?" X asked.

"Yeah, I subscribe to Christian, man."

"I'm sorry to hear that."

"Yeah, I guess it's just the lens you look through, you know what I mean?" Gordon said.

"Yeah, I was raised that way. I never really took to it. Too much faith. Not enough proof," X said.

"Have any kids?" Gordon asked.

"Luckily, no."

"No?"

"Maybe in the next life."

"You believe in the afterlife?" Gordon asked.

"Oh yeah," X said.

"But you're just not religious?" Gordon asked.

"Nope, but I believe in spirituality," X said.

"Okay," Gordon said.

"When I was about eight years old, I saw—well, back up," X said. "My babysitter, she got shot in the head by her husband, then her husband killed himself. Then, I don't remember how long later, no less than a year later, I was in the pool with my siblings, and I saw my dead babysitter who'd got shot in the head standing over there looking at us, clear as day. You can't tell me I didn't see it. I seen it, just as you see that blood all over the wall, and you see those dead bodies. I saw her. I saw her dead essence, her spirit, her energy, whatever the fuck you want to call it. I believe in the afterlife. No, I don't believe. I *know*. The afterlife is real. This is what gives me the courage to do this."

Gordon sat back, listening. X had just spoken more words in a row than he had all night. He'd told a story, gone back to a memory, pictured himself in another time and place. It was exactly what Gordon wanted, for X to momentarily leave the stress of the hallway. As long as he was telling a story, he wasn't thinking about shooting them.

"Did she say anything to you?" Gordon asked.

"No, she just smiled," X said.

"What, she just appeared in the room where you were or what?"

"Nah, I looked at my sister . . . that will never be taken away from me. That was my proof of the afterlife."

"So your sister saw her, too?" Gordon asked.

"Yep," X replied.

"Where were y'all living?"

"Uh-uh," X called back. "Not going there."

Damn, Gordon thought. He'd pressed too soon, broken the spell.

23

The Wives

Shan Gordon lay on the bed, the phone to her ear as she and a friend chatted, both watching *The Jeffersons* on television. One of George Jefferson's schemes was unraveling, and Louise was cutting him down to size. The scene had Shan and her friend laughing. Shan had already washed her face, put on pajamas, and placed a bonnet over her hair. Her thirteen-year-old daughter, Don'Yel, and her eight-year-old son, Christian, were asleep in their rooms.

A Facebook message flashed up on her phone's screen. "Hey girl, I was just checking on you and your family with all this police stuff going on. Just saw the news. Love you." Shan puzzled over that for a moment. Then another message popped up: "Is Larry okay?" A cousin called, and Shan clicked over. "Where is Larry? Is he working tonight?"

"Yes," Shan said. "What is going on?"

"You need to turn on the news," her cousin said.

Shan flipped the channel and watched for a couple of minutes, realizing the seriousness of the situation downtown. Officers had been shot, and the death toll was rising. Larry couldn't be down there, though, because he hadn't called her. She and her husband had a specific protocol for whenever he was going on a dangerous scene. He'd give her a quick call to let her know he'd be tied up.

Shan had met Gordon when she was eleven years old. Her cousin played sports with Gordon, and they ran into him at a track meet. He was a couple of years older, and after talking with him for two hours, she left with a crush. Before it got serious, Shan moved with her mother to California. But a few years later, Shan moved back, and she spotted Gordon with a friend one afternoon as she walked on a dirt path between apartment complexes. She recognized him and felt a flutter. Trying to be nonchalant, she kept walking. A moment later, she turned her head back to look. He'd done the same, breaking into a wide smile. She started clipping his photographs out of the sports section in the local newspaper and found reasons to walk past his family's apartment. They started talking and hanging out. Shan got a spot on the high school drill team as a Tigerette. One evening after a game, she found Gordon, the team's starting quarterback, leaning against a friend's red Camaro. She approached, and he pulled her close for their first kiss.

About six years later, just before they married, Gordon told her he wanted to be a cop. She was a worrier and didn't love the idea. But both hated being poor. They were surrounded by men who'd chosen life on the street, who cycled in and out of prison. Gordon's two older brothers already were behind bars. A career as a cop came with a regular paycheck and health insurance and a chance to raise their own children differently. During Gordon's early career in patrol and narcotics, Shan mostly bit her tongue about her fears and tried to be supportive. But that became more difficult once he joined SWAT. She thought constantly about what awaited her husband as he crashed through doors in the city's most dangerous neighborhoods. And the schedule was brutal. He got called out at all hours. He rarely was home on Thanksgiving or Christmas Eve. He missed birthday parties and dance recitals. When they went out to dinner, he drove his police Tahoe in case he got summoned mid-meal. Shan and the kids were always waiting for him to get a call, and it had gotten old fast. But Gordon had never seemed happier. He loved being on SWAT, and his career, along with hers as a teacher, had taken them out of poverty and into the life she'd grown up dreaming of.

The protocol had become their compromise, the quick call to let her know he wouldn't be reachable for a while. Gordon followed it religiously to avoid her wrath. But tonight he hadn't called. As Shan's phone kept buzzing with messages, she called Gordon's cell. It rang a couple of times, then went to voice mail. She called again. Still nothing. On the news, the tally of dead officers kept rising. She called again and left a message. *Please call.*

As the minutes ticked past, she kept calling. Eleven times, twelve, now thirteen. Shan waited half an hour, pacing the bedroom. In her twenty years as a cop's wife, she'd never feared her husband was dead. She didn't want to wake the kids, but she couldn't just sit there, either. She washed her face, pressing a cold washcloth over her eyes, trying to remove any trace of tears, and got dressed. She'd take the kids to Aunt Carolyn and Uncle Tommy's house, and she'd go look for him.

She sent Gordon a text. I'M WAKING THE KIDS AND TAKING THEM TO TERRELL. That would get his attention, she thought. If he was just busy and ignoring her, he'd stop everything and tell her not to do that. She kept watching the phone. Nothing.

She opened the door to her daughter's room, letting the light flood in along its turquoise walls. She stood there for a moment, stifling an urge to cry. She walked over to the bed and stroked her daughter's hair. "Hey, Mama," the girl said. Shan smiled at her. "I'm taking y'all to Terrell. I need to go be with Daddy for a while." Her daughter looked confused. "Baby, come on," Shan said. "Help me wake Christian."

Her daughter rose, wrapped herself in a blanket, and walked into her brother's room. She reached down to shake him. He opened his eyes, then rolled over. Don'Yel shook him harder. "Christian, get up. Mama's going to meet Daddy. We gotta go."

As Shan got ready, her son asked, "Where's Daddy?" "I don't know," Shan said. "But I'm sure he's okay." That was a lie. *He did not follow the protocol*, she thought. She sent him another text: I'M LEAVING THE HOUSE. I WOKE THE KIDS.

As they drove through the dark streets, Shan felt certain Gordon was dead. She looked in the rearview mirror and saw her daughter watching her. *How am I going to tell them he isn't here anymore? How am I going to say that?*

She walked the kids inside. She told her uncle she was going to drive downtown. "Hold on," her uncle told her gently. "You need to wait and stay put."

"No, I have to go find him."

"Where are you going to go?" he asked.

"I don't know," she said. "But I can't just sit here and wait."

Her uncle, who'd treated Gordon as his own son, told her he was certain there was nothing to worry about. If Gordon had been injured, Shan would have gotten a call, he said. "I don't think it's wise for you to go to Dallas with all this going on."

"He's not answering me," Shan said, raising her voice. "He hasn't answered for over an hour."

Shan knew she needed to calm down and keep it together. But the thoughts kept coming. Would she have to identify his body? Plan a funeral? She might need to be gone overnight or longer. She second-guessed her decision to bring the kids to her aunt and uncle's house. They were not in good health, not in a position to keep the kids as long as she might need. She decided to take them to her cousin's house around the block.

"I'm going to take the kids to Sharraine's house," she told her uncle. He nodded, made her promise to come back and talk before she drove downtown. When she returned, her uncle looked at her with concern.

"What's your plan?" he asked.

"I don't have a plan," she said. "I just want to go."

She tried Gordon one more time. Still nothing.

A few seconds later, her phone lit up. The name she'd given Gordon in her contacts, "Love of my life," flashed on the screen. The ringtone, "There Goes My Baby," filled her uncle's living room.

It was what Shan had been waiting for all night. But she was suddenly seized with panic, not wanting to answer. What if Gordon wasn't on the other end? What if it was someone else, calling with horrible news?

She picked up. "Hello?" she said. She got no response. She thought she heard something in the background. It was another man's voice. It sounded far away. Then she heard Gordon speak, not to her, but to someone else. "Hey, X," she heard him say.

That's when Shan understood. He was busy negotiating. She fell to her knees, still listening to his voice. She had no idea what he was in the middle of. But for now he was okay. She broke down sobbing.

"What's going on?" her uncle asked.

"It's Larry," she said. "He's okay."

After she got herself together, she went to get the kids and told them what was going on. "I brought you over here because I wanted to go find Daddy. He wasn't answering me, and I was worried."

Christian asked, "Did you talk to him?"

"Yes," she said.

"Why didn't you tell us?" Don'Yel asked.

"Because I didn't want you to worry," she said. Christian started crying and crawled into her lap.

They returned home, and the kids climbed into their parents' king-size bed. Shan sat in a window seat that looked out over the backyard.

"Can we call Daddy?" Christian asked.

"No," Shan replied. "He's talking to that man, the one who shot the cops."

Christian paused, then asked, "Is he shooting at Daddy?"

"No," Shan said, not wanting them to worry. But she felt herself starting to cry again and fought back the tears.

* * *

Emily Thompson woke in bed. Her son, Cameron, whose second birthday was a few days away, was sleeping next to her with an empty bottle of milk at his side. She could hear the comforting sound of his deep breaths over the hum of the humidifier. She looked at the clock and saw it was 10:30 p.m. already. She was surprised; her husband should have been home. Maybe he'd gotten stuck on a late call.

Emily, who'd been married to Brent Thompson only two weeks, understood the late calls better than most wives. She, like Brent, was a DART officer. She'd finished her shift at two o'clock that afternoon, just as he'd started his. They'd spoken briefly during the shift change and kissed good-bye. "Be careful," she told him. "I love you."

That night, as she was getting Cameron ready for bed, Brent had called. He told her the protest downtown had been uneventful and he'd be home soon. After they chatted, she texted him a funny cat meme. She left him a dinner plate in the fridge. She put her phone on silent and drifted off.

They'd met at work. After moving from the Midwest to Dallas, Emily waited tables for a couple of years, put herself through the police academy, then joined DART in 2009. One day, while picking up something from the equipment room, a colleague made her laugh. She was petite but her laugh was huge and guttural. Brent poked his head out of the quartermaster's office to see who was making that sound, and there was Emily with her emerald eyes and chestnut hair.

She worked days and he worked nights and their paths crossed only occasionally over the next couple of years. But when Emily picked up overtime shifts, Brent asked a sergeant to pair them. They laughed their way through the hours as Brent constantly pulled pranks. He'd put pepper spray on a colleague's door handle, then collapse in hysterics when the officer kept rubbing his eyes. A practice session at the shooting range began to feel like a date when Brent, a former Marine, stepped behind Emily and readjusted her grip.

Both were recently out of serious relationships. Brent had ended a twenty-five-year marriage with his first wife. Emily had broken up with a serious boyfriend, the father of her son. She'd given up on the idea that she'd ever find a good man. In the spring of 2016, she and Brent decided to move in together. He unpacked in Emily's brick house in one of Dallas's northeastern suburbs.

Emily would come home from work and find that Brent had fixed the hinges on the bathroom door or mowed the grass. He'd put Cameron in his cowboy boots and walk him around the house as the boy giggled. Some nights he'd turn on country music and try to teach Emily the two-step. "I'm a Yankee!" she'd protest, but he'd grab her hand and dance her around the living room.

They were sitting on the couch one night when Brent said, "I'm going to marry you." And then one day in June he said, "Let's do it today." She put on sandals and a green and white floral dress. He put on his Mason's belt and cowboy boots. They got married on a Tuesday in traffic court.

In the days afterward, she stopped by the records building several times to file the marriage license, but the line was always too long. That morning, July 7, the crowd was light, so she'd filed, making their marriage official. They'd fly to New Orleans for their honeymoon in ten days.

Now, as Emily woke and realized Brent wasn't home yet, she picked up her phone from the nightstand and saw she'd missed dozens of calls. The last had been from a sergeant, and she dialed him back. When he picked up, he sounded like he was crying.

"What's wrong?" Emily asked.

"Something happened," he said. "Brent's at Baylor."

"What happened?" she asked.

He told her a couple of sergeants were on the way to pick her up, then said he had to go.

Emily walked into the living room and Googled "DART police" on her phone. She learned of the shooting and saw that several officers were injured and one DART officer had been killed. The news didn't say much more. What Emily read shocked her, but she knew Brent must still be alive. If he were dead, the chief would have come himself. She woke Cameron, grabbed his car seat, and saw that a patrol car had arrived. Her colleagues drove with lights and sirens to Baylor hospital. She asked what was going on, but they said they didn't know.

At the hospital, Emily was led to a room filled with officers, many of them crying. A female officer outside the door offered to take Cameron. Emily hesitated, and the officer insisted. They told Emily to sit down. A social worker sat beside her and touched her knee. "There was a shooting," she said. "Brent didn't make it." Emily sat there confused. She felt a flash of anger, remembered the pistol in her purse, and briefly thought about grabbing it. Was the shooting still going on? Should she go to the scene? Then she started to cry.

She sat there for a couple of minutes staring at nothing. Someone brought Cameron into the room, and he sat in her lap. The social worker asked her gently, "Do you want to see him?" She pointed to a curtain covering a window on the wall. Emily nodded. The curtain opened slowly, showing another room. There was Brent, lying on a table. His body lay faceup, a bandage covering his head. His eyes were closed, as if he were sleeping.

Cameron looked up and saw him. He pressed his hands together, excited, as if expecting Brent to get up and come play. Emily hugged her son. As she stared at Brent, she realized she was looking at a shell. Whatever made him Brent was gone.

She hadn't yet told her relatives in the Midwest that she'd gotten married. Now she'd have to tell them she was a widow.

24

Mind-set

Canete crouched behind a row of black ballistic shields, steadied his M4 on top of one, and leaned over to look through his sight.

He worked to empty his mind, aiming for a place of focus but not overfocus, the way he'd once done during performances of Chopin's Polonaise. From just behind him, Gordon was carrying on the long negotiation. Canete listened to the gunman's words and his sounds, the snap of a pants pocket opening, the unwrapping of a snack, the gulping of water. As Canete listened, he visualized what it would look like if the gunman came out. If he emerged standing, Canete would raise his rifle and shoot him in the head. If he popped out low, Canete would adjust downward as he slid off the safety. He looked through the optic on his rifle, taking in the small circle of information. Then he moved his head back to survey the panorama. He felt like a hunter in a blind. He cycled through each possibility but tried not to get too attached to any particular one. He needed to be open-minded and calm, to react naturally as information presented.

Thoughts flitted through his mind with stubborn persistence, though. The two shootings he'd been involved with earlier in his career had been over in minutes, prompting ruminations only later about danger and death. But tonight he felt as if he were living in a suspended state, inside a cliff-hanger that wouldn't end. He tried to recognize excess thoughts and send them on their way. One kept circling back, the idea that this gunman was different from any other criminal he'd ever encountered, in his readiness and willingness to die.

Canete felt certain his training and skills were better than the gunman's. But Canete's desire to live would work against him. The only way he could beat this guy, Canete thought, was if he matched his mind-set. Canete finally understood what he'd read about in all those books about ancient samurai, how they strove to fight as if they were already dead.

He thought about his wife, blue-eyed Emily, pictured her standing in the kitchen in her Lululemon leggings. The house smelling of almond-crusted chicken and fresh kale. He saw three-year-old Hannah twirling around in her Elsa dress. Would they be okay without him?

25

Preparations

With the plan half-blessed by his sergeant, Borchardt needed to do two things: find a robot and build the most powerful device in the team's history. He needed help. He knew all the breachers' strengths and weaknesses, which explosives they preferred, whether they cut their tape sloppily or in neat strands. Tonight he grabbed the team's newest breacher, a former Marine nicknamed Short Dog.

Short Dog was of average height with a wiry, muscular build, short blond hair, and intense blue eyes. His teammates called him Rain Man because of his extraordinary capacity for numbers. He could remember their drill scores for months, down to a hundredth of a second. He could focus forever on jigsaw puzzles, crosswords, Escape the Room games. Short Dog was also one of the team's most athletically gifted, one of the few capable of running a six-minute mile. He held the unofficial speed record on the team's obstacle course, and he did it with such grace that one teammate couldn't resist pulling out his phone to film. With his history as a Marine and impressive shooting skills, he'd made it to SWAT on his first try in 2013.

Short Dog had turned into something of an explosives savant. He knew the mathematical breaching formulas by heart. His biggest weakness, Borchardt thought, was that he was too meticulous. A breacher needed to work quickly, be able to create a charge on the fly for whatever they encountered. Short Dog could overthink anything and become paralyzed by options. Sometimes he'd take too long building a charge because he wanted it perfect rather than merely functional. He believed in the breacher's saying: "A pretty charge is a happy charge is a successful charge."

While so much of SWAT came easy to him, Short Dog was quickly rattled by negative feedback and came off as fragile at times. No one was harder on Short Dog than himself. One sideways glance could send him spinning in self-doubt. He had such a loud internal critic that when he got to SWAT, where new guys were mercilessly derided, he routinely called Borchardt on his way home to confess to his latest fuckup. Sometimes Short Dog would get so knotted up that he'd wonder if he should quit. "Maybe I don't have what it takes," he'd say. But Borchardt would just tell him, "Quit being so hard on yourself."

Now, Borchardt found Short Dog in a hallway. "We need explosives," he said.

Short Dog slipped his breaching bag off his shoulder. "Bro, I got stuff," he said. He opened the bag and listed what he'd brought: water impulse charges, fire hoses, strip charges, a couple of blasting caps. "What kind of door is he behind?" Short Dog asked.

"No, just explosives," Borchardt said.

"What do you mean?" Short Dog asked.

"Not for the door," Borchardt said. "For him."

Short Dog puzzled over that for a moment. "*Oh*," he said.

The men knelt outside the college library, piling all their premade charges on the floor, while Borchardt explained. They needed to disassemble them and collect all the raw explosive material. They gathered detonating cord, a rope-like plastic tubing filled with explosive, often used in mining.

Short Dog was showing another officer how to puncture the tape on a water-bag charge, so they could neatly extract the det cord. It was taking forever. Borchardt looked over, annoyed. He wasn't a believer in the "pretty charge, happy charge" saying. He had another one: "No one's taking the charge on a date, so no one gives a fuck what it looks like." He pulled out his pocket knife, raised it high, and plunged it into a water bag, sending saline across the carpet. Short Dog looked over in surprise but appeared to take the hint. Borchardt assembled all the det cord—strands of pink, yellow, and white—and rolled it into a doughnut about seven inches wide. "We need something to put this on," Borchardt said. "Let's go get a book."

They walked through the aisles of the library and picked a light-blue hardback off the shelf, without noting its title. The plan was to fasten the bomb to one flat side of the book. On the other side, they'd create a ridge that would fit into the robot's claw. Short Dog cut a length of fire hose and taped it to the back of the book to make the ridge.

While Short Dog worked, Borchardt studied their doughnut of det cord. He was keeping a rough tally of how much they had— about fifty-two feet—and calculating how much explosive that amounted to.

"This ain't enough," he said.

In truth, Borchardt didn't know how much they'd need. His goal as a breacher was always to use the smallest amount of explosive possible—enough to blow in a door, without hurting anyone on the other side. Here he needed enough to incapacitate a person. How big a bang did that require? He wasn't necessarily trying to kill the guy but needed to at least ring his bell hard.

In theory explosives were a precise art, governed by a half dozen equations involving weight, heat, and distance. But in practice it was part guessing game. Officers rarely had all the information they needed—room dimensions, what doors were made of, how much electrical interference they'd encounter. They had to make educated guesses. If they used too little, they might not take out the gunman, allowing him to escape. If they used too much, they might blow up a piece of the college—and themselves.

"We need more explosives," Borchardt said, and picked up his phone.

26

The Gullah Wars

An assistant squad leader tapped Gordon on the back, then knelt and said quietly, "I see a bunch of blood on the wall. I think he's hit. I don't know if you can use that."

Gordon nodded and called out.

"Hey, X, are you injured at all?"

"You see a lot of blood all over the place?"

"Not here. I was just wondering if you were injured at all. I see a lot of shell casings."

"I'm good."

"I understand you might be good, but I'm saying, are you injured?"

"It's just the body. None of this matters. This world is not the real world."

"You don't sound like you're from Texas," Gordon said.

"I'm not."

"I can tell. I can tell by your accent."

"Where do I sound like I'm from?"

"I don't know. I'm yelling at you, so I really can't hear."

Around Gordon, SWAT guys were moving about, whispering.

X called out, agitated, "Is that a white man talking in your fucking ear?"

Gordon's pulse picked up. "Naw, man, it's just me," he said. "It's just me, X."

Gordon kept on about the gunman's accent. "What about California?" he said.

"Nope."

"Midwest?"

"I'm not going to tell you where I'm from. You'll try to do a background check on me."

"I can't. I don't know your name, bro."

"Let's keep it that way."

"I don't know your name, X," Gordon repeated, "so I can't do a background on you."

"You'll find out over my dead body."

"I don't want to find out over your dead body. I want to hear your story, man."

After another moment, X called out, "Hey, what kind of M4 you got? Is it an M4 or an AR?"

"It's an M4," Gordon replied, then regretted saying it. He didn't want X to perceive him as a threat. "I don't have it. I'm the negotiator. I felt I didn't need it."

"What? That's not very smart, but all right."

"What kind do you have?" Gordon asked.

"I already told somebody. It makes no difference."

Gordon suspected X was wondering, as he was, what waited on the other side of the wall, trying to picture the weapon that would kill him.

"I just want to know, X. We're talking, having a good conversation right here."

"Uh-huh."

"Think we're having a pretty good conversation?" Gordon asked.

"I've had better," X said.

"You've had better?" Gordon said. *Asshole*, he thought. "I bet. A guy as smart as you, you probably had a good few conversations."

"I've had some good conversations. I wish I could have more."

Gordon lifted his head. Was X having second thoughts?

"You can," Gordon said.

"Watch some TV," the gunman continued.

"You can, X."

"But naw, this needed to be done. This is my sacrifice for the people."

Nope, Gordon thought. No change of heart.

"Hey, you ever heard of the Gullah Wars?" X asked.

"Have I heard of what?"

"The Gullah Wars."

Gordon struggled to place Gullah—he thought he'd heard the term in an old Denzel Washington movie, *Glory*.

"You mind if I Google it right now?" he asked.

"I'm not doing anything," X said.

"You gonna give me time?" Gordon asked.

"Go ahead. I got my finger on the trigger though in case someone comes around this corner."

"Nah, nobody is coming there. I'm telling you, X. I've got control out here."

Gordon opened Google on his phone and typed in "Gullah Wars." Wikipedia popped up.

During early American history, the Gullah were slaves who lived along the coastal islands of South Carolina and Georgia. They were able to preserve a creole culture with heavy influences from their African roots. In the late 1700s, groups of Gullah slaves escaped rice plantations and fled to Spanish Florida, then a tropical wilderness of swamps and jungles. The Gullah established free settlements there alongside Native Americans, and both viewed the encroaching U.S. government as a common enemy. The Gullah and Seminole fought together against the U.S. Army in a series of battles called the Seminole Wars. They proved themselves to be fierce, formidable warriors. Later, during the Civil War, when Union forces arrived in South Carolina, the Gullah slaves there were eager to fight for their freedom.

The popular version of Civil War history was that moral, benevolent whites from the North marched in to rescue slaves from their masters. Schoolbook history left out the efforts at rebellion by many enslaved blacks, including the Gullah.

The Native Americans had their war heroes—Crazy Horse and Geronimo and Osceola. Who did African Americans have? They lacked a legacy of warriors who fought to the death for freedom. Their heroes had died anonymous deaths on the battlefields, a casualty of history's refusal to valorize fighting blacks as honorable. In recasting the Second Seminole War as the largest slave rebellion in history, activists hoped to reframe the narrative of slavery's end as less emancipation, more self-liberation.

After skimming the Wikipedia page, Gordon called out, "This basically says Gullah was enslaved Africans that lived in the Low Country, like Georgia, South Carolina. Is that about right?"

"Yep."

"You know they were also called Geechee?" Gordon added.

"Uh-huh, I know. I'm trying to teach *you*, brother."

"Pretty good, man. I told you, you were smart. I thought 'Geechee' was a Louisiana term."

"Yeah?"

"That shows what I know," Gordon said.

"We all got to learn someday," X said.

"Yeah, you're right."

"No one knows everything."

Gordon kept reading, feeling as if he and X were connecting. He wanted to reach out further, draw X closer.

"You need anything, X? You all right? You thirsty, you hurt?"

It was a standard negotiator tactic, showing compassion and care. It also played on a social behavior theory called reciprocity. *I do something for you, you do something for me.* If Gordon could get X to accept something, he might feel compelled to give something in return.

"I told you. I got a CamelBak and a first-aid kit. I'm good, man," X said.

Gordon leaned back against the wall. X was the rarest of negotiating subjects, a one percenter, a real-deal extremist. Most people wanted something—food, water, freedom, life. X, it appeared, did not want even his own life. The only thing X wanted was the thing they wouldn't give, their deaths. More bloodshed.

"You came prepared," Gordon said.

"Fuck yeah. If you gonna do it, do it right."

"That's true."

"Actually, I wasn't prepared for the protest. I had a little something else planned but, ah, you know, no time like the present."

"You say you weren't prepared for the protest?" Gordon asked.

"Naw," X said.

"What did you have planned?"

"Well, it will never come to pass. Maybe in the next life. . . ."

"You're educating me, X. I appreciate that."

Again the hallway fell quiet, until Gordon thought of something else to say.

"Did you drive here, X?"

"What?"

"Did you drive here?"

"Y'all will find out."

"I can't hear you, man. You got to speak up, bro," Gordon said.

"Y'all will find out everything you need to know," X said.

"Why can't we find out now?"

"Now, later, then. Time doesn't exist."

"It exists for me, X," Gordon said. "It exists for me."

27

Calculations

Borchardt descended the stairs, stepped outside the college, and found the team's explosives guru, Jude Braun. He'd arrived in an equipment truck with supplies the team might need. The men had been talking by phone; Braun knew the plan.

Borchardt told him he needed more explosives. He asked for Detasheet, which came in thin, rubbery sheets stored as rolls. Braun told him he didn't think that was the best choice. Its smoky residue tended to linger in the air, which might make it more difficult for the team to see afterward. "I've got something else," he told Borchardt.

At fifty-eight, Braun was the squad's resident old-timer. He'd joined SWAT in 1987, when the team's armament consisted of an old bread truck and five submachine guns. He was tall and stocky with brown eyes. He practiced the martial art of Shuai-chiao, one of the oldest forms of Chinese kung fu. The point was to throw the opponent to the ground—hard. He called the SWAT guys "young bucks" and was always asking them to help with some manual task on his to-do list—mow the grass at the range, pick up donated cinder blocks and railroad ties. He'd played a critical role in building the team's breaching program over the years. Two disastrous calls prompted its evolution.

The first was the one in 2006 when Borchardt got shot outside the Radisson hotel room. When Braun arrived, he was shocked by the amount of blood on the lobby's floors. It looked like someone had gutted an elk. And what happened next was, to Braun's mind, also a disaster. SWAT set up a perimeter around the suspect's room but felt they had few options. They weren't experienced enough with explosives to try blowing out a wall, and no one wanted to get close to the door after what had happened to Borchardt. After a couple of hours, the suspect shot his girlfriend, then shot himself. The injured woman fled the room after the suspect died, rescuing herself. They'd failed this woman as the gunman controlled the situation from start to finish, Braun thought. It was unacceptable. He vowed to himself that the team would get better.

A year later, SWAT was called to another hostage situation. A middle-aged man arrived home one night in a drunken rage, waving his .44 Magnum. His wife fled the apartment with their two-year-old daughter but hadn't been able to rescue her three-year-old son. SWAT circled the apartment, and a negotiator began talks with the man. Braun worked on a plan to breach the front door with an explosive. By then they'd done only about half a dozen outside of training.

After about an hour, the negotiator signaled to the team that they needed to enter right away—he thought the father was about to start shooting. Braun and the breachers hustled to create a charge but felt ill prepared. Braun had several options but did not pick his most powerful, nervous it would cause injury to those inside the apartment. A teammate crept to the door and placed the charge between the frame and the lock.

Braun stood by. As the charge blew, the door flexed, then bowed back to normal. Braun's heart sank. An officer shot the lock, and the men tried to push inside, slowed by two couches propped against the door.

As they worked, shots rang out from inside the apartment. By the time officers reached the bedroom, the man, a hole in his temple, lay crumpled on top of his son. SWAT lifted the three-year-old into their arms, cradling him as they passed him one by one out a back window, down to a waiting ambulance. His body was ash gray. When paramedics lifted his shirt, they saw he'd been shot in the chest.

Braun looked at the dead toddler and felt wholly responsible. His fail at the door, he thought, had caused a fail in everything else. If the team had deployed a more powerful charge or better tactics, could SWAT have reached the boy in time? It happened on Braun's birthday. He would never pass another birthday and not picture the boy's face.

In the debate over modern policing, the public narrative blamed police departments with becoming militarized. But from Braun's perspective, every escalation in force had been a proportional response to the acts of violent men. Dallas police officers, and those they were sworn to protect, had paid a painful price over the years for not keeping up, Braun believed. It was tragic mission failure, not bloodthirst, that had expanded their arsenals.

After the child's death, Braun vowed yet again to become better at explosive breaching. He reenacted the call, tweaking explosives until he found the right mix to collapse a wooden door barricaded with couches. He sought experts across the country, spent his own money on training seminars, and came back to teach the men what he'd learned.

By the summer of 2016, the Dallas Police Department had one of the best explosive breaching programs in the country. But on this and every other call, the reel of past failures played through the back of Braun's mind.

Outside the college, Braun handed Borchardt a rectangular block, about eleven inches by two inches, wrapped in army green plastic. "We should use this," he told Borchardt. It was a brick of C4.

* * *

Borchardt studied the block, about a pound and a quarter. He didn't have much experience with C4, which is so stable it's hard to detonate. You can shoot it with a rifle and it won't explode. Neither Borchardt nor Braun knew how much they should use. Two veteran agents with the Bureau of Alcohol, Tobacco, Firearms and Explosives had arrived on scene, and Borchardt went over to ask their advice.

He shook hands with the men and told them the plan. "We need your no-shit assessment," he said. How much C4 should they use? How close did they need to get to the guy? Would the plan work?

The men listened, wide-eyed, but said little. Finally, they said they thought the plan was badass but couldn't help. "Do what you have to do," one said, "but the ATF can't have anything to do with this." Borchardt walked off, annoyed. Those guys knew more about explosives than anyone. Dallas SWAT was about to make the mother of all breaching charges, and it appeared the team was on its own.

* * *

Over the years, police have flirted with explosives as a tool for more than breaching. One of the most noteworthy incidents happened in 1985 in Philadelphia, with a result so disastrous that federal authorities remained reluctant to help the SWAT team in Dallas three decades later. That situation had capped years of tension between the Philadelphia Police Department and a black activist group called MOVE.

MOVE was described as a combination of black power and flower power. Its members lived communally, believed in animal rights, and fought for racial justice. When police tried to evict leaders from a house in 1978, a firefight erupted, leaving one cop dead. Nine members of the group were sent to prison. The group later moved to a row house on Philly's west side and quickly became at odds with their neighbors, mostly middle-class African Americans. They mounted a bullhorn on the house and blared profanity-laced lectures at all hours. They built an unsightly bunker on the roof. The neighbors repeatedly appealed for help from the police and politicians, including the city's first black mayor.

One morning in 1985, police evacuated the neighborhood and ordered MOVE members to come out, announcing arrest warrants for four members. The city's white police commissioner urged them to come out peacefully. They refused.

Police shut off the house's electricity. They shot water cannons at it and tossed in tear gas. A gunfight followed, and police fired thousands of rounds of ammunition, until they ran out. Finally, the FBI supplied the police with explosives, dropped by helicopter onto the house's roof.

The explosion started a fire, which the mayor ordered firefighters to extinguish. But the police commissioner ignored him and told officers to let it burn. As flames leapt ten stories high, eleven group members, including five children, died. The fire destroyed a city block, including dozens of houses. A city investigation later denounced the police actions as "reckless, ill-conceived and hastily approved." The report said, "Dropping a bomb on an occupied row house was unconscionable." No one from city government was charged in the attack. But some began calling Philadelphia "The City that Bombed Itself."

What happened in Philadelphia influenced how federal authorities approached the siege in Waco, Texas, eight years later. After four ATF agents were killed while trying to storm the compound, authorities pulled back, attempted negotiations, and waited. A *Washington Post* columnist at the time mused about what might have happened if the Davidians were black. Would reporters be counting bodies instead of days spent in negotiations?

The fallout from the MOVE bombing stalled the use of explosives by police departments across the country. Then came the Oklahoma City bombing in 1995, when an ex–Army soldier, Timothy McVeigh, parked a Ryder truck full of fertilizer in front of a federal building in Oklahoma. The explosion killed 168, including nineteen children. Afterward, police departments reinvested in bomb squads. From there, they experimented with explosive breaching.

* * *

About 11:00 p.m., after the first press conference, Chief Brown called Commander Bill Humphrey, who was at a command center near the college. The men had been on SWAT together in the 1990s. Brown respected Humphrey's skills and his judgment, honed over decades of supervising officers.

"So what's your plan?" Brown asked.

Humphrey began running through options. "We could charge down the hallway, confront him, and take him down," he said.

Brown didn't like the sound of it. He'd gone down some long hallways on SWAT and knew how risky it was.

Another possibility, Humphrey said, was for officers to advance behind a shield. The department had steel barriers with a bar that two officers could hold as they came behind it. The problem, Brown knew, was that the barrier wasn't big enough to protect the officers' limbs. If the gunman's assault rifle got an officer in the arm or leg, he'd lose it, or worse.

What else? Brown asked.

"We could use an explosive," Humphrey said, explaining the idea of delivering a bomb with one of the robots.

Brown paused. He'd asked for creativity, but this was another idea filled with risk. What if they used too much explosive and accidentally took out officers, too?

"We'll use just enough C4 to contain the blast at the end of the hall," Humphrey said.

Up to that point, DPD's robots had served several roles: to retrieve explosives so bomb techs could dismantle them, to deliver cell phones and other items to barricaded suspects, to breach walls and doors, and for surveillance. DPD had never used a robot offensively. Humphrey was now suggesting that they "weaponize" one. As they talked through the idea, Brown considered how controversial it could be. He thought about the .50-caliber rifles Humphrey had persuaded him and the former police chief to buy a few years earlier. At first, Brown, who was second in command at the time, had refused. "You're never going to use a fifty-caliber rifle in a city," he said. But the manufacturer sent them a rifle to try, and SWAT had smartly invited Brown to the range. He lay on the grass three hundred yards downrange from the target and squeezed. The rifle was so powerful that when Brown fired, the force lifted him from the ground. He was sold. A couple of years later, SWAT faced the standoff with a man in an armored van who shot up police headquarters. The .50-cal had been the only weapon in their arsenal capable of piercing its bulletproof windows and killing the guy, ending the standoff. As far as Brown knew, his SWAT team was the only one in the nation to have sniped someone with a .50-caliber.

Brown didn't think any other police department had used a robot bomb, either. But then no other department had been so boldly attacked by a shooter who was still fighting, still holding the city hostage. Brown thought about the families who were getting word that their husbands, fathers, brothers, and sons weren't coming home. He'd soon have to face them. Then he'd have to start planning funerals. He needed a plan that would avoid more officer deaths.

Brown told Humphrey he'd think it over. "You all work on that while the mayor and I go out to do another press conference," he said. "When I get back, be ready."

Brown decided not to tell the mayor and other officials about the idea just yet. He didn't want the politicians, who might be overly concerned with optics, weighing in. Already some city leaders were suggesting they turn over the call to federal authorities. Brown had refused.

Brown soon stood behind a podium in the lobby of city hall, updating reporters. Officers had arrested a woman in the area of the college and were questioning her. Other officers had followed a Mercedes with two suspects carrying camouflaged bags. They, too, were being questioned, Brown said. And negotiations continued with the shooter on the second floor of the college, who told officers he'd planted bombs across downtown. "This suspect we're negotiating with for the last forty-five minutes has been exchanging gunfire with us and not being very cooperative in the negotiations," Brown said.

The press conference dragged on, and Brown struggled to pay attention to reporters' questions as he turned the robot bomb over in his mind.

Afterward, Brown called Humphrey, who said his team felt confident it would work. "Your plan is approved," Brown said. "Just don't blow up the whole building. Call me when you're ready to roll."

28

Tying In

C. T. Payne, a longtime member of the bomb unit and SWAT team at the Garland Police Department near Dallas, was sitting on the couch watching *Perry Mason* with his wife when the telephone rang. He was startled by Short Dog's question.

"How much explosive does it take to kill a man?" the younger officer asked.

"Hold on," Payne said. He rose from the couch and walked back to the bedroom.

Payne had a big, round frame and drove one of the biggest pickup trucks around. Many Garland officers took pride in their reputation as rednecks. Payne, a man colleagues described as "backwoods country," fit right in.

Payne had been one of the first law enforcement officers in the region to experiment with explosive breaching. After the Oklahoma City bombing, Garland police wanted to expand their bomb unit. They entered the field wanting to learn about explosives from the other end—how to disable them. Garland's department tapped Payne to head it up. Around 2000, when the city's tactical team wanted to expand its capabilities, he began to learn about explosive breaching as well. He attended a few training seminars, mostly held at off-the-grid properties owned by former military guys, and he did most of his experimenting in old country fields. He and a couple of the tactical guys made beer bets as they blew hundreds of doors, figuring out how to place charges. Members of Dallas SWAT came out and videoed the explosions. They'd play them back in slow motion, studying how much shrapnel each door produced, learning how to manage flying hinges and doorknobs.

Payne had learned early on to make firm rules about when to deploy his skills. He considered explosive breaching a last resort. All other means should be considered, and discounted, before using explosives, Payne believed. For him it wasn't an ethical issue; it was a legal issue. He wanted to keep his team out of trouble.

During one drug raid Payne was involved in, a gunman barricaded himself inside a house and shot at officers. SWAT members wanted Payne to breach a wall with explosives, but Payne worried the blast would kill the suspect inside. Payne had no qualm using explosives for lethal force if it was justified. But at that moment, they couldn't justify it. And he wanted no part of using explosives to "accidentally" kill someone. He declined to do the breach. The suspect eventually came out of the house and was shot by an officer.

Now, Payne registered Short Dog's question carefully. The Dallas team wasn't looking for his counsel on the advisability of their plan. If asked, Payne would have suggested using the robot to fire a shotgun at the suspect. He knew of cases where that had been done, and he thought the public would take it better than blowing someone up.

But Short Dog, for all the legal and ethical issues embedded in his question, was asking only for a simple mathematical calculation.

"What's your proximity to the target?" Payne asked. The closer they could get, the less explosive they'd need.

"I think I can get it within a foot or two of the guy," Short Dog said.

Payne thought it over. He knew that sixty to seventy pounds per square inch of pressure could be lethal to the human body. He calculated how much C4 it would take to produce more than double that from a foot or two away.

"I'd use about half a pound," Payne said finally.

But Payne cautioned Short Dog: it probably would not be instantly lethal. The team should not rush up on the suspect immediately. Even after detonation, the guy might still be able to move, and to kill.

"Thank you, sir," Short Dog said.

Payne added: "I can't believe they're buying off on this plan."

"I think we're good to go," Short Dog replied.

Payne hung up, worried about Short Dog. *That poor guy*. It was a risky operation. If it went south, Payne hoped the administration wouldn't hang the young officer out to dry.

* * *

Short Dog sat in the hallway, keeping an eye on their pile of detonation cord. Borchardt walked toward him, holding the brick of C4. He tossed it to Short Dog. "Throw this in there." Short Dog caught the block in his hands. He usually worked with small amounts of less powerful explosives. Now he was staring at more than a pound of C4. The only thing he knew about C4 was that it worked better if tight and compact. "Cut it in half," Borchardt told him. He did, then kneaded it into a ball like Play-Doh, placed it in the center of the det cord doughnut, and spread it out so the edges of both materials touched. Rub, push, rub, push. If the C4 didn't connect with the det cord, or if it had too many air pockets, it might not detonate.

Just a couple of hours earlier, Short Dog had been sitting in his living room, watching *My Little Pony* with his two young daughters. When he'd gotten the call, he turned on the news to see what was happening. As he'd geared up, he felt frustrated. He'd been troubled by the recent animus toward cops and thought it mostly unwarranted. Now people were shooting them? He kissed his wife and daughters good-bye and climbed into his Tahoe.

Short Dog loved everything about SWAT—shooting guns, slamming doors, hurling flash bangs. The new-guy excitement usually wore off after a couple of months, but Short Dog's hadn't. While handling explosives was dangerous, Short Dog didn't worry much. He hoped to die in his sleep as an old man, after he'd walked his daughters down the aisle and spoiled his grandchildren. But if he died honorably in the line of duty, he thought that was the "greatest fucking way you could ever die, going out with your boots on." What he feared more than death was making a mistake, disappointing the guys, being unworthy. "As long as I don't die because I did something stupid," he said. That was his vision of hell, an eternity rewatching some mistake he'd made, causing a teammate or victim to get hurt.

Tonight Short Dog felt the pressure as he worked. If the bomb didn't detonate properly, it would put the whole team at risk. Once he'd molded the C4 with the det cord, he fastened it tight to the book with duct tape.

* * *

While Short Dog finished up the bomb, Borchardt looked for a robot. The one SWAT typically used, Johnny 5, had been out of commission since a suspect had attacked it with knives months earlier. Borchardt went to find officers from DPD's bomb squad, who'd just arrived on scene.

"This is what we're going to do," Borchardt said, explaining the plan.

The bomb squad supervisor stared at him. "What?"

Borchardt felt impatient, not wanting to explain the plan to one more officer. And the bomb squad commander was looking at him as if he had lost his mind. Borchardt asked him for a robot.

"No," the commander said. They were in the business of diffusing bombs—not detonating them. His guys were not trained to use any of their robots offensively. Borchardt shouted at him, "I'm not trained to use this robot at all."

Borchardt told him to go ask whoever he needed to ask, but their plan had been approved, and he needed a robot. Now.

"None of my guys are driving it," the commander said. "And we're not pushing the button."

"Just give me the fucking robot," Borchardt said. "I'll drive it myself." Borchardt walked away, furious. He found Braun, who set about smoothing things over with the commander.

The bomb techs rolled their smaller robot off the truck. It looked as if its back tire was skipping. "The back tire sometimes locks up," the tech explained. Borchardt was growing more annoyed by the minute. "I can't have a robot that might lock up. It has to work."

So the officers drove their eight-hundred-pound Remotec Andros off the truck. They guided it up the stairs and onto the second floor. Borchardt studied it, amazed by its size.

After many calculations, Short Dog had built a bomb that was about three-quarters C4 and one-quarter det cord. If they could get the robot within a few feet of the gunman, Short Dog thought the plan would work. He placed the MacGyvered book into the robot's claw and secured it. Long after it looked solid, he kept adding tape. He didn't want the bomb falling off on its way down the hallway.

When Short Dog finished, another breacher, Officer Mark Michaels, arrived to help. Michaels was a big former Division I defensive tackle and U.S. Marine. Teammates called him the "Blue Hulk."

As Short Dog put finishing touches on the device, Michaels picked up a piece of duct tape and stuck it uselessly on top. "I just want to be part of history here," he said. Short Dog laughed, then returned to deep concentration. Michaels began wiring the bomb to an ignition system. In a few minutes, he called out, "I'm tying in." Now it was live. If someone transmitted a signal to create a spark, it would race through the shock tube at sixty-five hundred feet per second, hit a blasting cap, and set off a small explosion. That explosion would ignite the det cord, and that explosion would detonate the C4.

They'd also created another parallel ignition system. If the first failed, they'd have one more shot. Michaels was about to wire in the second system when Johnnie Green, one of the ATF bomb techs, spoke up. Stocky with a thick mustache, Green had been working with explosives for two decades all over the world, from the jungles of Colombia to the battlefields of Iraq. He'd stayed quiet all night, but now he intervened. He thought SWAT was about to make a critical error. The robot's ignition system, which transmitted wirelessly, might not work in the college, with stray Wi-Fi signals and radio noise from fluorescent lights, Green told the team. They were in danger of delivering an undetonated bomb, gift-wrapped, to a suspect who might use it against them. They needed a better backup, in case the robot's ignition system failed. At the very least, they needed a way to make the thing self-destruct.

Green had a less temperamental, top-of-the-line Zeus ignition system. It's what Navy SEALs used in the field, and Green said he'd never seen one fail. His partner grabbed a kit from his truck, and Green helped Michaels wire in the backup. He showed Michaels how the controller worked. "If the primary doesn't go, push it, and you're done," Green told him. Explosives people had a phrase for when a device did not go off: no joy. This ignition system would bring joy.

The officers stood back to look at the robot, with its claw

holding something covered in yellow tape and a tube hanging out. "It looks like a fucking bomb attached to a robot," Michaels said. They needed to disguise it. Michaels's eyes landed on a black trash bag lining a can in the stairwell. "Get me some garbage bag liners," he said. A couple of officers went around the floor, collecting bags. They ripped them into shreds, then wrapped them around the bomb, making sure to leave the robot's camera lens unobstructed. Now the device looked like a black blob. If nothing else, it might confuse the gunman. *What the hell is that?*

29

The Thin Blue Line

Gordon knew he'd have to figure out a way to get X to accept the robot. If he ran from it, or shot at it, their plan could fall apart. The gunman already had turned down a phone, and he didn't want food or water. Gordon thought maybe he could at least get X comfortable with robots moving around the hallway.

At the FBI Academy in Quantico, where Gordon had recently trained for a couple of weeks, he'd heard two negotiators talk about a scene they'd worked on a federal reserve in Oregon. Authorities contemplated launching an assault team off an armored personnel carrier to take control of the compound. They decided to get the suspects acclimated to the vehicle coming and going. Gordon wanted to do the same thing with the robots. He started with a Throwbot, a softball-size black device with a small camera. When an officer tossed it into the hallway, it popped open and could be wheeled around by remote control. Gordon told X it was just a tool they used to get a picture of the hallway. "You better not try anything," X called back. Gordon thought X might shoot it, but he didn't. The team moved the Throwbot and a couple of other small robots back and forth along the hallway, like remote control cars. X didn't complain.

Over Gordon's shoulder stood Huante, his M4 pointed down the hallway. Every so often another officer tried to relieve him, and he shook his head. "Not today, boys." Gordon knew that if the gunman came around the corner, Huante wanted the shot. Now, as Gordon and X talked, Huante loaded a different magazine into his rifle with a loud slap. The noise echoed down the hallway.

"Oooowee, I love that sound," the gunman said. "Y'all coming to get some?"

Gordon looked over at Huante, feeling tempted to punch him. He'd just gotten the gunman calmed down. Huante looked back at Gordon and shrugged. *What?*

"I told you, X. I got control over here," Gordon said. "I'm trying to make you understand. I got control."

"I'm a fucking vet. I know that sound. Don't bullshit me!"

"X, I'm not bullshitting you, man. I haven't bullshitted you in forty-five minutes. Not bullshitting you yet. Nobody is coming back there. We're just talking."

Gordon tried to change the subject. "All these people are talking in my ear, X, wanting to know why you doin' this."

"Tell them, Abedi Mahoya."

"Say it again?"

"Abedi Mahoya."

"What does that mean?"

"African liberation."

"Okay."

"Did you know that our brothers and sisters are still enslaved in Saudi Arabia and the Middle East? Yes, they still have slaves in the fucking Middle East."

"Uh-huh. Do they?"

"Yep, the Islamic—the Muslim, Arabs, they started the slave trade, over fourteen hundred years before the white man."

"Sounds like you don't like Muslims, either."

"Uh, no real experience with them, but from their history? Hell no."

"You know, people are probably going to try to say you're a member of ISIS or something."

"Sorry, not Muslims. I don't not like Muslims, just those who hate against my people," X said. "Not all whites are bad. Not all Muslims are bad."

"Not all police?"

X thought about that for a moment. "Most. About ninety-nine percent. If you are in a corrupt system, you are corrupted."

"What can we do about the corrupt system, X?" Gordon asked.

"Tear it down," X said.

"How do we do that?"

"Well, first there needs to be a little bloodshed; that's what I'm doing here. Then you need to hold accountable every action—" He stopped, midsentence, then snapped, "What the fuck was that?"

Gordon looked around. "What was what? What did you hear? We're over here, X. What did you hear?"

X made no reply.

"You okay?" Gordon asked, raising his M4.

There came no answer, and Gordon's heart raced, but soon X was talking again. "Hold everybody accountable for their actions," he said. "When a policeman beats, kills, shoots, or abuses anybody, y'all need to fucking arrest him. None of that thin blue line shit. Legal and illegal. If a cop breaks the fucking law, you arrest him. Y'all have his back. That's what's wrong with the system. Y'all keep looking out for each other, and I get that. As a vet, I get that, but y'all are corrupting the system. Y'all can't do that shit anymore.

Same thing with the judicial system, the DA and everyone who let y'all off, the juries, all that needs to be fucking torn down."

When X finished, Gordon asked, "You think the military is corrupt?"

"The people themselves? No. But all the wars, ever since . . . fuck, hell, even World War One, everything has been about money and controlled by the bankers."

"Uh-huh."

"World War Two, that was the last war for freedom. But even then, not really. There is always money involved. Iraq, Afghanistan, Vietnam, all bullshit. We didn't need to be over there."

Gordon thought he'd attempt a friendly debate. Could X see Gordon's service as a cop the same way he viewed his own military service?

"Did you fight in any war?" Gordon asked.

"Did I fight? No," X said.

"Did you help in any way?"

"I was there."

"That's what I'm saying. Did you help? Were you like a supply guy? I mean did you help in any way?" Gordon asked.

"Fuck no. I was in construction," X said.

"You were building things?"

"Yep. I built shit and I tore shit up."

"Were you in demolition?" Gordon asked.

"Nah, just with a hammer."

"Just with a hammer?"

"For the Army."

"You said the Army?"

"Yes sir. Y'all gonna run that. I know what you're doing. Don't think you're outsmarting me."

Gordon sighed. "X, listen to me, please."

"I'm listening."

"All I'm trying to do is find out some information about you. We don't know your name, so we can't find out anything about you. We're just talking. Trying to slow this thing down and just talk about it. So I'm getting to a point, X. You say you tore things down, right?"

"Uh-huh."

"You helped out the military, right?"

"Uh-huh."

"You were part of the military, correct?"

"Uh-huh."

"And you feel the military had some corrupt wars, right?"

"All our soldiers are fucking dying for no reason. They don't need to be over there," X said.

"Were you a corrupt guy?" Gordon asked.

"Nope."

"But you were part of a corrupt war."

"I believed in what I was doing, just like the others. We thought we were soldiers, being patriotic and fighting for our country, but I opened my eyes. Corrupt."

"So you're saying I'm—we're—part of a corrupt system as police."

"That's different. Y'all know what y'all are doing."

"You know what you were doing, too, right? You were trained, right? You went to basic, right?"

"I never pulled the trigger on anybody," X said.

"I never have, either," Gordon said.

"In SWAT? What the hell?"

"No, I never have."

"Well, I have today. I don't really know what else to say."

"All I'm saying, X, is we all have our battles to fight," Gordon said.

"And this is mine," X said.

"All right, you made your point, though."

"What?"

"You made your point. You have all of our attention, loud and clear. You have our attention, X. Where did you go to basic?"

"Man, you're getting deeper and personal."

"We already been personal, X. You told me you've seen a ghost."

The gunman laughed loudly. Gordon laughed, too.

"You told me you seen a ghost, man. You educated me about the Gullah, the Gullah Wars. We've already been personal."

"I'm trying to wake you up, brother."

"And I really, really appreciate it," Gordon said.

"Knowledge is power," X said.

"You're absolutely right. You're absolutely right, X," Gordon said.

"Do you know the power of your melanin?" X said.

"It is pretty powerful," Gordon said.

"Are you just saying what I want to hear?" X asked.

"Oh no, not at all, bro. I been black a long time. Mama used to say, the blacker the berry, the sweeter the juice."

30

The Toll Rises

Dr. Williams pushed open the heavy wooden door of a small waiting room. It was time to face the family of the first dead officer. By now Williams knew his name, Patrick Zamarripa. Williams was surprised by how many people were inside the room. As he entered, everyone grew quiet and all eyes turned to him. Williams saw an older man wearing a Navy baseball cap, sitting in a chair. He walked over and asked the man if he was Zamarripa's father. The man nodded. "Is Patrick all right?" he asked. Williams sat down in a chair beside him.

"I'm Dr. Brian Williams, the trauma surgeon on call tonight," Williams said. "I was leading the team that cared for your son. When he arrived, he was in critical condition. We did everything we possibly could. I'm very sorry, but Patrick died."

Williams let that sink in a moment. He'd had hundreds of these conversations over the years, and they never got easier. He followed a couple of rules he'd learned over time. He did not use euphemisms like "passed away" or "left us." He used words that left no room for interpretation. He tried to say "died" in the first couple of sentences, so as not to build suspense. Many doctors believed in saying it three times in three different ways. Dead. Died. Gone. It was important to talk slowly, giving information in small chunks. Most families wanted to hear three things. That it was quick, that their loved one felt no pain, and that they had not been alone. Williams said these things if he could. Most families wanted to know the basics of what happened, and he tried to talk in non-medical terms. *We put in a breathing tube. We pumped his heart. We gave him drugs. Nothing worked.* Williams wanted to get this conversation right every time. What he said in these moments would be remembered and replayed forever. His words marked the beginning of the grieving process, and he knew that if he handled them poorly they could cause much more pain. He could never predict how a family member would respond. Some burst into wails. Others shouted at him. This man stayed quiet and just looked down at the floor.

Williams asked if he wanted details. The father nodded.

"As I go through this, you can stop me at any time. You can ask me any questions. There is no rush," Williams said. He walked the man through the procedures his team had tried, as everyone in the room listened. "I'm very sorry for your loss," Williams said when he was finished. "If you have any questions, I'll be here all night. I will always be available to you." The man thanked him, adding that he knew Williams had done everything he could. Williams found himself comforted by the man's words. He rose and left the room. As the door swung shut behind him, he heard the silence give way to wails.

Patients were still waiting for him in the ER, but Williams couldn't go back yet. Three dead cops in one night. He swept his badge and entered a corridor between the ER and Psych Department.

He sank down beside a utility closet, put his head in his hands, and, for the first time ever at work, sobbed.

* * *

After midnight, inside the emergency operations center downtown, Mayor Rawlings watched as Chief Brown walked in front of the crowd and announced that Sgt. Mike Smith had died during surgery. That brought the death toll to four.

Rawlings felt deflated by the news. He'd been optimistic that all of the injured officers would survive. Three dead cops had seemed impossible. Four seemed unimaginable. Rawlings had learned that Smith was a veteran, close to retirement, with a wife and two school-age daughters.

After the announcement, Rawlings saw the chief approaching him. It was time for them to go to the hospital. Brown looked shaken. They attended a police memorial every year to commemorate fallen officers, and they'd been proud of the fact that none had died during their tenure. The suspect, Brown said, was still not cooperating. "This guy is motherfucking us," he said. Rawlings was surprised by the oddly phrased profanity; he'd never heard the chief curse before.

As the police chief and mayor prepared to head to the hospital in separate cars, Brown stepped away to take a call. Afterward, he walked back over to Rawlings.

"We're about to end this," Brown said. "We're going to blow him up."

Rawlings felt the color drain from his face as he waited for Brown to elaborate. But the chief offered nothing more, and Rawlings didn't ask any questions.

Riding through the city's deserted streets, Rawlings felt his mind drifting back to the philosophy lessons of his college days. He remembered Camus's assertions about the absurdity of existence.

Everything about this night had begun to feel unreal. The angry protesters, marching to decry police shootings, now fleeing fresh waves of gunfire aimed by some unseen attacker. The fallen officers, dying one by one. The cries of ambulances, rising over the desolate and barricaded streets. The heart of this great city, broken all over again. And now the police wanted to blow up the shooter with a robot bomb inside the shelter of a community college. Just hours earlier Rawlings had been watching the Rangers game, eating a tuna sandwich.

His mind struggled to find a purpose behind it all, any hint of a divine plan he could latch onto now for reassurance. Albert Camus, he realized, would have scoffed. Had he been seated beside him in the back of this SUV, the Nobel Prize–winning writer would have reminded the mayor that his longing for meaning and purpose was wasted. There was no benevolent hand guiding from above, no greater truth waiting to be discerned beneath the tawdry surface of these events. Camus had fixated on the myth of Sisyphus, the Greek king whose divine punishment had been to push an immense boulder up a hill again and again, only to have it roll back down. Camus had warned that there was "no eternity outside the curve of the days." The central struggle of life, he believed, was accepting mortality and other hard truths and learning to bear them.

With these thoughts churning, Rawlings gathered himself to face the tasks that awaited him. When the Suburban pulled up at the hospital's ambulance bay, the mayor stepped out to face the families.

31

Backup

Midnight had come and gone, and Gordon was still leaning against the wall, listening to the gunman's voice. The men had been talking for more than two hours. Now the gunman began singing.

Rollin'... Rollin'... rollin' on the river...

Gordon knew the song. A few months earlier he'd been on a Caribbean cruise with his family. He'd sat in the bar wearing a tank top and flip-flops, drinking Crown Royal and Sprite, playing music trivia with shipmates. One of the questions had been to name the song, which Gordon had gotten wrong.

"Hey X, I bet you a hundred dollars you don't know the name of that song," Gordon said.

The gunman paused. "Rollin' on the River"?

"Nope," Gordon said. "It's called 'Proud Mary.'"

The gunman laughed.

"That's pretty good, Larry," he said.

One of the Amigos, Ryan Scott, was holding cover in the stairwell. Every so often he put his phone in front of Gordon's face, showing him the latest tally of officers down. The first time,

Gordon had learned one officer had been killed and another five shot. Scott had done it again a little later: two officers dead, eight shot. Now, Scott came back a third time. Four officers dead, nine injured. Gordon fought the urge to slap the phone out of Scott's hand. He needed to show X empathy, and it was becoming more difficult as the numbers rose.

They'd settled into a comfortable back-and-forth. Gordon wanted to test the connection.

"X?" Gordon called.

"Yeah?"

"If I come around this corner and walk back there, are you going to shoot me, man?"

The gunman paused.

"I don't know, Larry," he said. "I can't like you too much, though, because I might have to kill you."

Gordon got word from his sergeant that it was time. He told X he was tired of yelling down the hallway. He wanted to send him a cell phone. They could deliver it to him with a robot. He wouldn't have to reach out into the hallway; it would be safe.

"You want me to have the phone, you can bring it to me," X shouted.

"I'm too scared to come down there," Gordon said. "I don't want to get shot. We can drive it to you on the robot, man."

"I ain't taking no cell phone from y'all. Y'all probably gonna try to blow me up or something."

Gordon saw the SWAT guys near him look at one another. *Damn, this guy is smart.*

"This is the city of Dallas, X," Gordon said. "That's some CSI shit you're talking about. The city of Dallas barely has enough money to buy police gear."

The gunman paused, as if he was thinking about it, then agreed. He had gotten used to the little Throwbot. X told Gordon to make sure the phone had Pandora on it. He wanted to listen to some music.

"I'll tell you what," X said. "I'm gonna listen to, hmmmm, twenty songs. Maybe twenty songs will be enough."

He paused.

"And then I'm coming out."

Gordon's heart pounded. He didn't think the gunman meant he'd surrender. To Gordon, it sounded like "huffing"—what people did right before they jumped off a building or a bridge. They took deep breaths in and out, trying to get up their courage. He thought X was gearing up to come out shooting.

* * *

Gordon kept talking, as fifteen minutes passed, then thirty. He was exhausted.

"Where's the phone, Larry?" X shouted.

"It's coming," Gordon said. "I've got it under control."

Finally, Gordon felt a hand on his shoulder. He turned and saw his sergeant, who leaned in close. "The robot is here," he said.

Gordon looked around and realized his teammates had left their posts in the stairwell. Only Huante remained, still pointing his M4 down the hallway. Gordon surveyed his distance from the safety of the concrete stairwell. He steeled himself.

"X, they're telling me it's ready," he called out. "It's done. The robot's here. It's about to bring you a phone."

"Okay, Larry," X said.

Gordon made a final overture. "Hey X, how about you put your rifle down, man?"

"I can't do that," X said. "I've got to do what I came here to do."

Gordon looked around the hallway behind him. All night, every time he'd glanced back, he'd been comforted by the sight of at least a dozen geared-up officers. Now the hall was empty except for a three-foot-tall robot, standing there facing him.

He stared for a moment, puzzling over how it looked. Like some kind of space-age Clint Eastwood. A camera eye peered out from the center of its metal head. Its claw, sticking straight out, held an amorphous black shape. The bomb. Seeing the thing, Gordon felt a sort of affection for it. It was the same feeling that flooded him on a dangerous call, when he could hear an approaching siren in the distance. Backup.

"Hey X, I'm gonna need you to guide this robot in, man."

"I know y'all have cameras on it," he said.

"Yeah, but they only capture at ninety degrees."

"Okay, but don't try anything," X said.

"Where are you back there?"

"Tell them to make a left at the door and come straight back, all the way to the back."

Gordon reached down and grabbed a black ballistic shield. He tucked it beside his body, covering himself as best he could, ready to run. He called out one last open-ended question to X. He didn't know what he was saying anymore, just anything to keep X talking.

The robot rolled forward slowly, squeaking across the carpet. The sound reminded Gordon of the motorized car his kids used to drive around the neighborhood.

As the robot moved closer, Gordon looked over at Huante, who nodded. Then Gordon took a couple of large steps, shield raised high, launching himself toward the stairwell. With Huante's large frame leaning out, the men briefly got stuck together in the door frame. Gordon wiggled free. Then Huante stepped back into the stairwell, M4 still raised, and pushed the door shut. Just before it closed, they heard X call out. "Larry. Larry? Where'd you go, Larry?"

Fuck, Gordon thought. *He's coming out.* Gordon stepped down a flight of stairs, joining the team. Huante lingered on a higher step, and a sergeant ordered him to move back. Huante shook his head, and the men started whisper-shouting. "I am giving you a direct order," the sergeant snapped, and Huante finally relented. The men stood along a wall, waiting for the count.

32

The Mother

Greg Weatherford, the undercover officer who'd shielded protester Shetamia Taylor in the street, was at police headquarters filling out paperwork. Now supervisors approached him with another task. They'd run the tags on a black SUV left outside the college with its hazard lights flashing. They thought it might belong to the gunman, and they gave Weatherford an address. They wanted him to go knock on the door.

Weatherford and his partner climbed into a Tahoe and headed east on I-30. The home was in a town called Mesquite, a short drive east of Dallas, so they called the local police department. Four officers met them in a grocery store parking lot, then they caravanned to the two-story brick house along a quiet street.

The officers stepped out of their patrol cars and approached the house in the dark, taking positions around the front yard; one went around back in case anybody ran. Once they were set, Weatherford walked up to the front. He was still wearing his jeans stained with Taylor's blood, along with his heavy ballistic vest. He was nervous. What were they walking into? Weatherford knocked. After a few moments, the porch light flipped on. The door cracked open, and a woman wearing pajamas appeared.

"I'm sorry to bother you, ma'am," Weatherford said, pulling out his badge. "I'm with Dallas Police. Do you have a black Tahoe?"

"Yes," she said.

"Is it here?"

"No, my son has it," she said.

"Where is your son?" Weatherford asked.

"He went to some protest in Dallas," she said.

Weatherford nodded. "I need you to come to Dallas with me and talk to detectives," he said.

"Is my son okay?" the woman asked, looking bewildered and fearful.

"I don't know, ma'am," Weatherford said. The woman invited the officers inside as she went to change. She asked if she could bring her other son, who was autistic. Soon, they all climbed into the car and drove toward police headquarters.

The woman was kind and polite. On the way, she asked again if her son was okay. Weatherford knew that her son wasn't likely to survive the night, but he again said he didn't know. They talked about their kids. Weatherford's daughter had just graduated high school; his son was a Dallas firefighter. As the woman asked about his children, he thought about how nice she was. He felt a tug of sympathy for her and rising anger at the suspect. *This guy has just absolutely shattered his mother's life, too. Now she's that mom, of that guy, and she always will be.* He knew that no matter how hard you tried to teach your kids, sometimes they did things you did not understand and could not control.

33

Ready, Ready, Now

Borchardt sat at a desk in a classroom about forty yards away from the gunman's hiding spot. It was about 1:30 a.m., four and a half hours after the shooting started. The two ATF officers had helped them pick the spot, which they believed was a safe distance away. Borchardt looked at the picture on a color monitor before him, coming in live from the robot's camera. A half dozen officers stood behind him, watching.

Borchardt looked at Sergeant Hertel and nodded. The sergeant would talk into his radio, updating officers through their earbuds. The other breacher, Michaels, held the backup detonator. He cradled the small, black device gently, making sure his finger stayed away from the button on top.

Borchardt pressed his joystick slightly forward, directing the machine down the hall. He prayed he wouldn't get the giant metal creature stuck on a corner or a door frame. He reminded himself to stay wide on the turns. The robot clicked and creaked loudly as it rolled down the carpet. It coasted to the end of the hallway, then slowly turned the corner. It glided past Gordon's empty chair, moving closer to the gunman. It crossed the final doorway, entering the gunman's hallway. Borchardt didn't know exactly where the gunman was or what kind of angles the robot would face. He feared the guy had tucked away in some corner and the robot would pass him.

As soon as Borchardt turned the droid into the hallway, a figure appeared on his monitor. There was X. He stood in the alcove, his rifle pointed toward the robot. The machine was about thirty feet away from him. Then twenty-five. Then twenty. *Don't move,* Borchardt thought. If the gunman ran, the robot wouldn't be able to catch him. But the gunman stayed there. He took a knee, then lay prone on his belly, rifle still pointed. He seemed to be staring at the robot, puzzling over what he saw. As it crept closer to him, he appeared to look beyond it, as if waiting for SWAT to charge in.

Fifteen feet. Ten feet. As Borchardt drove closer, the screen flickered. *Shit*, Borchardt thought. *We're losing the signal.* One more foot, and they'd be in the target zone. Borchardt drove a little farther. Short Dog put his fingers in his ears. He'd never been this close to C4 going off, and particularly not in such a confined indoor space. *Holy crap, this is going to be bad.*

"I have control, standby for the short count," Sergeant Hertel said into his radio. Borchardt placed his right hand on the keylike lever, ready to switch from vehicle mode to armed mode. Officers across the college listened through their earbuds and braced for the wave of overpressure. The sergeant began a short count: "Ready. Ready. Now."

With his hand turning the key, Borchardt pressed the button. Silence. Borchardt quickly reset the control, turned the key, and tried again. Still no joy. SWAT officers in the stairwells looked at each other, lifting their fingers from their ears. Why wasn't it going off? Borchardt began to reset the control a third time.

Michaels didn't wait. He pressed the button on the backup detonator.

A boom thundered across the college. The building seemed to expand, then contract. Borchardt stared at his screen. The picture had frozen, and he could still see the gunman lying prone, staring at them. Then the screen flashed blue. Borchardt looked over at Michaels, who still held the backup detonator. "Did you do that?" he asked. "Yep," Michaels said. The remote in his hands had a digital readout that said "Success."

But the pressure boom wasn't as big as Borchardt had expected. "That was way too light," he said. He worried only half the bomb had exploded. Maybe the det cord had gone off but not the C4. Then came another sound, a burst of semiautomatic rifle fire.

Borchardt and Michaels looked at each other. *This guy is still alive.*

* * *

Short Dog and a teammate had stayed in the classroom with Borchardt, assigned to protect the team in case the gunman emerged shooting. After the detonation, Short Dog kicked the door open. His teammate took a couple of steps out into the hallway and dropped to a knee. Short Dog snapped around the corner to cover him, peering down the hallway. It looked like a war zone, dust swirling, wires dangling, heating pipes exposed. Then Short Dog heard gunfire. He had two simultaneous thoughts: *How did he survive that?* And, *Here he comes.*

He was worried about his teammate, who seemed too exposed in the hallway. "Let's get high low," he said. Short Dog dropped to a knee and his teammate leaned over him, both with M4s ready. They waited for the gunman to come charging, but the hallway stayed quiet.

SWAT, positioned in stairwells and the library, had been instructed to hold back after detonation. The gunman bragged about having explosives, and the team worried he'd booby-trapped himself or his lair. They knew the first robot would lose its camera feed, so they'd planned to send one of the FBI's robots down the hall behind it. As the backup robot traveled toward the blast site, the team watched the picture from its monitor. Ceiling tiles hung from above, lighting fixtures dangled, and drywall was strewn all over the floor. Borchardt desperately wanted the gunman to be dead. No trial, no months of media coverage exploring the gunman's childhood and philosophies and motives. That was one of the things that bothered him after his fellow patrol officer Nix got shot. That the cops hadn't ended it. The suspect survived and stood trial as Nix's family sat in the gallery, having to listen to him talk.

Halfway down the hallway, the backup robot got hung up on debris. They tried to back it up and go forward again, but it was stuck. They'd have to send some guys in. A team of several officers crept across the carpet, M4s raised. As they got closer to the gunman's hiding spot, they found the walls had been blown apart. They looked through newly opened gaps, searching for the gunman. One officer, Senior Cpl. Chris Webb, heard a muffled sound. He looked through a hole, scanned a pile of debris, and spotted the gunman. He lay curled on his left side, head down, his body covered by slabs of drywall. A bloody tourniquet covered his muscular right arm, and his finger was still laced through the trigger. A blossom of blood spread from the gunman's head. His chest heaved slightly as he took a breath. Webb looked through his sights and steadied for a headshot. But he could tell the gunman's body was shutting down, making its final gasping sounds. Webb rolled his finger off the trigger.

"Suspect is down," another officer, Senior Cpl. Matt Smith, said over the radio.

The officers believed the final gunshots had been a reflexive motion by the gunman after the blast.

After the ATF checked for bombs, many of the SWAT guys came in to look. They needed to see the man who'd tried so hard to kill them. Banes stared at the gunman's body, twisted in a pile of Sheetrock and dust. It was strange, seeing him in the same tactical trousers cops wore. Banes had an overwhelming desire to pee on him. He decided that wouldn't go over well with commanders. He wanted to feel vindicated somehow, but he didn't. He just stood there looking, wondering why.

34

After

Chief Brown had just arrived at Parkland hospital and met up with Mayor Rawlings when his telephone rang at around 2:00 a.m. It was Humphrey.

"Chief, we got him," Humphrey said.

Brown turned to Rawlings. "It's done," he said. "The plan worked."

The men began a walk through the hospital, going from room to room. In one they met the wife of Sergeant Smith, the officer who'd been shot outside the 7-Eleven. Heidi Smith stood there with her two teenage daughters, Victoria and Caroline. Rawlings sensed a consuming loneliness from the newly made widow, a woman realizing she would now carry the family on her own. He told the daughters how proud he was of their father.

Soon, Rawlings and the chief got word that Lorne Ahrens, the big officer whose last words had been exhorting protesters to run, had died at another hospital across town. *Five officers killed*, Rawlings thought. *This just doesn't happen in the United States of America.*

The mayor and chief walked out into a large waiting room filled with officers, some of them wounded. Nurses and doctors. Family and friends. Rawlings looked around the room, noting its diversity—black, white, Hispanic, young, old, men and women.

The chief stepped in front of the room, talking to officers and hospital staff. "We just used explosives to kill the man who we believe is the lone suspect. We have lost so many officers, and we're all heartbroken."

* * *

Dr. Williams was attending to patients when he saw dozens of police officers walking toward the ambulance bay. The medical examiner's office had arrived to take the bodies to the morgue. Williams fell into the throng headed toward the hospital exit.

He stepped through a pair of sliding glass doors out into the night. He saw that the officers had formed two lines, creating a passageway. They stood at parade rest, feet spread, arms folded behind their backs. Williams knew he didn't belong in the formation, but he stepped forward and joined the line. He looked across to see if his presence was offensive to the officers. In their eyes, he saw only grief.

A commanding voice broke the silence. "Attention." Officers snapped their feet together, arms at their sides. "Present arms." Officers raised their arms in salute. Williams placed his hand over his heart.

Nurses pushed out three stretchers, each carrying a black body bag. Relatives of the men walked alongside, their hands resting on the bags. The bodies were loaded into three waiting vans. Motorcycle engines roared to life, and the procession pulled out of the bay, on its way to the morgue. For the second time that night, Williams wept.

* * *

Sgt. Ivan Gunter caught up with the police chief once he'd made his way across town to Baylor hospital, where two of the dying officers had been taken. Gunter spotted Brown in a hallway and prepared himself for what he needed to say. He'd been among the last to speak with Lorne Ahrens, the huge officer who'd been among the first to be targets. Gunter had spent the intervening hours stewing over the last order he'd given the man—that he couldn't wear his heavy ballistic vest.

Three of the dead officers and three of the wounded were from the Foxtrot unit Gunter commanded. After helping load the injured into police cars, he'd rushed inside the community college and spent much of the night guarding a stairwell just below the gunman. He'd pointed his Glock at the stairwell door for hours, waiting for the man to pop out, scared he would, hoping he would. He'd gripped his gun so long and hard that his hand ached. In the stairwell he'd learned that Zamarripa was dead. And Krol. And Ahrens.

Gunter had come to the hospital to see Ahrens one last time. Now, when Gunter saw the chief, he let loose. He'd asked for permission for his men to wear their heavy vests, and he'd been denied. The department had protected its image, he believed, over its officers.

"This was a motherfucking shit show," Gunter shouted. "How the hell did this happen?"

As Gunter went on, Brown returned Gunter's blazing look with one that was stoic and steady. In his unflappable way, the chief stood there and took it.

"It's all right," Brown said gently when Gunter had finished. "It's all right."

Gunter and the only other uninjured Foxtrot, Brian Fillingim, ·alked through the hospital to Ahrens's room. His giant, tattooed me stretched across the hospital bed, still hooked to a ventilator, ·ines still beeping. His skin had turned blue. It seemed impos-
·hat this powerful man, who'd once commandeered a cab to
·bad guy, was gone. Both men approached, touched his hand,
·good-bye.

35

Daybreak

Banes descended the stairwell, still painted with the shooter's blood, and stepped into the college's atrium. SWAT guys were taking seats beneath a large television screen to watch the news. Representatives from the police association were passing out McDonald's cheeseburgers. As Banes stood there, Huante walked toward him and stopped an inch short of his nose. *What now?* Banes wondered briefly. Then Huante flung his arms around Banes and pulled him into a bear hug, lifting his feet off the ground. "I'm proud of you, buddy," Huante said.

Soon, Banes, Huante, and the other SWAT team members walked out of the college into the night. They'd never seen the city so still and quiet. They drove through the empty downtown streets to police headquarters and rode elevators to the fifth floor. They joined dozens of officers, some still covered in blood, some weeping, waiting in lines to type their statements. It marked the beginning of a long investigation. Everything they had done would be examined and second-guessed.

After officers used deadly force, it was customary for detectives to take their weapons, examine them, and count the bullets. A crime scene tech approached Borchardt and asked for his gun. "But I didn't shoot," Borchardt said. "I drove the robot." The tech, puzzled, turned to a colleague. "What are we supposed to do with him?" They let him keep the gun.

Then it was Banes's turn. He unholstered his handgun. "No, your rifle," the crime scene tech said. Banes shook his head. He was still in threat mode. "You're not taking my rifle."

Canete saw what was happening and put his hand on Banes's shoulder. "Just give him the rifle." Grudgingly, Banes handed it over.

The tech asked Banes to stand next to the wall for a photograph. He was given a whiteboard with his name and badge number. Banes stared into the camera, hurt and angry. He'd just risked his life, and now he had to stand for a mug shot? It felt like a betrayal. *I thought I was the good guy here.*

Banes drove home in silence as the sun rose, the beginning of a bright, blue-sky day. His was one of the only cars headed east from Dallas on I-30. Looking at the sunrise ahead, he was hit by the thought that others were not seeing this sunrise and would never see one again. He was driving home to a wife who he knew had been through something god-awful. He realized a slightly different man was returning to her than the one she'd last seen.

As Banes drove, he thought about what he and his teammates had been through. He could see Canete and Scott and Berie standing in that hallway with bullets ricocheting off door frames and walls, knowing that the odds of death were high. Banes thought about how no one had run. Each stood there and took it, staying because the guy next to him stayed.

Finally, Banes neared his driveway, and he looked around at his tidy neighborhood, lawns trimmed, basketball goals upright. Mothers and fathers were waking, rousing children from bed. Maybe

36

The Press Conference

Several days after the shooting, Parkland hospital called a press conference. That morning, Dr. Williams texted his wife. CAN YOU PLEASE CALL ME? Williams still felt emotional. In the preceding days, he'd tried to slip back into normal life. He'd attended his daughter's disco dance party, making small talk with the other parents. He and the family went to see *The Secret Life of Pets*. But he kept seeing the dead officers in his mind. He could recall their faces in perfect detail. This hadn't been the case with other patients who'd died on his table.

As Williams thought about whether to attend the news conference, his mind replayed the shooting videos of Sterling and Castile. He felt he needed to say something, but he wasn't sure what. Those conversations tended to polarize quickly. You were either for the cops or against them. Williams supported law enforcement but thought the videos still demanded answers. Part of him wanted to retreat once again behind the cover of his surgeon's coat. But his wife, Kathianne, urged him to speak up. He was the only black trauma surgeon at Parkland. He had not been they'd see what happened on the news. But to them it was just another Friday.

Banes felt out of place. He'd just helped kill a man. Had nearly been killed himself. He sat in the driveway, not wanting to go inside. He thought seeing his wife and sons would upset him, and he didn't want to cry in front of them. His cell phone rang, and he heard his fourteen-year-old son's voice. "Dad, are you okay?"

It took Banes a moment to respond. "No," he said, still sitting behind the wheel. "No, I'm not okay."

* * *

Gordon walked inside his house and found Shan in her pajamas. They looked at each other and hugged for a long time. Gordon took off his gear, showered, and put on a T-shirt and shorts. He lay in the bed and turned on *SportsCenter*.

He'd poured everything he had into that hallway. All his concentration, his words, his energy, his fear. Now he felt nothing. No sadness or sense of loss. Just exhaustion. He knew he'd have a couple of hours of numbness before his feelings started to leak out. He wanted to put the whole night into what he called his "forgetter," an internal system he'd developed over the years to purge the things he witnessed.

That afternoon, Gordon climbed onto the treadmill in his office and started running. Through the open door, he saw his wife and son playing tag in the house. She chased him and he squealed and laughed. Something about the noise became distorted and frightening, as if his son were screaming for help. He called out for them to stop. He saw Shan look at him with concern.

scheduled to work that night. He'd been placed there, she believed, for a reason.

That afternoon, Williams joined a line of colleagues along a table inside a hospital conference room, in front of a bank of microphones and dozens of news cameras. As his colleagues spoke about the events of that night, Williams felt his hands clenching beneath the table. No one was addressing the elephant in the room. His mind kept going back and forth. *This is not the time and place*, he told himself. Then, *You need to speak up.*

As the cameras turned to Williams, he audibly inhaled.

"I'm Dr. Brian Williams," he said, trying to order his thoughts. "I want to state first and foremost I stand with the Dallas Police Department. I stand with law enforcement all over this country. This experience has been very personal for me and a turning point in my life."

He continued, saying, "The preceding days of more black men dying at the hands of police officers affected me. I think the reasons are obvious. I fit that demographic of individuals. But I abhor what has been done to these officers, and I grieve with their families."

He paused, struggling to keep his voice steady. "I understand the anger and the frustration and distrust of law enforcement. But they are not the problem. The problem is the lack of open discussions about the impact of race relations in this country. And I think about it every day, that I was unable to save those cops when they came here that night. It weighs on my mind constantly. This killing, it has to stop. Black men dying and being forgotten. People retaliating against the people that are sworn to defend us. We have to come together and end all this."

A long silence filled the room. Then Williams's boss opened it up to questions. When a reporter asked about the emotional impact of the shooting later in the press conference, Williams again found himself speaking.

"There's this dichotomy, where I am standing with law enforcement, but I also personally feel and understand that angst that comes, when you cross the paths of an officer in uniform, and you're fearing for your safety. I've been there, and I understand that. But for me that does not condone disrespecting or killing police officers."

A reporter asked if he had children, and Williams said he had a daughter. When he was out with her, he picked up police officers' tabs at restaurants. Once, when they got ice cream, he'd paid for a Dallas police officer in line behind them.

"I want my daughter to see me interacting with police that way, so she doesn't grow up with the same burden that I carry, when it comes to interacting with law enforcement. And I want the Dallas police to also see me, a black man, and understand that I support you. I will defend you. And I will care for you. That doesn't mean that I do not fear you. That doesn't mean that if you approach me, I will not immediately have a visceral reaction and start worrying for my personal safety. But I will control that the best I can and not let that impact how I deal with law enforcement."

After he spoke, he sat back in his chair. He was aware of his boss sitting beside him. *Oh shit*, he thought. He wondered how his words had come out. He felt dread. He also realized he felt something else. Relief. The mask was off.

37

The Memorial

Mayor Rawlings stood behind a podium, looking out at hundreds who had gathered at the city's Meyerson Symphony Center. It was five days after the shooting, and onstage along with Chief Brown sat President and First Lady Barack and Michelle Obama. Beside them sat former president and first lady George W. and Laura Bush. Lining the stage were easels holding photographs of the five fallen officers. In the balcony to one side were five empty chairs with hats and folded flags.

"The past few days have been some of the darkest in our city's history, there's no question about that," the mayor told the crowd. "As we bury these men in the coming days, it will not get easier, I know.

"I've searched hard in my soul of late to discover what mistakes we have made," the mayor said. "I've asked, 'Why us?' And in my moments of self-doubt, I discovered the truth. That we did nothing wrong. In fact, Dallas is very, very good."

After prayers and singing, President Bush rose to the microphone. "At times it seems like the forces pulling us apart are stronger than the forces binding us together," he said. "Argument turns too easily into animosity. Disagreement escalates too quickly into dehumanization. Too often, we judge other groups by their worst examples, while judging ourselves by our best intentions."

Applause filled the room, and soon President Obama walked to the podium.

The mayor sat in his chair, wondering how the nation's first black president would navigate this moment. Hours before the murder of Dallas's officers, Obama had called a press conference during a summit in Warsaw to speak about the deaths of Sterling and Castile. The comments had angered many police officers.

Now, Obama looked out at an auditorium filled with cops. Gordon and several of his SWAT colleagues sat about halfway back in their dress blues. Misty McBride, the injured DART officer, sat with her arm in a sling. Shetamia Taylor, the protester, sat in a wheelchair, her leg propped up. The police widows and their children were there.

"Scripture tells us that in our sufferings, there is glory, because we know that suffering produces perseverance; perseverance, character; and character, hope. Sometimes the truths of these words are hard to see," Obama said.

He eulogized each of the dead officers. How Lorne Ahrens took his kids fishing and liked to show up at their school in his uniform. How Michael Krol had traveled a thousand miles from his home in Michigan to become a Dallas cop. How Michael Smith loved playing softball with his two girls. How Patrick Zamarripa had been an altar boy and dreamed of becoming an officer. How Brent Thompson had married two weeks earlier and looked forward to a new life.

"All of it has left us wounded, and angry, and hurt," Obama said. "It's as if the deepest fault lines of our democracy have suddenly been exposed, perhaps even widened. And although we know that such divisions are not new, though they've surely been worse in even the recent past, that offers us little comfort. Faced with this violence, we wonder if the divides of race in America can ever be bridged."

He continued: "We see all this, and it's hard not to think sometimes that the center won't hold and that things might get worse. I understand. I understand how Americans are feeling. But Dallas, I'm here to say we must reject such despair. I'm here to insist that we are not as divided as we seem. And I know that because I know America. I know how far we've come against impossible odds."

His words drew applause from the concert hall. Then he returned to the bravery of Dallas police officers, how they did not flinch when the bullets flew.

"We mourn fewer people today because of your brave actions," he said.

More applause.

Obama continued: " 'Everyone was helping each other,' one witness said. It wasn't about black or white. Everyone was picking each other up and moving them away. See, that's the America I know."

Obama mentioned Shetamia Taylor by name. "She said she wanted her boys to join her to protest the incidents of black men being killed. She also said to the Dallas P.D., thank you for being heroes. And today, her twelve-year-old son wants to be a cop when he grows up. That's the America I know." Taylor smiled from her wheelchair as the crowd rose to their feet and their applause filled the room.

And then, Obama's speech pivoted.

"But America, we know that bias remains," he said. "We know it, whether you are black, or white, or Hispanic, or Asian, or Native

American, or of Middle Eastern descent, we have all seen this bigotry in our own lives at some point. We've heard it at times in our own homes. If we're honest, perhaps we've heard prejudice in our own heads, and felt it in our own hearts."

"None of us," he continued, "is entirely innocent. No institution is entirely immune, and that includes our police departments. We know this. And so when African Americans from all walks of life, from different communities across the country, voice a growing despair over what they perceive to be unequal treatment, when study after study shows that whites and people of color experience the criminal justice system differently. So that if you're black, you're more likely to be pulled over or searched or arrested; more likely to get longer sentences; more likely to get the death penalty for the same crime . . ."

As Obama delivered these lines, Gordon felt the mood in the auditorium shift. His SWAT colleagues moved restlessly, some shaking heads, others rolling their eyes. Officers who had been clapping now sat stone-faced, hands clasped.

"Can we do this?" Obama continued. "Can we find the character, as Americans, to open our hearts to each other? Can we see in each other a common humanity and a shared dignity, and recognize how our different experiences have shaped us? And it doesn't make anybody perfectly good or perfectly bad, it just makes us human."

Obama paused. "I don't know," he said, shaking his head. "I confess that sometimes I, too, experience doubt." He looked out at the crowd. "I've been to too many of these things."

Obama continued. "Even those who dislike the phrase 'black lives matter,' surely, we should be able to hear the pain of Alton Sterling's family," he said. "Just as we should hear the students and co-workers describe their affection for Philando Castile as a gentle soul."

Obama continued, urging the audience to look at the world through one another's eyes, until he arrived at his closing.

"We cannot match the sacrifices made by Officers Zamarripa, Ahrens, Krol, Smith, and Thompson. But surely we can try to match their sense of service. We cannot match their courage. But we can strive to match their devotion. May God bless their memory. May God bless this country that we love." Obama turned and walked back to his seat.

The organist waited for the room to fall silent. Then she began the familiar notes of one of America's most enduring anthems, "The Battle Hymn of the Republic." The words had been sung across centuries and generations, in every corner of America. It was a popular Civil War song, the rhythm sung by Union soldiers drinking around campfires, extolling the exploits of the revolutionary abolitionist John Brown. *He captured Harpers Ferry with his nineteen men so true. He frightened old Virginia till she trembled through and through.*

Black soldiers sang their own version. *We are done with hoeing cotton, we are done with hoeing corn. We are colored Yankee soldiers as sure as you are born.*

A white female poet from New York, who'd heard the song while visiting soldiers, had woken in the middle of the night with new words. *Mine eyes have seen the glory of the coming of the Lord.*

The same words had been quoted by Martin Luther King Jr. in his famous mountaintop speech, the day before he was killed.

As the choir joined in, the march's cadence picked up momentum, and hands reached out along the stage. The politicians sang and swayed, and the audience began to clap, first softly, then louder, until applause filled the room. Audience members, too, joined hands.

As their voices sang together, Rawlings experienced the same feeling that had made him suspicious of Camus throughout the years, and he looked upward and smiled.

* * *

Afterward, Gordon and the SWAT guys filed out of the auditorium. They had not been moved by the battle hymn or the politicians or what they viewed as a canned display of unity for the cameras.

"That was fucking bullshit," Huante said. "He should not have said their names." He was referring to Obama's mention of Sterling and Castile. A couple of his teammates nodded in agreement.

"Why?" Gordon said, growing angry. He'd agreed with everything Obama had said. "Those are two people who died. They got killed. They have families, too. Philando Castile—he didn't do a damn thing."

38

X

As the dead were buried and the living grieved, photographs began to appear online of the gunman, Micah Xavier Johnson. There he was wearing a dashiki, his fist raised in the air. There he was with Professor Griff, who'd been a member of a hip-hop group known for calling out police brutality. There he was behind the wheel of an Army vehicle, wearing desert fatigues, spreading two fingers in a peace sign.

So, too, emerged fragments of Johnson's life before July 7, 2016. He was born in a small town in Mississippi about an hour from Jackson. When he was about four, his family moved to Texas. Around that time, his father divorced his mother, but he remained in his children's lives. Johnson grew up alongside a sister and an autistic brother in a diverse, working- and middle-class neighborhood in Mesquite, a city near Dallas. His father remarried to a white woman, who formed a close relationship with Johnson.

The most startling fact came from his mother, who said in an interview that when Micah was little he had wanted to be a cop. As he grew up, Johnson still gravitated toward a career in uniform, joining the JROTC at John Horn High School in Mesquite, and asking his mother to sign for him to join the Army Reserve before his eighteenth birthday. He wasn't much of a student—he'd graduated near the bottom of his senior class in 2009—and he hung out mostly with the "gamers," spending long hours playing *Call of Duty* and *Halo.* Classmates described him as goofy, outgoing, and funny. Two years after graduation, he registered for several courses at Richland College, a community college in north Dallas. He dropped out after a couple of weeks.

An early suggestion that Johnson was mentally unwell was soon documented in a police report. Late one night, Johnson walked into Mesquite's police headquarters visibly upset, "bouncing from side to side," and asking to talk with somebody. He was nineteen and had served in the Army for about two years. He told an officer he was distraught because a female friend had lied to him, and he didn't have anywhere else to go. Though he'd come in part because he "did not want to get into trouble," the officer noted, Johnson was adamant that he didn't feel like hurting himself or anyone else. He didn't want to call his mother, with whom he was living, nor did he want to see a mental health professional. But he did call a friend in his reserve unit, who picked him up. The friend assured the officer he'd notify someone in Johnson's chain of command the next morning. Johnson's behavior struck the officer as erratic enough that he took care to write up a report, which noted Johnson's "unstable mental faculties."

Another incident that happened about that time would come up much later in an Army report, which charted Johnson's relationship with a young woman he would be accused of sexually harassing. The report describes an evening during which Johnson said he'd gotten so angry he punched through a car window. "I was stuck at a dead-end minimum-wage job that I loathed," Johnson would tell Army investigators in a statement. He'd also been in a wreck and had to borrow money to buy another car. "While living with my mother, her and I fought almost every day and I had nowhere else to live, because of no friends and not enough money. Nothing at all was going my way."

Johnson wrote that he and a female friend had planned to see a movie that night. At the last minute, she backed out and decided to go home. "I was just frustrated at the events from before and I needed to let out the stress," Johnson wrote, explaining why he'd smashed the window. The friend told investigators the glass cut Johnson so badly she took him to a hospital.

Johnson and his friend had met during training in Hawaii, where they were assigned to the same platoon, according to Army records. Not long after, while riding in an elevator, Johnson asked her if she wanted to be "friends with benefits," she later told investigators. She said no, but the pair became close. The young woman described Johnson as her "Best Army Friend." She gave him a nickname, "Cookie Bear." They went out together frequently. Sometimes, when they played beer pong, he'd give her a "good game" smack on the butt, she told investigators. She'd tell Johnson to stop, that her boyfriend wouldn't approve. Sometimes Johnson would comment on her breasts, or how her hips swayed when she walked. She said she'd grown up around boys and always had plenty of guy friends; she took it more as playing around than harassment. On drill weekends, she'd spend the night at his mother's house, and they'd drive to drill together in the morning. They were close enough that some people assumed the relationship was romantic. It wasn't, both would later tell Army investigators, but it seemed Johnson longed for more. At one point in a washateria, he asked the young woman for a pair of her underwear. "I immediately told him no," she told Army investigators.

In 2013, the pair deployed to Afghanistan. They were sent to a forward operating base in Logar Province, where Johnson served as a carpentry and masonry specialist. They didn't see combat, but they lived at a base soldiers called "Rocket City" because of frequent mortar attacks. They hung out with friends they'd trained with, a group that was mostly white and Hispanic. Other soldiers viewed Johnson as a loner, describing him as "odd" and "off." Some soldiers thought he was lovesick over the woman; they worried he wouldn't be able to take the rejection they believed was coming. After arriving, things between Johnson and the woman became strained. She was promoted to a higher rank, and he chafed under her authority. His sexual advances grew more insistent, forcing her to defend her boundaries in stronger terms. Finally, they quit talking to each other.

A few weeks after they parted ways, the woman was inventorying her laundry bag and realized several pairs of panties had gone missing. She told a fellow soldier she suspected Johnson. Upon learning of the potential theft, supervisors announced "health and welfare" searches, without telling the soldiers what they were looking for. When they got to Johnson's room, he opened his door and stood by as they entered. He asked them what they were looking for and was told platoon leaders were worried about drugs, alcohol, and contraband. Moments later, a supervisor lifted Johnson's mattress and saw the panties.

Before a supervisor had a chance to pick them up, Johnson snatched the panties and stuffed them into his hoodie's front pocket. "What was that?" one of the supervisors said. Johnson replied: "Don't worry about that." Supervisors told Johnson to report to a nearby room. Instead, he hurried into the night, past the smoking area and out toward the trash bins. When supervisors found him, Johnson said he'd gotten the panties from a woman he'd dated years before. Questioned further, he changed his story, saying they came from a different woman he'd slept with.

Supervisors found the panties in a trash bin. They summoned

Johnson's female friend to identify them. Seeing they were hers, she began to cry. The supervisors relieved Johnson of his firearm and ordered another soldier to keep an eye on him. Less than forty-eight hours later, he was flown from the base to Bagram Airfield, en route to an early return home. The victim of the panty theft told Army investigators her friendship with Johnson would not recover. She also requested a protective order against him. Still, she asked that he be "treated rather than punished."

Johnson waived a hearing on the allegations to avoid a less than honorable discharge. He was released from active duty "with an Honorable characterization" during the summer of 2014. Humiliated and distanced from friends, at twenty-three years old, he moved back in with his mother, who he told the Army had run him out unjustly.

He was different when he came home, his mother would tell an interviewer for TheBlaze. "The military was not what Micah thought it would be," she said. "He was very disappointed, very disappointed. But it may be that the ideal that he thought of our government, what he thought the military represented, it just didn't live up to his expectations."

Once home, Johnson sought help at the VA. He told an intake worker he'd been excited about returning, thinking about the places he'd eat, the friends he'd reconnect with. But instead he'd been irritable, depressed, and anxious. He'd had panic attacks at busy places like Dave & Buster's and Walmart. "I feel like I can't trust all of these strangers around me," he said. While in public he felt on high alert, scanning for danger, noting the exits. Talking to people was hard. "I have actually asked people to stop talking to me," he said. He'd been drinking to make himself feel better. He'd gained twenty pounds. "My heart feels like someone is pinching it," he said.

Johnson said that during his deployment he'd begun having trouble sleeping. Now at home, he was sleeping only four to five hours a night. He'd lie down, and his mind would spin. He'd wake at every noise. "The AC kicks on . . . I wake up . . . a dog outside barking . . . I wake up." When he did sleep, he'd have nightmares, seeing images of things he told the VA worker he'd witnessed in Afghanistan—a soldier blown in half, another shot in the chest. He'd jolt awake, drenched in sweat.

He was hearing things, he said. Mortars exploding and sirens going off. He'd hear his mother calling his name in the house. He knew she was at work, but he'd walk around, making sure. He saw shadows out of the corner of his eye. While driving, he'd see debris along the road and wonder if it was an IED. He'd change lanes, his heart thumping. He could no longer play *Call of Duty*. Now the video game's mortar strikes, battle cries, and shooting were too disturbing, he said. He hoped one day to become a self-defense instructor, but he lacked motivation. "I just feel kinda insignificant," he said.

The VA intake worker described Johnson as well groomed, cooperative, easily engaged, and of above-average intelligence. He was not in danger of hurting himself or others, the worker wrote. Johnson was given initial diagnoses of depression and PTSD. He was prescribed cyclobenzaprine, sertraline, and trazodone. A nurse gave him a tip sheet on managing anger and directed him to a mobile app, PTSD Coach.

When a caseworker called Johnson a few weeks after his visit, he said he was busy remodeling his mother's house and wanted to put further PTSD assessment on hold. He didn't show up for his next appointment. His VA records show no further contact after the fall of 2014.

The next spring, Johnson had what he'd tell family members was a bad experience with police. Johnson had just finished a self-defense class and was behind the wheel of his mother's black Chevy SUV, with his brother in a passenger seat. They were parked at a strip mall eating sandwiches, waiting for their father to pick up Johnson's brother. Someone called the police and reported a "suspicious person," and two officers arrived. It's not clear what happened during the encounter, but Johnson left angry.

While living with his mother, Johnson rarely left the house. He helped take care of his brother. He stopped drinking and started eating healthy and working out. He studied black history and asked questions about his heritage. He clicked "like" on Facebook pages connected to the New Black Panther Party and the Black Riders Liberation Party. He was upset over the recent police shooting videos. "He was outraged at what could happen in this day and age," his mother told TheBlaze. "He was angry that in 2016 we were still being treated like 1816."

In May 2016, two months before he would kill five police officers, Johnson spent a week with his grandparents in Mississippi. His grandfather, too, noted a change. "He had gone from a fun person to someone who was just all to himself," the Reverend Havard McDonald told his local newspaper after Johnson's rampage. "Having to leave the military was one of the most devastating things that ever happened to him. When he was with me in May, he had no job, no desire to go to school, no desire to have a family . . . no reason to live."

McDonald said the police shooting videos profoundly affected his grandson.

"People see police killing black men and nothing is done about it," he said. "What Micah did—in his mind—was about injustice."

McDonald made it clear he was not trying to justify his grandson's violence. "What he did was wrong," he said. "We do not support what he did. We are so sorry for those other families."

After the shooting, Army investigators went back to interview the woman who'd accused Johnson of harassment. She offered additional details about her concerns. She said she'd asked years earlier that he not deploy with the unit. Though he was her friend, she'd been worried about his anger issues, and she'd feared he might snap. She described how the unit would be practicing combat tactics, and Johnson would be choking someone. The person would tap out, signaling for him to stop, and he wouldn't; other unit members would have to pull him away. She was shocked when she learned what Johnson did in Dallas. But also, in some ways, not surprised, she told investigators.

Cops would never know the meaning of the cryptic message, R.B., that Johnson drew with his own blood in the hallway that night. Some speculated it was a reference to the red, black, and green Pan-African flag, a symbol of black power.

An autopsy concluded that Johnson had died from "blunt and penetrating injuries of the head following bomb detonation by a police-controlled robot." It appeared the robot's claw had blown off and possibly struck him after detonation, SWAT officers said. According to the autopsy, Johnson had three gunshot wounds, one from a medium-caliber bullet to his arm, and two others from small-caliber bullets on his left wrist and forearm. Though the autopsy could not determine who fired those bullets, SWAT officers believed the medium-caliber bullet came from a handgun, and the small-caliber bullets might have come from the team's M4s or Henry Edwards's AR-15.

39

The Long Night

In the days after the standoff, Larry Gordon was gripped with paranoia. Pulling into his neighborhood one night on his way home from another shift, the negotiator noticed car lights looming behind him. Was he being followed? Had he and his family been targeted? He drove past his house, just in case. It turned out to be a neighbor, who soon pulled into a driveway down the street. Gordon felt the neighbor's eyes on him as he made a U-turn, back toward his own home.

Gordon had learned a little about the man on the other end of the hallway. He learned that X had lived near his house, and the thought unsettled him. Gordon began to feel unsafe much of the time. His house had a basic security system that in years past he'd never bothered to turn on. Now he upgraded. He walked a technician around the rooms, explaining where he wanted cameras—one on the front door, one on the back, one in his living room. He downloaded an app so he could watch the camera feeds live on his phone. If anyone came near his house, a voice called out, "Visitor." He'd never before paid to have his alarm monitored by police—he was, after all, the police—but now he did. Gordon had long enjoyed uncapping a Blue Moon beer after work. Now he often opened a second or a third. He'd begun to dread climbing into bed at night to face the quiet darkness. He started tucking a gun beneath his mattress—not his service revolver but his personal weapon, a Glock 9 mm—a precaution he'd never taken before. He positioned the Glock right below his head, its butt slightly sticking out. As he watched *Big Bang Theory*, he'd run his hand along the side of the bed, memorizing exactly where the gun was waiting. He never told his wife about the Glock under the mattress, and if she noticed on her own, she did not say anything.

Larry often woke hours before dawn and would lie beside Shan as she slept on, and he'd hear the knocking of the ice maker in the kitchen. He'd reach for his phone and pull up the security system's camera views. As he waited for the picture to emerge, he'd prepare for the sight of X walking through his living room. Gordon knew X was dead—he'd seen the man's limp, bloody body—but paranoia played tricks at 3:00 a.m. As he listened to Shan breathe, he'd run through scenarios in his mind. If X was near their bedroom door, he'd reach for his gun and shove Shan off the bed. If X was already in his bedroom, he'd roll over and yawn, pretending to be asleep as he reached for his pistol. If he had time, he'd run to his closet, where he'd hidden his loaded AR-15 behind clothes.

One morning, Larry sat down on his living room couch and pulled up an audio file on his phone. He'd recorded twenty-seven minutes of his negotiations with X. Shan and the kids were gone, and the house was quiet. Gordon put on his earbuds and pressed play. He heard his own voice calling out down the hallway.

I'm just concerned for our safety. I'm concerned for your safety. You have a compelling story, though. You know what's going to happen, X?

Then the voice of the dead man played in Larry's ears.

Malcolm X, Martin Luther King, Kwame, there's been too many people talking. Revolution, that's what I want. The talking is over. It's time for revolution, brother.

Larry heard himself asking, *Are you injured at all? . . . I see a lot of shell casings.*

I'm good.

I understand you might be good. I'm saying, are you injured?

It's just the body. None of this matters. This world is not the real world.

Larry couldn't listen for long. Heart pounding, he pressed stop. But in the weeks that followed, he found himself returning to the tape again and again. Often he listened in the car.

Larry heard X explaining about the Gullah Wars, heard him shouting, evading, refusing to be analyzed. Larry found it puzzling how calm X was, and painful to hear the fear in his own voice.

If you are in a corrupt system, X was saying again, *you are corrupted.*

What can we do about the corrupt system, X?

Tear it down.

On and on it went, like a call-and-response without end.

Hey X, how about you put your rifle down, man.

I can't do that. I've got to do what I came here to do.

Larry's memories of the night always ended the same way, when the bomb team was sending in the robot and Larry went silent and X called out one last time.

Larry. Larry? Where'd you go, Larry?

40

Breathe

One cold and gloomy day at a dusty gun range outside the city, Shetamia Taylor held a 9 mm. She'd bought it after the shooting, and now she was ready to fire it for the first time. She stood on the firing line looking down at a fresh paper target. She picked up her weapon, inserted bullets into her magazine, and stared downrange. She tried to steady her hands, but they kept shaking.

"I can't do this," she told the instructor. She'd been fine all day in the classroom, but she was nervous about pulling the trigger and hearing the sound. She wanted to leave. The instructor put his hands on her shoulders. "You can do this," he said.

She focused again on the sights and got control of her breath. She inhaled, exhaled, then slowly squeezed.

After being named in the speech by President Obama, after the funerals, after getting interviewed by Anderson Cooper, and after healing enough to stand from her wheelchair, Taylor had tried to resume normal life. But she jumped at every loud sound. When the garbage trucks came around slamming trash cans, her heart raced and she felt like she might pass out. She felt scared all the time. She didn't want to let her kids leave the house. She couldn't shake the feeling that what had happened to her was not finished, that the gunman was coming back.

A sadness had descended on her. She'd rushed her recovery trying to get back to work, putting pressure on her leg months before doctors said she should. She had a metal plate and a dozen screws in her leg, and she felt daily pain. The family still owed thousands in medical bills. They struggled to pay rent. The shooting had put distance between her and her husband, because she felt the experience was something he could not understand. She wasn't the wife she'd been, nor the mother. One of her sons began skipping school and experimenting with drugs.

She began to feel like everyone knew about that one day, July 7, but had no clue about all the days after.

She felt like the only people who truly understood what she was going through were the cops. She'd become close with the officer who had shielded her that night on the street, Greg Weatherford. He was a white guy from a small town south of Dallas, and she couldn't imagine another circumstance in which they would have met. But now they talked often. Another new cop friend, SWAT officer Chris Webb—the one who'd first spotted Johnson in the rubble after the blast—had suggested the gun range as a sort of therapy. He'd called a friend and set her up for a shooting class. Having a gun and knowing how to use it, he thought, might make her feel safe again. If she were the one controlling the bullets, he told her, it would lessen her fear.

So here she was, learning sight alignment and trigger control, getting used to holding the piece of steel in her hands. She'd never shot a gun and had never planned to own one. As she held it, all she could think about was how much death and destruction they caused. But she was tired of being afraid.

When the gun first fired, she jumped. Then she looked around.

All the other students were focused downrange, firing. She inhaled deeply and fired again, this time nailing the target. By the time she loaded her second clip, she felt calmer. *You're okay*, she kept telling herself. Though she wasn't.

She went back to the range the next week, and the week after. She'd walk to her assigned lane with her gun box. She'd unpack her pistol and her two magazine clips. She'd put on safety goggles and slide on her shooting gloves. Before she picked up the gun she'd breathe. In and out, in and out.

41

Loss

After her husband's death, DART officer Emily Thompson was patrolling on foot near the Martin Luther King Jr. train station south of town. It was a cool fall night, and the area was crowded with people coming and going from the State Fair of Texas. Two women flagged her down, asking for help with a homeless woman who was splayed out on a bench sleeping. The women, one of them elderly, wanted to sit down. All three women were black. Emily shook the homeless woman's arm and told her she needed to get up. The woman walked away, then turned back to curse Emily. Just then, a car passed by, and the driver yelled out a window, "Leave that lady alone. You're just fuckin' with her because she's black."

Emily felt angry as she watched the car drive away. She wanted to shout back, "I'm out here helping two black women. And, by the way, my husband got killed because he was white."

For eight years, Emily had loved her job so much that she couldn't believe she got paid. She loved working the streets, loved interacting with people, loved colleagues who'd become family. Now she didn't trust herself. *I'm too angry to be out here*, she thought. She feared someone would say something and she'd lose her temper. It would be recorded on a cell phone, and she'd end up back on the news, Brent Thompson's widow getting revenge for her husband's death. That's who she was now, Brent Thompson's widow.

At the memorial service, Emily had felt offended when Obama started talking about "the pain of Alton Sterling's family." Why did the president feel the need to opine on race in America next to her dead husband's picture? What was he trying to say, exactly? That police had caused her husband's death? It made her so angry that she had looked around for the nearest exit. But she didn't think she could escape the television cameras, and she didn't want to create more news by walking out.

Later, at another memorial service, she'd vowed that she would continue as an officer. The gunman had taken her husband; he wouldn't take her profession. She'd seen a counselor to get cleared for duty. During the session, she mentioned it was the first time in her life she'd "wanted to go out and get somebody," but catching the counselor's look of concern, she'd quickly reeled the comment back in.

She grew close with two widows of other officers who had been murdered that night. They met at memorials and events and started a group text. Heidi Smith was raising two teenage daughters alone. Officer Zamarripa's partner, Kristy, was raising their young daughter, Lyncoln. A dozen kids were growing up without their fathers. The women talked about living in "the Fog." They drove carpool and stood in the grocery checkout line, there and not there. Heidi told someone about the family turtle, then remembered they hadn't had a turtle in years, and she blamed the Fog and Emily knew exactly what she meant.

More than a year after the shooting, Emily still couldn't pull herself out of bed sometimes. She had run through all her vacation and sick days. She started to think about a different career, of becoming a counselor for police officers. After giving two weeks' notice, she cleaned out her desk and turned in her Glock. She drove home that afternoon, feeling naked without the gun.

42

Beginnings

Dr. Brian Williams walked onstage and pulled note cards from his suit pocket. He'd been invited to speak at an annual symposium at the U.S. Air Force Academy, his alma mater. He stood in silence for a moment, then read a list of twelve names. "James Means. Alfred Olango. Keith Scott. Terence Crutcher. Philando Castile. Alton Sterling. Freddie Gray. Walter Scott. Eric Harris. Samuel DuBose. Tamir Rice. Michael Brown."

Pacing onstage, he said, "Now I'm confident that everyone in here recognizes at least one name on that list. And there are those that will debate the justifications for their killings. They will debate the value of their lives. But one thing you cannot debate is their humanity."

Since the shooting, Williams had opened up about his experiences as a black man, and things he'd kept to himself for too long came rushing out. He talked to friends, to family, to Don Lemon and David Muir. In coming months, he would keep talking. He felt it was no longer enough to be just a surgeon; he'd become an activist. He launched a podcast called *Race, Violence & Medicine.*

He chaired the city's citizens police review board, where people could lodge complaints about officers. Later, he accepted a job as a trauma surgeon on the south side of Chicago, a city devastated by gun violence.

He told the crowd of Air Force officers and cadets that working in the emergency room that night in Dallas had changed his life. "And now I'm on a mission to change all of yours," he said. "But to do that, we have to talk about race. And racism. And I know it's difficult, and it makes people uncomfortable. But I'm asking you when you feel uncomfortable today, to sit there and don't dismiss that feeling."

At the end of his talk, he read another list of names, struggling to keep his voice steady as he said each one. "Michael Smith. Michael Krol. Brent Thompson. Patrick Zamarripa. Lorne Ahrens."

He looked out at the crowd. "When you hear those names, do you feel differently about those names than the others that I read? Because I don't—I feel sick about all those deaths. But if you do, that is where the work begins."

43

Unease

After the national media left Dallas to follow gunfire in other towns, the city retreated into a quiet uneasiness. On balance, Mayor Rawlings thought his city had fared well in the aftermath. There had been criticism and handwringing over the robot bomb, fears about what it meant and where law enforcement was headed. Rawlings had mostly stayed out of the debate, but his police chief, David Brown, had been unapologetic. "I'd do it again," he said more than once. Brown retired a couple of months after the shooting, wrote a book, and joined ABC News as a contributor.

The mayor believed his city, and the country, was still suffering from the repercussions of America's original sin, slavery. Rawlings planned to do his part to make amends. He appointed a task force to evaluate the city's Confederate monuments, leading to the removal of a fourteen-foot statue of Robert E. Lee from a city park, where the Confederate general had been installed on horseback in 1936 while President Franklin D. Roosevelt watched.

As Rawlings's second term as mayor came to an end, another incident tested racial bonds in north Texas. In the fall of 2018 a young accountant, Botham Jean, was sitting in his apartment watching television and eating ice cream. A police officer, Amber Guyger, was getting off a long shift and heading home. She lived on the floor below Jean but had mistaken his door for her own. It had been left ajar. As she entered, she would later tell authorities, she thought Jean was a burglar, unholstered her gun, yelled, "Let me see your hands!" and then shot him dead. Guyger was white; Jean was black. The case prompted more anguished questions. Was there any place in the world where a black man was truly safe? Protesters marched, and reporters returned to town. To many people, the case illustrated the deepest and most troubling aspects of racial bias, how quickly the officer's mind appeared to have reflexively thought, *Black man, threat, danger, shoot.* Would she have done the same to a white man?

Jean's death was very different from other cases of officers shooting unarmed black men but, in some ways, simpler. He was a church-going, college-educated professional—and in his own home, no less. As many saw it, there was no reason, other than skin color, for Guyger to have perceived Jean as a threat. It was almost as if the universe had choreographed the case to say, "Okay, how are you going to explain this one?"

A jury convicted Guyger of murder and she was sentenced to ten years in prison. Five of the jurors were black, five Hispanic or Asian, and two white. It was a stunning verdict in many ways, a departure from high-profile officer acquittals of recent years, decided by mostly white panels. Outside the courtroom, attorney Benjamin Crump told reporters, "This verdict is for Trayvon Martin. It's for Michael Brown. It's for Sandra Bland. It's for Tamir Rice. It's for Eric Garner."

Still, many activists thought the sentence was too light. Their chants echoed through the corridors of the courthouse, "No justice, no peace."

For Rawlings, who'd retired from city hall by the time of the trial, the verdict provided more evidence of just how fragile racial relations remained. One officer's bad judgment—a split-second act on the back of centuries of injustice—and tension barreled back into the open.

44

The Bunker Barn

Matt Banes sat in the air-conditioned cab of his new tractor, a bright green John Deere front loader with a 55-horsepower engine. Wearing his cowboy hat and listening to Waylon Jennings, he worked the controls to scoop up another load of gravel. He'd bought 165 acres of west Texas land filled with mesquite and hackberry trees. Now he spent most of his weekends on his ranch. He and his three sons hunted for deer, pigs, turkey, and doves, and passed afternoons driving four-wheelers around the dirt roads.

His latest project was building what he called a "bunker barn." He was spreading gravel to create a foundation, back-dragging his tractor's bucket to level the rocks. He could spend hours on the project, forgetting about everything, enjoying the cool air and the unbroken sky. He'd had two large steel shipping containers delivered, and when he finished with the foundation, he'd sit them on top. Inside one, he'd already built custom racks for his fishing rods. Next, he'd build a metal roof over them to create his own base camp. He and his wife sketched out plans for an eight-hundred-square-foot log cabin. Its windows would look out over a pond and fields of sunflowers. They would be self-sufficient, with solar power and their own water well.

Months after the shooting, Banes left SWAT and returned to narcotics as a trainer. He spent his days telling young officers war stories, showing them how to make undercover buys, teaching them pistol skills, trying to make it harder for the bad guys to kill them. He had a few more years until he could retire, and he was counting the days.

He felt like he could no longer provide what the police department wanted of uniformed officers—patience, lenience, community building. There was no glory in risking your life to protect a public that demonized you.

His trainees, Banes believed, would never know the honor of being a police officer the way his generation had. He thought it was no coincidence that crime had spiked in Dallas. As he saw it, that's what happened when police weren't allowed to police. All the no-chase policies and use-of-force constraints had undermined the men and women tasked with protecting people. Banes had thought X's rampage, five dead cops in Dallas, might change some of that. And for a while it had. But before long the public narrative vilifying police seemed to take hold again.

In the November 2016 presidential election, Banes voted for Trump. He was a little embarrassed to admit his support, but he most of all believed the new president was pro–law enforcement.

Banes hoped the public knew what they were asking of cops now. He hoped that when the next active shooter showed up, mowing down schoolkids or churchgoers, the new generation of nicey-nice cops could take care of it. He might have retired to his tractor by then. To hell with all the people in the city.

The work on his bunker continued. Once he finished flattening the gravel, he drove his tractor back into the barn, headed to the fire pit, and poured himself a whiskey. As the sun disappeared over the western horizon, he sat in front of the pit. In the falling light, he could see the bass jumping in his pond, their silver bodies rising above the water, then disappearing. He looked forward to an evening sipping his drink, listening to the owls hoot in the oak trees. In the distance, coyotes yipped and howled.

45

Call It Out

Negotiator Gordon left SWAT not long after the shooting and joined the mayor's security detail. After the November 2016 election, he was driving Rawlings, a Democrat, to events. Gordon had voted for Hillary Clinton and, like pretty much everyone else, assumed she would win. Gordon felt both shocked and deeply unsettled by the election of Trump.

For all of Gordon's thoughts about racial injustice, for all the horrible things he'd seen human beings do to one another, he still believed that deep down most people were good. Everyone had flaws. Everyone got tripped up in their own biases, their frustrations and disappointments, their own fragmented assumptions about America. But wasn't that the point of it all? Weren't we all supposed to talk and learn from each other?

Trump's election shattered the few certainties Gordon had left. How could millions of people vote for a man like that? Suddenly Gordon felt as though he were living in a country he no longer recognized. The president wasn't just a man. He was supposed to be the living, breathing embodiment of what America stood for.

"This is white people's fault," Gordon told the mayor, who could only nod in agreement.

Trump's election seemed to Gordon a resounding statement from white America, an attempt to swing back the pendulum after its first black president. Gordon knew that many of his SWAT teammates had voted for Trump. But when he confronted them, they insisted their support of the man had nothing to do with race. His teammates had despised Obama for being "divisive." And yet they supported a man who had proposed mandatory registration for American Muslims, mocked a Latina former Miss Universe as "Miss Housekeeping," and talked about grabbing women "by the pussy." Obama had been given endless grief for the most trivial of things—a tan suit had become evidence of his "lack of seriousness." Gordon told his teammates, "I'm not saying you're a racist if you voted for Trump. But all the racists voted for Trump."

Gordon continued doing training sessions on de-escalation tactics for police officers across the country. How to slow down an interaction to allow more time, space, and flexibility, how to calm moments rather than escalate. He focused on the skills he'd used as a negotiator, discussing empathy, respect, and restraint. People wanted to be treated with dignity, he told officers. Know the power of respect. "Be nice," he'd say, "until it's time not to be nice."

Gordon would flash police shooting numbers on an overhead, how black people make up 13 percent of the population but a quarter of those shot. "This is what Black Lives Matter is talking about," he'd tell the officers in the audience. "This is what the hoopla is about. This is why X shot at us that day in Dallas." Gordon played the video of Sandra Bland getting pulled over by a Texas state trooper, showing how the cop had shouted at her. He played a video of Philando Castile's death recorded from the officer's dash cam. He went through it step by step, explaining how he thought the officer had drawn his weapon too quickly.

Gordon also played parts of his recording of the negotiation with X. The recording was a trapdoor back to the longest night of his life. By now he had memorized every word, every sound.

Officers in Gordon's training sessions would laugh when they heard X tell him, "You gonna keep kissing my ass or shoot me?" The officers would gasp when X told Gordon to put down his rifle and kill the cops behind him.

Gordon always played one particular part. "When a policeman beats, kills, shoots, or abuses anybody, y'all need to fucking arrest him. None of that thin blue line shit."

Gordon paused the recording and looked at the audience.

"That was just a seminal moment when I was sitting there talking to this guy," he'd tell the crowd. "I'm thinking, what did we do as police to cause this to happen? What did we do? I mean, and I remember thinking, 'Damn, he's right.'

"When a police officer does something bad, we got to call it out," Gordon would say. " 'Hey, that's a bad shooting.' I mean, this is just one guy. And he shut down Dallas. One guy. What if we had ten guys?"

Over time, Gordon began to shake his feeling, upon waking at night, that X was still waiting for him. But he still activated his alarm system, still slept with his gun beneath the mattress.

46

The Prairie

One of the most replayed videos from the night of July 7, 2016, was the death of DART officer Brent Thompson. It was recorded by a bystander with a cell phone from a hotel balcony near the college. The bystander zoomed on the street below, where Micah Johnson's black Tahoe was parked, its hazard lights flashing. The video showed Johnson slinking among the college's stone pillars and ducking behind a trash can.

By this point, Johnson already had ambushed three officers—Lorne Ahrens, Michael Krol, and Patrick Zamarripa—men he had never met, had no sane reason to want dead, and who without question would have come to his aid, in their capacity as first responders, had he found himself in need. He attacked these fathers, husbands, and sons by sneaking up from behind, leaving them no chance to fight back.

Then came transit cop Brent Thompson. He wasn't equipped for combat. He wasn't wearing a military-grade bulletproof vest, like his opponent, and he had only a pistol. Still, he ran toward the gunman and fired. The two adversaries converged, and as Thompson went around one side of a pillar, Johnson came around the other and shot Thompson from behind. Many officers believe that Thompson's actions saved their lives that night. He mounted the police's first serious challenge to the gunman, distracted him, and helped drive him off the street.

In a small town south of Dallas a little while later, Thompson's parents were sitting in their living room, watching the news. Sam and Paulette Thompson had lived in Corsicana for thirty years and raised three sons there. Sam spent all those years as a high school football coach and athletic director. Although he'd retired, people around town still called him "Coach."

The newscasters, who'd been reporting on the protest, suddenly broadcast live footage of police officers lying in the street. Sam looked at Paulette, and neither said a word, but he knew her thoughts: *Brent is gone.*

They called their oldest son, the county's district attorney, who said he couldn't talk and hung up. Then they got into their car and drove toward Dallas. Minutes into their ride, the son called back. "It was Brent," he said. "And it was fatal."

For a long time to come, Sam couldn't sleep through the night. He'd pull the sheets up to his chin, drift off for a while, then get up and discover it was only 10:00 p.m. He'd watched the video taken by the bystander on the balcony, and he kept seeing images of his son's death in his mind.

Sam had followed coverage of the Black Lives Matter movement, and he understood. "If you say there are not racial problems in this country," he'd told others more than once, "you've got your head buried in the sand." He'd always been up for a discussion about race, and he knew there was plenty to talk about. He thought there were problems with how the country policed itself, but he felt his son was part of the solution, not a cause.

Sam couldn't shake the image of this gunman shooting his son. First in the head. Wasn't that enough? But then the man stood over his son and fired a dozen more times. That was overkill. That, Sam thought, was something evil.

Years earlier, Sam and his sons had decided to build a family cemetery on a patch of prairie he owned outside of town, across the street from a wooden church and around the bend from a lake where he'd proposed to Paulette. He imagined the cemetery laid out in the shape of a family tree: he and Paulette buried at the top, beneath a big oak. The plots of their sons and their families would spread across the land from there.

When the hearse brought Brent from Dallas, people lined the highway three-deep. Firefighters parked their trucks on overpasses and hung American flags. The mourners laid Brent to rest in the new cemetery, which had not been meant to receive him for many more decades.

The pain the gunman caused this family, just this one of many, did not end there. The following year, on November 20, 2017, Sam and Paulette's oldest son knocked on their door at dawn. They answered in their pajamas. "The shooter got another one," their son said. Sam learned his grandson William, who was Brent's youngest son, was dead. He had called 911 to warn dispatchers, walked to a park, and shot himself. He was nineteen. He'd been close with his father and had not been the same after July 7. The family didn't consider William's death a suicide, as much as a son wanting to see his dad again.

Now, once every week or so, Sam and Paulette load a mower into the car and drive out to their land. They step onto the ancient prairie and listen to the cows lowing and the cardinals singing. Sam unwraps a chain lock, and they walk through a gate into the cemetery. They stop at Brent's headstone, where cops have left cans of beer and quarters and pennies, a military tradition meant to show the family that Brent has not been forgotten. Paulette bends beneath the live oak to pull weeds. Sam cranks the mower and pushes it beneath the endless Texas sky, weaving carefully around his son's and grandson's graves.

IN MEMORIAM

Remembering the five officers killed in the line of duty the night of July 7, 2016:

Lorne Ahrens

Dallas Police Department

The 48-year-old father of two children and husband of a DPD detective, the 6-foot-5 Ahrens loved tattoos and heavy metal and asked to be buried in a T-shirt, shorts and no shoes.

Michael Krol

Dallas Police Department

Krol, 40, a Michigan native, moved to Dallas in 2007 to become a police officer. Fellow officers called the 6-foot-4 Krol "B.W.G." — Big White Guy.

Mike Smith

Dallas Police Department

Smith, 55, was a former Army Ranger who served nearly three decades in the Dallas Police Department. He was married and had two daughters and loved making them pancakes.

Brent Thompson

DART Police

An officer with Dallas Area Rapid Transit, Thompson, 43, was the father of six and had one stepchild. He married a fellow DART officer two weeks before he was killed.

Patrick Zamarripa

Dallas Police Department

A Navy veteran who did three tours in Iraq, Zamarripa, 32, had a young daughter and a stepson. He loved baseball and rooted for the Texas Rangers.

Illustration by Michael Hogue/*Dallas Morning News*

Source Notes

After the shooting of July 7, 2016, Dallas Police Department investigators retrieved more than 170 hours of footage from cameras fastened to officers' uniforms and their patrol cars. None of that footage has been publicly released, nor is it expected to be. The department has fought nearly every public records request seeking information about the ambush, the standoff, and its resolution.

Most of what we know about the night comes from the men and women who were there. During the past three years, I have spent hundreds of hours interviewing them. I started the morning after the shooting, while reporting for the *Washington Post*. It was months later before I persuaded the first SWAT officer to speak with me. I continued writing about the event for *D Magazine* and the *Dallas Morning News*. Work from some of those articles has been reprinted here. I got to know the officers by riding along in their patrol cars, watching their CrossFit workouts, spending time at the shooting range, watching them set off a pound of C4, and going to their homes and meeting their wives and children.

Many officers spoke to me without the knowledge or permission of the police department. Many felt as if they'd been unfairly forbidden from talking about one of the most traumatic and important nights of their lives. It is a story they wanted told, not only for posterity but for other officers who might find themselves facing similar threats. Toward the end of my reporting, I obtained access to various nonpublic videos and recordings, granted on background by people who wanted this book to be as accurate as possible. The recordings have helped transform this account into a clearer and more precise record of what happened that night. While many scenes in this book are based on officers' recollections, others are based on actual footage.

Negotiator Larry Gordon used his cell phone to record twenty-seven minutes of his negotiations with the gunman and shared his recording with me on the record. I lightly edited some portions of that dialogue to omit muddled words and repetitions. Below I've detailed which segments are from the tape and which are reconstructed from Gordon's memory.

Thoughts I ascribe to the gunman are based on my interviews with Gordon, who spent hours talking with him before his death. The gunman's relatives did not respond to interview requests.

Police Chief David Brown declined to be interviewed. His chapters rely heavily on his memoir, *Called to Rise* (New York: Ballantine, 2017), his personnel file, and hundreds of his e-mails, obtained through public records requests.

I asked the characters in the book to review sections portraying them prior to publication. I did this not to seek their approval, but to check for accuracy, particularly in places where the narrative was told from the characters' interior points of view. All of them, except Chief Brown, agreed. Where possible, I corroborated interviews with information from records, including the police department's internal report on the night, released only because of the tireless efforts of reporters Tanya Eiserer and Jason Trahan of Dallas's WFAA-TV (Channel 8).

Five police officers—Larry Gordon, Matt Banes, Danny Canete, Brandon Berie, and Ryan Scott—share in a portion of this book's proceeds. All gave up their own creative projects to tell their stories to me instead. They had no editorial control over the work and did not see the manuscript in full prior to publication.

Prologue

Descriptions of the gunman's mind-set come from interviews with police negotiator Larry Gordon. Physical descriptions of the gunman come from his autopsy report, obtained through a public records request, and from photographs taken by officers after his death. Details from the gunman's journal come from public officials and police officers briefed on its contents. Details about the gunman's last conversation with his mother, Delphine Johnson, are from the only interview she's given, to TheBlaze in July 2016, shortly after the shooting.

Chapter 1

The jumper scene was reconstructed from interviews with Larry Gordon and his partner on the call, SWAT officer Brent Jones. I also used details from a photograph of the woman on the ledge, provided by Gordon. Details about Gordon's law enforcement history come from Gordon and his personnel file. Details about the police headquarters shooting come from Gordon, multiple *Dallas Morning News* stories, and records provided by police officers, including a copy of the shooter's 911 call and crime scene photographs. See also Tristan Hallman and Naomi Martin, "One Year Later: Police in Peril," *Dallas Morning News*, June 11, 2016, http://interactives.dallasnews.com/2016/dpd-shooting/.

Chapter 2

Former Dallas police chief David Brown declined requests for interviews. Information in this chapter comes from his memoir, *Called to Rise*, as well as his personnel file and hundreds of his e-mails, obtained through public records requests.

Dallas shooting statistics come from the police department's Officer Involved Shootings Database, which can be found here: https://dallas police.net/ois/ois.

Information on Dixon Circle comes from the department's investigative file, obtained through a public records request, and from various articles in the *Dallas Morning News*.

Information on Dallas comes from these books:

Harvey J. Graff, *The Dallas Myth: The Making and Unmaking of an American City* (Minneapolis: University of Minnesota Press, 2010).
Molly Ivins, *Molly Ivins Can't Say That, Can She?* (New York: Vintage, 1992).

Darwin Payne, *Big D: Triumphs and Troubles of an American Supercity in the 20th Century* (Dallas, TX: Three Forks Press, 2000).

Michael Phillips, *White Metropolis: Race, Ethnicity, and Religion in Dallas, 1841–2001* (Austin: University of Texas Press, 2006).

Jim Schutze, *The Accommodation: The Politics of Race in an American City* (Secaucus, NJ: Citadel Press, 1986).

Chapter 3

This chapter is based on multiple interviews with Shetamia Taylor.

Chapter 4

This chapter is based on interviews with Matt Banes, Gerry Huante, Larry Gordon, Misty VanCuren, Garret Hellinger, and other current and former members of Dallas SWAT.

Information on officer reaction times came from several studies, including this one: J. Bumgarner, W. J. Lewinski, W. Hudson, and C. Sapp, "An Examination of Police Officer Mental Chronometry," *Journal of the Association for Crime Scene Reconstruction* 12 (July 2006).

Chapter 5

This chapter is based on interviews with Dr. Williams; his wife, Kathianne; and other nurses and doctors at Parkland Memorial Hospital.

Chapter 6

This chapter is based on interviews with Misty McBride and Emily Thompson. Dallas information comes from *Dallas Morning News* articles and the books listed in notes for chapter 2.

"Why Has Downtown Dallas Taken Off? A Failure to Land Boeing in 2001," *Dallas Morning News*, July 7, 2016, https://www.dallasnews.com/business/2016/07/07/why-has-downtown-dallas-taken-off-a-failure-to-land-boeing-in-2001/.

Chapter 7

This chapter is based on interviews with Larry Gordon.

Police shooting statistics: "Fatal Force," *Washington Post*, https://www

.washingtonpost.com/graphics/2019/national/police-shootings-2019/. Joe Fox, Adrian Blanco, Jennifer Jenkins, Julie Tate, and Wesley Lowery, "What We've Learned About Police Shootings 5 Years After Ferguson," *Washington Post*, August 9, 2019, https://www.washingtonpost.com/ nation/2019/08/09/what-weve-learned-about-police-shootings-years -after-ferguson/?arc404=true.

Chapter 8

This chapter is based on multiple interviews with Sgt. Ivan Gunter. He is the source for details about his last conversation with Ahrens. Details also were drawn from the department's internal investigation into the shooting, obtained through a public records request. I also interviewed members of the Foxtrots, including Jorge Barrientos, Brian Fillingim, Ivan Saldana, Ruben Lozano, and Gretchen Rocha, who is the source for the details on Zamarripa's encounter with the homeless man.

Chapter 9

Details about the march come from Shetamia Taylor and various news videos. This video in particular was helpful: G. J. McCarthy, "Video of Black Lives Matter Protest and Police Shooting in Dallas," *Dallas Morning News*, YouTube, July 8, 2016, https://www.youtube.com/ watch?v=n5alejF5k7c.

Other details, such as the path of the marchers, the time line, and details about Johnson's weapons come from the police department's internal investigation into the shooting. Excerpts of radio traffic come from the police department's audio recordings. Other details were provided by police officers Ivan Gunter, John Abbott, and others who worked the protest.

Details about the DART bus driver are from the *Dallas Morning News*.

Jennifer Emily, " 'Our Worst Nightmare': Heroism, Devastation and the Story of How 1 Man Killed 5 Dallas Cops," *Dallas Morning News*, July 31, 2016, https://www.dallasnews.com/news/2016/07/31/our-worst -nightmare-heroism-devastation-and-the-story-of-how-1-man-killed -5-dallas-cops/.

Chapter 10

This chapter is based on interviews with Ivan Gunter, Jorge Barrientos, Ivan Saldana, and Gretchen Rocha. I supplemented their accounts with affidavits and internal statements they and other officers gave to the Dallas Police Department, obtained through a public records request.

Details about the interaction on the street between Taylor and Weatherford come from my interviews with both. Their account was corroborated by a bystander's cell phone recording, which captured part of what happened.

Quotes from radio communications come from police department recordings.

Portions of this story first appeared in my account of the Foxtrots for the *Washington Post*: Jamie Thompson, "Inside the Deadliest Day for U.S. Law Enforcement Since 9/11," *Washington Post*, September 26, 2016.

Chapter 11

This chapter is based on interviews with Henry Edwards, Jake Deloof, Bob Craig, and John Abbott.

The information on AKs is from C. J. Chivers, *The Gun* (New York: Simon & Schuster Paperbacks, 2011).

Chapters 12 and 13

These chapters are based on interviews with Danny Canete; Canete's mother, Kim Canete; Brandon Berie; Ryan Scott; Henry Edwards; Joe Lopez; Daniel Diaz; Kelvin Johnigan; Mike Rawlings; Scott Goldstein, then the mayor's spokesman; and Clay Jenkins, then the Dallas County judge. Details about Brown are from his book *Called to Rise*. Radio traffic is from a police department recording of Channel 12. Details about the Yanez traffic stop are from episode 2 of Minnesota Public Radio's Peabody-winning podcast *74 Seconds*, which aired May 23, 2017.

Chapter 14

This chapter is based on interviews with Cesar Soto, Misty McBride, and Shetamia Taylor.

Chapter 15

This chapter is based on interviews with Matt Banes, Danny Canete, and Brandon Berie.

Chapter 16

This chapter is based on interviews with Matt Banes. Quotes in the scene of his first shooting are from Banes's recollection. Details were corroborated with a Dallas police incident report dated May 23, 2012. Details of the second shooting are from Banes and a police report dated January 7, 2013. Dialogue between Banes and X, starting with "You firing up a little weed over there?" to the end of the chapter, was transcribed by me from recordings from that night. Some words were too muffled to be heard, and I did not always mark those spots with ellipses. Other dialogue was reconstructed based on the memory of Banes and other officers.

Chapter 17

This chapter is based on interviews with Dr. Brian Williams. The Florida doctor's comments are from Heather Sher, "What I Saw Treating the Victims from Parkland Should Change the Debate on Guns," *Atlantic*, February 22, 2018.

Chapter 18

Negotiations between Gordon and X are reconstructed based on Gordon's memory and other SWAT officers. Dialogue starting with "X, I think you have a valid point" to the end of the chapter comes from a recording that captured part of the negotiation.

Factual details about Attica come from *Attica: The Official Report of the New York State Special Commission on Attica* (New York: Praeger, 1972), available online at https://nysl.ptfs.com/data/Library1/Library1/pdf/14815273.pdf.

I also drew from this excellent book: Heather Ann Thompson, *Blood in the Water: The Attica Prison Uprising of 1971 and Its Legacy* (New York: Vintage Books, 2017).

Information about the Downs case is summarized from court records of the original lawsuit (382 F.Supp 713 [M.D. Tenn., 1974]) and its appeal

(522 F.2d 990 [6th Cir., 1975]). I also drew details from "Hijacker Kills Wife, Pilot and Himself," *New York Times*, October 5, 1971.

Information on Cambria is from Pervaiz Shallwani, "Life Lessons from the NYPD's Top Hostage Negotiator," *Wall Street Journal*, August 28, 2015.

Information on Waco comes mostly from "Report to the Deputy Attorney General on the Events at Waco, Texas: The Aftermath of the April 19 Fire," United States Department of Justice, February 14, 2018, https://www.justice.gov/archives/publications/waco/report-deputy-at torney-general-events-waco-texas-aftermath-april-19-fire.

Information about the history of crisis and hostage negotiations comes from these books:

Michael J. McMains and Wayman C. Mullins, *Crisis Negotiations: Managing Critical Incidents and Hostage Situations in Law Enforcement and Corrections*, 5th ed. (New York: Routledge, 2015).
Gary Noesner, *Stalling for Time: My Life as an FBI Hostage Negotiator* (New York: Random House, 2018).
Chris Voss and Tahl Raz, *Never Split the Difference: Negotiating as if Your Life Depended on It* (New York: Harper Business, 2016).

Chapter 19

This chapter is based on interviews with Mike Rawlings. Information from the Kennedy assassination comes from Bill Minutaglio and Steven L. Davis, *Dallas 1963* (Boston: Twelve, 2014).

Rawlings's speech can be found here: "Dallas Mayor Mike Rawlings Speech—JFK 50th Anniversary Dallas," YouTube, uploaded May 8, 2014, https://www.youtube.com/watch?v=_ho88_e8XOw.

Chapter 20

Information in this chapter comes from interviews with Jeremy Borchardt; Borchardt's wife, Patricia; Josh Hertel; and other SWAT officers, including Scott McDonnold, Brent Jones, and Jude Braun. I also viewed recordings relevant to this chapter. Information about

Borchardt's previous shootings comes from multiple *Dallas Morning News* articles reported by Tanya Eiserer, Jason Trahan, Holly Yan, and Tiara Ellis.

Chapter 21

Information in this chapter comes from interviews with Larry Gordon. The dialogue between Gordon and X, starting with "I'm just concerned for our safety," was transcribed by me from a twenty-seven-minute recording taped by Gordon on his cell phone. I lightly edited the conversation, mostly to remove repetitions, and at several points X's voice is too muffled to make out what he is saying. I did not note all of these spots with ellipses.

Chapter 22

Details in this chapter come from interviews with Gordon. Dialogue between X and Gordon is from Gordon's tape, lightly edited. Information on Ferguson is taken primarily from these two reports: US Department of Justice Civil Rights Division, "Department of Justice Report Regarding the Criminal Investigation into the Shooting Death of Michael Brown by Ferguson, Missouri Police Officer Darren Wilson," March 4, 2015, https://www.justice.gov/sites/default/files/opa/press-releases/attachments/2015/03/04/doj_report_on_shooting_of_michael_brown_1.pdf; and "Investigation of the Ferguson Police Department," March 4, 2015, https://www.justice.gov/sites/default/files/opa/press-releases/attachments/2015/03/04/ferguson_police_department_report.pdf.

Chapter 23

Information in this chapter comes from interviews with Shan Gordon and Emily Thompson.

Chapter 24

Information in this chapter comes from interviews with Danny Canete.

Chapter 25

Information in this chapter comes from interviews with Jeremy Borchardt and Short Dog. Short Dog is a nickname. He agreed to be interviewed on the condition that his real name not be revealed.

Chapter 26

Dialogue in this chapter comes from Larry Gordon's twenty-seven-minute recording, lightly edited.

Information on Gullah comes from Joseph A. Opala, "The Gullah: Rice, Slavery, and the Sierra Leone–American Connection," Yale University, https://glc.yale.edu/gullah-rice-slavery-and-sierra-leone-american-connection.

Information on reciprocity comes from Robert B. Cialdini, *Influence: The Psychology of Persuasion* (New York: HarperCollins, 2007).

Chapter 27

Information on the SWAT callout involving the three-year-old comes from interviews with Jude Braun, former SWAT officers Chris Webb and Rich Emberlin, and *Dallas Morning News* stories, including Matthew Haag and Tanya Eiserer, "Man Kills Young Son, Himself as Police Try to End Standoff," *Dallas Morning News*, June 21, 2007.

Information about the MOVE bombing comes from "Excerpts from Commission's Report on Bombing," *New York Times*, March 7, 1986, https://www.nytimes.com/1986/03/07/us/excerpts-from-commissions-report-on-bombing.html. Additional information from Selwyn Raab, "Philadelphia Officials Vary in Explaining Siege Tactics," *New York Times*, May 19, 1985, https://www.nytimes.com/1985/05/19/us/philadelphia-officials-vary-in-explaining-siege-tactics.html; and Kitty Caparella, "Cop's Death in '78 Clash Was a Spark," *Philadelphia Inquirer*, May 10, 2010, https://www.inquirer.com/philly/news/special_packages/dailynews/20100506_Cops_death_in_78_clash_was_a_spark.html.

Details about Chief Brown and Bill Humphrey's phone call come from an interview with Humphrey and from Brown's book *Called to Rise*.

Chapter 28

This chapter is based on interviews with C. T. Payne, Short Dog, Mark Michaels, and Johnnie Green. Interaction between Jeremy Borchardt and bomb squad officers is as told by Borchardt.

Chapter 29

This chapter is based on interviews with Larry Gordon and Gerry Huante. Dialogue is transcribed from Gordon's twenty-seven-minute tape, lightly edited.

Chapter 30

This chapter is based on interviews with Dr. Brian Williams, Mike Rawlings, and Chief Brown's memoir.

Chapter 31

This chapter is based on interviews with Larry Gordon, Gerry Huante, and other SWAT members. Dialogue reconstructed from Gordon's memory.

Chapter 32

This chapter is based on interviews with Greg Weatherford.

Chapter 33

This chapter is based on interviews with Jeremy Borchardt, Short Dog, Sgt. Josh Hertel, Mark Michaels, Johnnie Green, Mel Williams, Chris Webb, Matt Smith, Alex Eastman, Matt Banes, and Danny Canete. There is also a photograph of the gunman as the robot approaches.

Chapter 34

This chapter is based on interviews with Bill Humphrey, Mike Rawlings, Scott Goldstein, and Chief Brown's memoir. It also relies on interviews with Dr. Brian Williams, Sgt. Ivan Gunter, and Brian Fillingim. Exchange between Gunter and Chief Brown is as told by Gunter.

Chapter 35

This chapter is based on interviews with Jeremy Borchardt; Danny Canete; Gerry Huante; Matt Banes and his wife, Melissa Sue; and Larry Gordon and his wife, Shan.

Chapter 36

This chapter is based on interviews with Dr. Brian Williams and his wife, Kathianne.

Chapter 37

Information in this chapter comes from interviews with Larry Gordon, Gerry Huante, Misty McBride, Mike Rawlings, and Shetamia Taylor.

Full video of the memorial service can be found here: *New York Times*, "Memorial Service for Dallas Officers," YouTube, uploaded July 12, 2016, www.youtube.com/watch?v=wOTW6ldED5c.

I have offered a greatly condensed history of "The Battle Hymn," which is thoroughly explored in John Stauffer and Benjamin Soskis, *The Battle Hymn of the Republic: A Biography of the Song That Marches On* (New York: Oxford University Press, 2013).

Chapter 38

Details about Johnson's life prior to July 7, 2016, were drawn from the only interview his mother, father, and stepmother have given, which aired on TheBlaze a week after the shooting.

Army investigation details come from two reports obtained by the *Dallas Morning News*: a 131-page redacted copy of an AR15-6 Investigation, Equal Opportunity Task Force Rugged, completed May 29, 2014, which focused on the panty theft allegations, and a second Army investigation, a 15-page redacted copy of a Law Enforcement Report, completed August 23, 2016, which also provided additional details of the Army's sexual harassment investigation.

Details from Johnson's visit to the Mesquite Police Department come from a copy of the police report dated January 26, 2011. Details about Johnson's interaction with two police officers while he ate outside a sandwich shop are from a Richardson Police Department report dated May 8, 2015. Additional information about that encounter was given by Johnson's grandfather Havard McDonald, in an interview with his local newspaper in Mississippi: Donna McLean, "Family of Dallas Shooter, a MS Native, Say Johnson Was Not Racist," *Magee Courier*, July 13, 2016. McLean's story also is the source for McDonald's quotes and his impressions of Johnson in the weeks before the shooting.

Details about Johnson's medical treatment come from seventy-two pages of redacted medical records from the Veterans Administration. Information on Johnson's wounds are from his autopsy report.

Special thanks to *Dallas Morning News* investigative reporter Sue Ambrose for sharing her files with me.

Chapter 39

This chapter is based on interviews with Gordon and his twenty-seven-minute recording.

Chapter 40

This chapter is based on interviews with Shetamia Taylor, Greg Weatherford, and Chris Webb.

Chapter 41

This chapter is based on interviews with Emily Thompson.

Chapter 42

This chapter is based on interviews with Dr. Brian Williams and his wife, Kathianne. His full talk is here: U.S. Air Force Academy, "Dr. Brian H. Williams, MD, FACS__24th Annual National Character and Leadership Symposium_2017," *YouTube*, uploaded February 24, 2017, www.youtube.com/watch?v=ojNKPTKImRU&t=2107s.

Chapter 43

This chapter is based on interviews with Mike Rawlings and media coverage of the Guyger case, particularly the *Dallas Morning News* and the *New York Times*.

Jennifer Emily, LaVendrick Smith, Dana Branham, and Charles Scudder, "Amber Guyger Convicted of Murder for Killing Botham Jean; Sentencing Phase to Continue Wednesday," *Dallas News*, October 1, 2019.

Marina Trahan Martinez, Sarah Mervosh, and John Eligon, "Former Dallas Police Officer Is Guilty of Murder for Killing Her Neighbor," *New York Times*, October 1, 2019.

Chapter 44

This chapter is based on interviews with Matt Banes.

Chapter 45

This chapter is based on interviews with Larry Gordon and Mike Rawlings. I also attended several of Gordon's training sessions.

Chapter 46

This chapter is based on interviews with Sam and Paulette Thompson and also articles from the *Corsicana Daily Sun*, including "Son of Slain DART Officer Found Dead," *Corsicana Daily Sun*, November 20, 2017.

Acknowledgments

I owe my greatest gratitude to the men and women whose names appear in these pages. Thank you for the hours you spent with me, for inviting me into your homes and lives and minds. Not one day of interviewing any of you felt like work. Getting to know you all has been a joy and an honor. Special thanks to Larry Gordon, Matt Banes, Danny Canete, and Dr. Brian Williams, who went above and beyond to help me get it right.

Two brilliant editors, Tom French and Tim Rogers, guided this book in essential ways. Thank you for sprinkling your magic throughout. Another amazing editor, Chris Weston, offered valuable feedback on the manuscript, as he has throughout my career on so many stories. Thank you for staying in my life. Yet another gifted editor, Mike Wilson, laid the foundation of this book over breakfasts at Cindi's. I'm so glad I finally got the chance to work with you.

Thanks also to Rudy Bush, Jenny Liberto, Ken Nolan, Katherine Ogburn, Grant Thompson, and Kathianne Williams. Your close reads and contributions were generous and invaluable.

I owe much to Richard Abate and Erwin Stoff, who loved this

story from the start and helped find it a home. Thanks also to the team at Holt, most importantly editor Serena Jones, for believing in me and this book. Her thoughtful guidance greatly improved this work. Thanks also to Madeline Jones for helping with every detail.

My mother and father, Cindy and Kelly Jones, drove carpool and cooked dinner and folded clothes and supported me in every conceivable way. Thank you, Mom and Dad. I couldn't have done this without you.

My friends Sarah Hepola and Lauren Schneider provided literary wisdom, laughter, and support the whole way through. Thank you for making my days less lonely. Thanks also to these women, all vitally important to me: Amy Crowell, Katie Kellett, Hayden Hilke, Mindy Sturm, Pamela Southerling, and Marjorie Kreppel.

My kids, Carter and Benjamin, put up with my absences and inattention for the good of this book. Thank you for filling my life with joy, laughter, snuggles, meaning, and pure boundless love. (You're welcome for my contributions to the swear jar during this project. And, yes, the book is finally really done now.)

Most important, I want to thank my husband, partner, and best friend, Steve Thompson. He was this book's first and most devoted editor, and it would be hard to overstate his contributions. Thank you for climbing into every trench. Without you, nothing else works or matters. All my love.

Index

About the Author

Jamie Thompson covered the Dallas police shooting for the *Washington Post*. Her later account of that night for the *Dallas Morning News* won an Edward R. Murrow Award for excellence in writing. She has been a contributing editor for *D Magazine* and an associate professor of journalism at the University of Dallas. Her work also has appeared in *Texas Monthly* and the *Tampa Bay Times*. Twitter: @ThompsonJamieL